Student-Focused Coaching

The Instructional Coach's Guide
to Supporting Student Success
Through Teacher Collaboration

by

Jan Hasbrouck, Ph.D.

JH Educational Services
Seattle, Washington

and

Daryl Michel, Ph.D.

Be A Change, LLC
San Antonio, Texas

·P A U L·H·
BROOKES
PUBLISHING Cº®

Baltimore • London • Sydney

Paul H. Brookes Publishing Co.
Post Office Box 10624
Baltimore, Maryland 21285-0624
USA
www.brookespublishing.com

Typeset by Lumina Datamatics, Inc.
Manufactured in the United States of America by Versa Press.
Foreword © Jim Knight 2022.

The individuals described in this book are composites or real people whose situations are masked and are based on the authors' experiences. In all instances, names and identifying details have been changed to protect confidentiality.

Library of Congress Cataloging-in-Publication Data

Names: Hasbrouck, Jan E. (Jan Elizabeth), author. | Michel, Daryl, author.
Title: Student-focused coaching : the instructional coach's guide to supporting student success
   through teacher collaboration / by Jan Hasbrouck and Daryl Michel.
Description: Baltimore : Paul H. Brookes Publishing Co., [2022] | Includes
   bibliographical references and index.
Identifiers: LCCN 2021029150 (print) | LCCN 2021029151 (ebook) | ISBN
   9781681254944 (paperback) | ISBN 9781681254951 (epub) | ISBN
   9781681254968 (pdf)
Subjects: LCSH: Student-centered learning. | Effective teaching. |
   Teachers—In-service training. | Mentoring in education. |
   Employees—Coaching of. | BISAC: EDUCATION / Professional Development |
   LANGUAGE ARTS & DISCIPLINES / Literacy
Classification: LCC LB1027.23 .H375 2022 (print) | LCC LB1027.23 (ebook)
   | DDC 371.39/4--dc23
LC record available at https://lccn.loc.gov/2021029150
LC ebook record available at https://lccn.loc.gov/2021029151

British Library Cataloguing in Publication data are available from the British Library.

2025   2024   2023   2022

10   9   8   7   6   5   4   3   2

Contents

About the Online Materials

To support coaching efforts, purchasers of this book may download, print, and/or photocopy the forms and appendices for professional and/or educational use. The forms include worksheets, checklists, tracking sheets, self-assessments, and more.

To access the materials that come with this book:

1. Go to the Brookes Download Hub:
   http://downloads.brookespublishing.com

2. Register to create an account (or log in with an existing account).

3. Filter or search for the book title *Student-Focused Coaching*.

About the Authors

Jan Hasbrouck, Ph.D.

Jan Hasbrouck, Ph.D., is a leading researcher, educational consultant, and author who works with schools in the United States and internationally. Dr. Hasbrouck worked as a reading specialist and coach for 15 years and later became a professor. Her research in reading fluency, academic assessment and interventions, and instructional coaching has been widely published. She is the author and coauthor of several books, curriculum materials, and assessment tools. She continues to collaborate with researchers on projects related to reading assessment and intervention.

Daryl Michel, Ph.D.

Daryl Michel, Ph.D., is the founder and innovator of Be A Change, LLC, and a lifelong educator who is passionate about engaging with others to learn, teach, and inspire while appreciating and advocating for voices and perspectives to be heard. Growing up in rural Iowa and moving to Texas to student teach was quite the leap. Experience led to opportunity for Daryl, however, as he went from being a classroom teacher in one school district to being nationally known as an instructional coach, area manager, and director to establishing international networks as a business owner. Each day, Daryl does his very best to live by his business tagline of "Many Individuals. Infinite Possibilities." He doesn't aspire to be "the" change. He aspires to be "a" change by being present, listening, and noticing.

Foreword

When my colleagues and I began studying instructional coaching back in the mid-1990s, we started from scratch. I did my dissertation on Partnership Learning, so we understood the importance of recognizing teacher professionalism, and we knew that anyone needs a lot of support to implement new strategies, but that was pretty much it. Each week, though, we learned more, and now after two decades of research, we have an efficient, adaptive, and easy-to-implement model for instructional coaching, which I refer to as The Impact Cycle.

We needed many years to arrive at our tight model of coaching. Between 1999 and 2009, I met with our coaching team each Friday, and we spent 2 hours identifying what was working, what wasn't working, and what we needed to do differently. We were all committed to creating an efficient and effective coaching model that had an unmistakably positive impact on student learning and well-being.

Those Friday conversations were life giving because we were all learning with each other. Sometimes our interactions got heated, but we were always learning. One thing we learned early on was that coaching needed to be guided by goals. Coaching without goals—to paraphrase Wayne Gretzky—is a bit like trying to play hockey without nets. You do a lot, but not much happens.

As we studied goals, we learned—as Jan Hasbrouck and Daryl Michel learned a long time ago—that the best goals are student-focused, not teacher-focused goals. What we found was that when teachers set teacher-focused goals (i.e., I want to use more cooperative learning), they usually don't keep using the new teaching strategies they try. In contrast, when teachers set student-focused goals (i.e., I want at least 90% of my students to be able to write a well-organized essay as measured by a single-factor rubrics), they usually continued to use the new strategies that they learned to help students reach those goals.

I believe that student-focused goals lead to continued use of new strategies, in part, because a strategy has to be implemented effectively for a student-focused goal to be hit. Students' learning or behavior won't change if a strategy is implemented poorly. Also, teachers are more inclined to keep using a strategy when their students succeed, simply because, for most educators, nothing is more motivating than seeing students succeed. Ultimately, of course, student-focused goals may be most important because they put the emphasis of coaching where it needs to be: on students.

This is why I am so grateful for this extremely powerful and useful book: *Student-Focused Coaching*. The book contains a wealth of valuable information gathered over more than two decades studying Student-Focussed Coaching (SFC). Dr. Hasbrouck has been either studying or working as a coach since 1985, and Dr. Michel brings a wealth of experience as a nationally recognized instructional coach and change leader. Together they have created a book that any coach will benefit from reading.

Even though Jan and Daryl's coaching model is significantly different than the one my colleagues and I have developed, I find myself continually grateful for this publication. There is, after all, plenty of room for more than one model of coaching. Indeed, no matter what approach you take to coaching, I feel confident stating that you will find many useful practices in this book that you can integrate into your coaching practice, and I'm sure many will find that the SFC approach works extremely well as the model for coaching in their setting.

As I read the book, I found myself nodding in agreement about many of the authors' fundamental assertions—that coaching is collaborative, nonevaluative, student focused, and guided by the issues that teachers are most interested in addressing. SFC, as it is described here, is what I refer to as "inside out," guided by the deepest concerns of the teacher about students' needs, and not "outside in," imposed by the coach, administrator, or others who are outside the classroom. In my experience, "inside out" coaching, which is driven by the teacher's passionate desire to improve students' experiences, is absolutely necessary for the complex work of changing classroom strategies, simply because the work is too complex and challenging to be accomplished without a teacher's passionate commitment—and most of us aren't committed to goals that are given to us by others.

I am also very grateful for the tools and expertise that Hasbrouck and Michel share in their book, which can all be downloaded, and used by any coach. The book contains powerful tools coaches can use for a wide variety of aspects of their coaching practice from forms for tracking how they use their time, to surveys that can be shared with teachers to assess teachers' instructional priorities. The book is also packed with advice on such topics as how to create a personal coaching vision, how to restart your coaching if it gets off on the wrong foot, and a framework for better understanding teacher readiness for coaching.

What I found most interesting and helpful, however, is the authors' clarification of the role of Student Focused Coaches, and the three main roles for these coaches—Facilitator, Collaborative Problem-Solver, and Teacher/Learner. Most people will find it very difficult to succeed if they do not understand what it is that they are supposed to do, and Hasbrouck and Michel's book will help any coach better understand exactly what it is that they do.

Coaching has come a long way in two decades. More and more we are clear on what works, what doesn't work, and how to get started. When coaches understand the beliefs, conversational framework, skills, and strategic knowledge of coaching, they have a much greater chance of making a difference in children's and teachers' lives. This book will help any coach move closer to the kind of clarity. And we need coaches who know what they are doing to create the kinds of schools we want for our students.

Jim Knight
Author, The Definitive Guide to Instructional Coaching *(2022)*
Senior Partner, Instructional Coaching Group

Acknowledgments

We must first acknowledge the major contributions to the original Student-Focused Coaching model by Dr. Carolyn Denton. This book would not have been possible without her. To Liz Gildea and Rachel Word for their feedback, recommendations, and guidance as we wrote this current edition of *Student-Focused Coaching*. And to the peer reviewers for their thoughts, feedback, and recommendation that this edition be published.

Introduction

Providing coaching support to colleagues can be a rewarding but challenging job. The purpose of this book is to help all coaches be successful in their work. Although Student-Focused Coaching (SFC) is the model of coaching we present here, we will use the term *instructional coaching* as a broader term throughout this book. In its generic form, *instructional coach* describes a person whose primary professional responsibility is to successfully bring proven research- and evidence-based practices into classrooms by working with teachers and administrators/supervisors. SFC is one way to provide instructional coaching. We describe other models of instructional coaching in Chapter 1.

Before we go further, we want to be sure that this book is going to be helpful to *you*, in your work as a coach. In our experience, many educators are given the title of "coach," but their primary responsibility is actually working directly with students, perhaps as an interventionist or tutor, or their work is actually more like that of an assistant administrator. Although a professional may have the title of "coach", they may not be coaching in the powerful and effective process described here. This book supports the work of instructional coaches at all levels, prekindergarten through high school, who spend at least part of their time in classrooms working in partnership with teachers or specialists to support the successful implementation of proven research- and evidence-based instructional practices. If this is the role you have, or the role you hope to create in a school, district, or region, then this book can be your guide to success!

Instructional coaching can have a significant impact on improving student outcomes if

- The right person has been selected

- The role of the coach is clearly defined, communicated, and adhered to

- The coach receives sufficient training in how to do their job effectively

- Coaching is focused on supporting teachers to successfully implement proven research- and evidence-based instructional practices, rather than supervising or evaluating colleagues

- The coach has ongoing support from the administrator/supervisor

We have witnessed the best of intentions from administrators/supervisors in wanting to implement coaching for their teachers. Funding is available, coaches are hired, and coaches start to work. Unfortunately, too often, coaches start their jobs without clearly defined roles or responsibilities. Without these, the coaching role often becomes a "catch all" position with quasi-administrative duties that may even include evaluating their colleagues, a role that only an administrator/supervisor should take.

We have also witnessed administrators/supervisors who hired a coach because that individual had good student assessment data, more years of experience in education than their colleagues, or perhaps were a well-liked colleague. These hiring decisions, coupled with coaches who receive minimal training about the coaching role or direction for using their time and expertise, too often result in a coach who is not as skillful and effective as they can be. Our goal with this book is to help you be a truly successful instructional coach who helps teachers and school leaders to effectively use proven research- and evidence-based practices in their classrooms and schools in ways that benefit every student.

As you continue reading this book, you will encounter application exercises and reflection questions in each chapter focusing on the SFC coach role, and the end of each chapter features tips for virtual coaching. We recommend that you complete the exercises as you read each chapter, use any prior knowledge to respond to the reflection questions, and make adjustments as you gain new knowledge or insights. As previously discussed, major challenges exist for coaches in our schools. This book provides strategies to address these challenges. Still, as you begin your journey to becoming an SFC coach, you may struggle to find the support you need or fulfill the role as we are defining it. Despite these factors, we encourage you to use the tools, resources, processes, and skills as you can, applying them to your context and work to help accurately and clearly define your role. If you find yourself in a role that does not actually involve coaching, we believe you will still learn about some new tools, resources, processes, and skills that you can apply in other contexts.

Developing a well-defined list of coaching roles and responsibilities is the first and most important step in becoming an effective instructional coach because it brings clarity to the position at the onset. The primary role of coaches is to support the teachers and specialists they work with, either through one-to-one consultation and strategic problem solving about students' needs or by providing differentiated, sustained professional learning experiences to small groups such as a grade-level team, a department, or to the entire faculty. All forms of professional learning (PL) provided by a coach should be coupled with ongoing support, feedback, and modeling as needed.

Several models or approaches to instructional coaching are discussed. Some are specific to a program or initiative, whereas others are broad. Some models are highly contextualized and subject specific; others are inclusive of all subject areas and grade levels. The SFC model shares some attributes with other models or approaches; however, the overarching goal is to create a process for providing coaching support to teachers in real-world schools that are both effective and functional. SFC is designed to be flexible, versatile, and focused on meeting students' needs to improve academic outcomes. In fact, the original title for the SFC model was "Responsive Consultation" as you will read in Chapter 1. We understand from decades of coaching work that the SFC is responsive and can be adapted to any identified academic, social-emotional, or behavioral student concerns. This book introduces and describes many processes or strategies in future chapters, and these strategies are meant to be useful in real-world settings. For example, Chapter 6 introduces the SFC Collaborative Problem-Solving Process for coaches that is conducted across four phases. Based on the teacher's need, a coach might work through each phase as described, shorten time spent in one phase, or spend more time in another phase. It depends on the need(s) of the teacher!

REFLECTION

Before reading any further, take time to complete the following exercise.
    What is your definition of an instructional coach? Begin by writing down what you believe are critical attributes of the instructional coaching role. Then reflect on and synthesize what these critical attributes mean. Finally, summarize by writing your definition of an instructional coach in one to two sentences.

We define *SFC* as a cooperative, ideally collaborative, professional relationship with colleagues mutually engaged in efforts that help maximize every teacher's skills and knowledge to enhance student learning. This definition includes several keywords and phrases: "cooperative, ideally collaborative"; "professional relationship with colleagues"; "mutually engaged"; "maximize every teacher's skills and knowledge"; and "enhance student learning". The definition of instructional coaching you created might include one or more of these keywords or concepts. Over the past several decades, hundreds if not thousands of coaches have used the SFC model in their schools. We have found that all the keywords and phrases in our definition are essential and must be the focus of the work of a successful coach. Following is our rationale for including each component in the SFC model.

COOPERATIVE, IDEALLY COLLABORATIVE

SFC is not a hierarchical, expertise-based model. Rather, SFC coaches act as colleagues who work with and alongside their peers to influence student achievement. Teachers have full control over the coaching process—they can choose to work with a coach or not. Administrators/supervisors can encourage this collaborative partnership but cannot mandate it. We discuss in depth how administrators/supervisors can provide this kind of support and encouragement later.

PROFESSIONAL RELATIONSHIP WITH COLLEAGUES

Positive and trusting professional relationships are essential to successful coaching. These relationships are not social friendships (although that might sometimes be an outcome), nor do coaches and teachers have to share the same philosophical beliefs about how students should be taught or a classroom managed. A successful SFC coach is not judgmental or evaluative and is always focused on supporting evidence-based instructional practices to increase student outcomes.

MUTUALLY ENGAGED

Coaches and colleagues work together to identify a concern and collaboratively determine a plan to address that concern. The plan always includes the support that the teacher might need to successfully carry it out as well as detailing how the coach will support the successful implementation of the plan throughout the process. The SFC coach and teacher are equal players in the process.

MAXIMIZE EVERY TEACHER'S SKILLS AND KNOWLEDGE

The SFC coach provides differentiated, sustained support to every teacher based on their needs. A teacher requesting support from an SFC coach is always included in identifying the concern and determining any intervention or next steps. Shared decision making provides a sense of ownership, and teachers' willingness to alter an instructional practice or classroom procedure is increased because of their ownership. Change is hard. SFC coaches do not do things to teachers, they accomplish great things with teachers!

ENHANCE STUDENT LEARNING

Coaching can be challenging and demanding. Sometimes we are not sure what next steps to take or how to spend our time. Making all coaching decisions based on what is best for students is a guiding principle for SFC coaches.

REFLECTION

Before proceeding, take time to consider our SFC definition. Write down words, phrases, or examples for the following items and how each is directly affected by the role of the coach. You can do this in the form of a list, table, word map, or other creative manner of your choosing.

Cooperative

Ideally collaborative

Professional relationship with colleagues

Mutually engaged

Maximize every teacher's skills and knowledge

Enhance student learning

SFC coaches play a critical role in developing and delivering PL opportunities and providing ongoing assistance to support colleagues with successfully implementing evidence-based instructional practices with their students. Although the day-to-day responsibilities may vary for an SFC coach, based on the needs and demands of a particular setting, the focus of the work remains the same—to guide and support the planning and implementation of effective practices to support optimal student progress.

We worked with a school district that planned to implement the SFC model. We collaborated extensively with various stakeholder groups (i.e., administrators/supervisors, current instructional coaches, teachers) to develop a definition of the SFC role that would work for them. Following is the list of activities they envisioned for their SFC coaches:

- Organize and deliver personalized and sustained PL opportunities for various stakeholder groups.

- Guide and support stakeholders in the collection and analysis of data to guide instructional decisions that improve student outcomes.

- Work collaboratively with colleagues to support student needs and an equitable learning environment.

- Help facilitate 21st-century learning and technology integration.

- Assist various stakeholders with planning and implementing the delivery of the instructional programs with fidelity.

- Collaborate with teachers and leaders to develop and successfully implement action steps outlined in campus improvement plans.

- Model lessons and/or activities as requested by colleagues.

- Participate in professional development activities or meetings to learn from each other and explore relevant topics of interest.

- Expand coaches' knowledge base and, in turn, share effective, proven strategies with stakeholder groups.

- Be knowledgeable about local, state, and federal rules, regulations, and policies.

In addition to the roles and responsibilities, these stakeholders also developed a list to describe the roles in which an SFC coach should not engage during their time working in the coaching role.

- Administrator, supervisor, or evaluator of teachers

- Substitute teacher or classroom cover

- Interventionist or tutor

- Classroom teacher

- Playground, bus, cafeteria, or hall monitor

- Test administrator, monitor, or coordinator

- Chaperone for field trips or discipline referrals

Certainly, we are not saying that SFC coaches should never teach an intervention class, monitor a test, or supervise the hallways. This should not, however, be their main role or take up a significant amount of time that should be allocated for coaching. Some teachers will view coaches as more credible when they are actively engaged in teaching. This seems reasonable provided there is sufficient time protected for the actual coaching role. If an SFC coach takes on additional roles or duties that do not directly support a teacher to enhance their students' learning, then you end up with what teachers may perceive as simply another administrator or teacher. If this happens, you really do not have someone working as a coach, despite their title. We have firsthand experience to show that when an SFC coach is able to commit to a clear set of responsibilities, relationships with teachers flourish, trust is established, and the coach is readily available to provide differentiated, sustained professional development and learning.

CONCLUSION

If the role of the SFC coach seems like a good fit for your work and you would like to learn more, we are ready to proceed! We believe the information provided in this book will help you feel more confident about your role as a coach and more effective in providing coaching services to your colleagues. Chapter 1 provides an overview of instructional coaching and discusses why coaching is valuable. We also discuss the SFC model in more detail. The remaining chapters are the true how-to guide for success as an SFC coach. Chapter 2 describes how to successfully get started as an SFC coach, and Chapter 3 further describes the Facilitator role. We next discuss the essential skills of coaching, including communication for collaboration (Chapter 4), time management (Chapter 5), and using collaborative problem solving in the Collaborative Problem-Solver role (Chapter 6). Chapters 7 and 8 address team problem solving and gathering information for problem solving, and Chapter 9 focuses on developing and implementing effective interventions. Chapter 10 discusses the third role of SFC coaches—Teacher/Learner—and describes how to design and provide effective PL. Chapter 11 focuses on effective instruction and intervention, including how coaching can fit into a multi-tiered systems of support/response to intervention (MTSS/RTI) framework, because the whole point of coaching is to support the successful implementation of evidence-based instructional practices. Chapter 11 also provides a framework for sustained school success called SAILS. We devote Chapter 12 to our partners in successful coaching—the administrators/supervisors—and include resources for successful coaching.

We look forward to being on this journey with you! See you in Chapter 1.

Note: This book builds on earlier work by Jan Hasbrouck and Carolyn Denton, including *The Reading Coach: A How-to-Manual for Success* (2005) and *The Reading Coach 2: More Tools and Strategies for Student-Focused Coaches* (2010). Although the framework of the SFC model remains the same, including some of the strategies and processes described here, this new book incorporates all that we have learned since 2012 as SFC has been implemented in schools across the country and internationally. In addition, research and ideas for successful coaching that have been developed over this period are included. We look forward to sharing this updated and expanded version of SFC with you in the coming chapters!

REFERENCES

Hasbrouck, J., & Denton, C. (2005). The reading coach: A how-to manual for success. Sopris West Educational Services.

Hasbrouck, J., & Denton, C. (2009). The reading coach 2: More tools and strategies for student-focused coaches. Sopris West Educational Services.

To the many students and colleagues I've worked with over the past 30 years at the University of Oregon, Texas A&M University, and in the many schools and districts around the United States who helped shape and refine the Student-Focused Coaching model. My profound thanks.

—*Jan*

Each day I am sincerely blessed with opportunities to engage in conversations with colleagues and family members to learn, teach, inspire, or be inspired; to be a collaborative thought partner; and to understand or appreciate others' perspectives. I am sincerely grateful to everyone who has been part of or supported me throughout my life's journey and want to give a special thanks to Jan for believing in me and giving me this opportunity to be her coauthor!

—*Daryl*

1

Overview of Coaching

Before reading this chapter, consider the following questions. Jot down some notes on your current understanding, and then at the end of the chapter, we will revisit these questions to assess the knowledge and insight you gained during your reading.

- How might a coach affect teacher development and student learning?

- What challenge(s) might a coach face?

- What goal(s) might you set for yourself as a coach?

- How might a campus administrator support a coach?

APPLICATION EXERCISE

List three verbs to describe the work of a coach. Then, in your own words, summarize what each verb means to you and how it will be reflected in your coaching (e.g., deliver: deliver differentiated, sustained professional development [PD] and learning targeting the needs of each teacher).

Here you are—ready to begin your learning journey into Student-Focused Coaching (SFC)! We are excited that after careful reflection during the introduction of this book, you are willing to take on this challenging, yet rewarding role. You probably have heard about coaching or maybe have direct experiences with it. Perhaps you have been coached by someone yourself, which may have been a valuable or positive experience. Some of you reading this book will already be experienced, veteran coaches. Some of you are stepping into this new role with only a vague understanding of what the coaching role entails.

We want to be clear from the start: Coaches do not just attend meetings, compile assessment data, make copies or organize materials, unpack shipments, or meet with the principal. The role of an instructional coach, if clearly defined and well executed, is hard work, and every minute counts. Successful coaching requires a great deal of planning, communicating, building relationships, working with all types of adults, and remaining positive even when facing inevitable challenges.

WHAT IS THE PURPOSE OF COACHING?

If coaching is this hard and potentially frustrating, then why even consider it? The answer is that the rewards of being a coach are worth it. Coaching is all about helping every teacher be as successful as possible so that every student achieves success. We can all agree that teaching is hard work, and we also know that high-quality instruction can make a lifelong impact on the success of students, with demonstrated academic, social-emotional, and even economic benefits. International, evidence-based research indicates that quality teachers and teaching (Chetty et al., 2014; Jackson, 2016) that are supported by strategic teacher professional development (PD) (Rowe, 2003) are what matters most for student success.

Professional Development

Providing coaching to teachers has become a widely used and effective way to provide strategic PD to teachers and specialists in schools (Kraft et al., 2018). PD for educators can be described as specialized training, formal education, team development, and more intended to help administrators, teachers, or other educators improve their professional knowledge, competence, skill, and effectiveness (Great Schools Partnership, 2014). PD might include taking college or university courses, participating in online webinars, attending conferences or workshops, or reading relevant resources. These options often inspire, motivate, and energize a teacher to try implementing new ideas based on this acquired knowledge. All these various PD formats can and do play a valuable role in supporting high-quality teaching; however, there is a clear downside to these traditional formats. Although PD can result in growth for the teacher, these traditional methods of providing PD are unlikely to alter the culture of an entire school or a classroom (Fullan, 2007). PD alone rarely results in sustained improved practice.

Professional Learning

Professional learning (PL) shares attributes with PD; however, PL focuses on "ownership over compliance, conversation over transmission, deep understanding over enacting rules and routines, and goal-directed activity over content coverage" (Martin et al., 2014, p. 147). PL might include reading and discussing professional literature, analyzing data with colleagues, or collaboratively planning curriculum. Teachers' effectiveness can steadily improve with effectively designed and implemented PL because of the shared depth and understanding of their work—to improve student learning. PL coupled with PD can optimally ensure continuous learning as an individual and with colleagues. Combining professional development and learning (PDL) addresses individual student needs across the school and encourages teachers to, "keep challenging and stretching [themselves] and each other to create the maximum benefit for all students" (Fullan & Hargreaves, 2016, p. 6). More details about effective PDL are provided in Chapter 10.

Professional Development and Learning and the Student-Focused Coach

What does PDL have to do with a Student-Focused coach? High-quality instructional coaching can provide the onsite, job-embedded, sustained PDL for individuals and groups that really makes a difference. Coaches have specific expertise and can assist individuals and groups of teachers to gain the knowledge and skills needed to improve instruction and student outcomes. Skillful, knowledgeable, trained, and well-supported SFC coaches can deliver an optimal form of PDL because SFC integrates two essential components—targeted support for individuals and groups that is sustained over time (Guskey, 2003; Ingvarson et al., 2005; U.S. Agency for International Development, 2014).

The PDL provided by SFC coaches has these characteristics:

- Content is based on evidence- and research-based best practices.

- Coaching efforts focus on student learning.

- Teachers have a voice in the development of PDL.

- PDL is collaborative, experiential, interactive, and engaging.

- Opportunities exist for reflection and inquiry.

- Content connects to the educators' day-to-day work with students, as well as to a larger plan for school improvement.

REFLECTION

What do you think about the list of characteristics of effective PDL? Reflect on each. Are there other things you would add to this list?

Write down ways in which you have attempted to enhance and improve your own professional practice. Did any result in positive and sustained changes in your classroom that resulted in improved student outcomes? Why or why not?

WHAT IS INSTRUCTIONAL COACHING?

Providing effective, strategic PDL to teachers that ultimately results in improved student outcomes is the overarching purpose of coaching. What should this strategic PDL actually look like when implemented in real-world school settings?

If we stopped some average people on the street and asked them if they had ever heard of someone who works in schools who is called a coach, we are guessing most people would say, "Sure! Basketball coaches, right? Or football coaches?" Or gymnastics, baseball, or even cheerleading. It would not surprise any of us to hear this response. Few people outside of schools have heard about the role of the academic coach—even though it has been a role in some schools for at least a few decades. If we went on to ask these same people to speculate about what someone who is called an instructional coach might do in schools, then they would likely suggest that these coaches watch teachers teaching lessons and give the teachers feedback, or they might hypothesize that coaches provide guidance and support to other teachers to help them provide the best possible instruction to students. And, of course, they would be right. This description seems like a common sense, practical view of the role of an instructional coach. As the coaching role has grown and expanded, however, we should recognize that there are other things that coaches are frequently asked to do with their time.

In fact, the number and types of tasks that coaches perform vary greatly (Denton & Hasbrouck, 2009; Deussen et al., 2007; Kraft et al., 2018; Scott et al., 2012). Although the fundamental purpose of instructional coaching should always be related in some way to PDL, several different approaches to coaching have been implemented in schools. We describe four of these approaches, or models, of coaching. As you read, think about the pros and cons of each if they were implemented in your real-world setting.

Four Models of Coaching

The four models of coaching discussed here are technical coaching, problem-solving coaching, reflective practice coaching, and peer coaching. We certainly recognize that this list is not exhaustive or complete. We are not recommending, or discouraging the use of, any of these models of coaching. We simply have observed these four different processes being used in schools to provide coaching services.

Technical Coaching   The primary function of the coach in the technical coaching model is to assist teachers in the accurate and high-quality implementation of a specific program or strategy (American Institutes for Research, 2004). Technical coaching is often used to support and extend training that has been previously provided to teachers in seminars or workshops. The relationship between the technical coach and the teacher is that of an expert and a novice.

For example, a school might adopt a new math curriculum or a new computer-assisted intervention program and hire coaches to provide support for teachers using these new materials. These technical coaches receive significant training to become highly knowledgeable about those materials or strategies. Their coaching is focused on helping their colleagues successfully implement them. Technical coaches can play an important and valuable role in achieving successful outcomes when educators use well-designed, research-supported materials with fidelity.

REFLECTION

Write down possible pros and cons of the technical coaching model.

Problem-Solving Coaching   Problem-solving coaching involves having the coach work with one or more colleagues to address specific concerns such as, "Malique is struggling with phonics," "Rory isn't making progress because he is so often off-task during our instructional time," or "There are a bunch of students in my fourth-period science class that can't write a report without a lot of help from me." Problem-solving coaching can address issues or concerns related to a single student, a small group of students, or even an entire class.

The basis for the problem-solving model of coaching in schools comes primarily from research that was conducted in the fields of school psychology and special education. Practitioners in both professions are frequently called on to collaborate with or advise colleagues about the academic, behavioral, and/or social-emotional concerns of a student. The process—typically called *consultation* in the research literature—has been studied since the 1970s as a triadic (three participants), indirect service delivery model in which a consultant (e.g., special educator, school psychologist, reading specialist) works with and through a consultee (often a general education classroom teacher or parent) to improve the outcomes of a client (usually a student with some learning, behavioral, or emotional challenges). Sometimes consultation can be collaborative; the consultant and the consultee pool their respective knowledge and skills to jointly attempt to solve the concern. Or, consultation can be more prescriptive, in which the consultant provides expert guidance to direct the resolution of the problem. The process has been studied extensively by researchers (Erchul & Sheridan, 2008; Idol et al., 1995; Kampwirth & Powers, 2016). The process of school-based consultation mirrors much of the work of coaches (Denton & Hasbrouck, 2009).

REFLECTION

Write down the possible pros and cons of the problem-solving coaching model.

Reflective Practice Coaching   When the primary function of a coach is to help teachers become more aware of thought processes surrounding their own instructional decision making, the coach is likely using strategies from the reflective practice model of coaching. Cognitive Coaching, developed by Costa and Garmston (1993) in the 1980s, is probably the most widely implemented version of this model. In this model, coaches receive extensive formal training in the cognitive coaching strategy, in which the coach serves as a mediator who initially works to establish rapport with the person being coached. The person receiving coaching is viewed as a trustworthy colleague, not someone who needs to change or be fixed in some way. The coach observes a teacher delivering a lesson and then meets, sometimes in a series of meetings, to encourage the teacher to reflect on the quality of their teaching. Having teachers keep a journal of their reflections is encouraged.

REFLECTION

Write down possible pros and cons of the reflective practice coaching model.

Peer Coaching   Peer coaching is likely the best known of all coaching models. Many acknowledge Beverley Showers and Bruce Joyce as the originators of the term *peer coaching.* These researchers started to look at coaching in the 1970s, exploring the hypothesis that schools could improve, and students benefit, if teachers provided each other with on-site guidance, support, and feedback. Their peer coaching process started by having teachers attend weekly seminars to study the teaching process. These seminars were followed up by encouraging teachers to watch each other teach and then discuss and share their ideas and reflections.

In 1996, after nearly 20 years of research on this process, Showers and Joyce reflected on what they had learned. A key conclusion they reached was that teachers should not provide verbal feedback to each other. Showers and Joyce's research clearly showed that when teachers used technical feedback techniques following an observation, it was difficult to prevent coaching from slipping into something that looked and felt like supervision, and the collaborative activity among the participating teachers was impaired rather than enhanced. Showers and Joyce continued to recommend that teachers have the opportunity to watch each other teach; however, they suggested that the debriefing after the observation should not include feedback. Rather, the observing teacher should simply comment on what they learned and how they might use what they learned in their own classroom. These researchers also found that a key to effective coaching involves teachers collaboratively planning lessons and developing support materials and instructional activities.

REFLECTION

Write down the possible pros and cons of the peer coaching model.

What are your thoughts on the recommendation that coaches not provide verbal feedback following an observation?

After reading about these four coaching models, which most closely resembles the coaching you have seen provided in schools?

HOW STUDENT-FOCUSED COACHING CAME TO BE

We asked you to identify possible pros and cons for each of the four models of instructional coaching presented in this chapter. Each model clearly has some positive aspects that would benefit teachers. SFC has evolved since the 1990s and combines elements of all four of the previously discussed models. SFC is very much rooted in the real world and based on real-world needs.

Jan Hasbrouck suddenly became a reading coach with no guidance, support, or training—likely a situation with which many of you can relate. In 1985, Jan was asked to leave her position as a reading specialist, her job for the past 15 years, and take on a new role that was vaguely described to her as "someone who would work with the other reading specialists in the district to help them . . . well, you know. Help them!" Her new role started the following Monday, and it soon became evident to Jan that 1) this role was completely different from teaching struggling readers and 2) she did not really know where to start or how to be helpful to her colleagues. She knew she needed help.

Jan learned that there were courses being offered to graduate students in education at the University of Oregon on school consultation. *School-based consultation* is generically described as a process involving a consultant (typically a special educator or school psychologist) and teachers as an effort to promote success in students who are struggling. The process is voluntary, and the consultant serves as a resource for ideas and suggestions rather than the provider of a solution. All participants are considered equally valuable and necessary in the process. There was a shared sense of ownership of the problem, the goals for the student, and the intervention developed to achieve the goals, which results in a greater likelihood of the teacher making changes to their practice. The personalized and sustained guided support provided by the consultant during the intervention implementation helps ensure that new skills can be adequately learned and used again in future situations (Denton & Hasbrouck, 2009; Erchel & Sheridan, 2014). Consultation has been extensively studied and found to be effective in not only successfully addressing the targeted concern of the client (the student) but also strengthening the skills of the teacher and thereby preventing similar problems in the future (Sheridan & Cowan, 2004).

The consultation courses Jan took proved to be very valuable and insightful to her, and she soon entered the doctoral program at the University of Oregon to study the consultation process more in depth. While there, she worked with her colleagues to develop the initial version of SFC, a process they originally called *Responsive Consultation* (RC; Hasbrouck, 1991; Hasbrouck & Garrison, 1990). The RC model drew heavily on the problem-solving strategies often used in educational consultation as an effective way to both improve student's outcomes (behavioral, academic, social-emotional) and, in the process, strengthen the knowledge and skill set of the consultee (teacher). The RC model continued to evolve and develop. It was later used in research conducted at Texas A&M University (cf. Hughes et al., 2001) in a process called *Responsive Systems Consultation* (RCS).

Around this same time, Jan, in collaboration with Carolyn Denton, began to think about how the RC/RCS model could work as a process to provide coaching to teachers. Jan and Carolyn incorporated research on peer coaching and effective PD strategies (Gulamhussein, 2013) into the original RC/RCS model, along with strategies from technical coaching. The model was now called SFC and continues to evolve and improve with the insight and expertise of Daryl Michel.

STUDENT-FOCUSED COACHING

In the Introduction, we defined *SFC* as a cooperative, ideally collaborative, professional relationship with colleagues mutually engaged in efforts that help maximize every teacher's knowledge and skills to enhance student learning. We described a few of these words and phrases in the Introduction and now want to dig a bit deeper into this definition. There are a lot of important words included here, and all are essential to understanding SFC.

We start with the last four words of the definition because this is the focus of our work: *to enhance student learning.* As you perhaps have experienced or can already see based on what you have read so far, coaching can sometimes seem quite complex and even intimidating to provide (and at times unpleasant to receive). Coaching can sometimes feel awkward and uncomfortable when, for example, you are coaching a veteran teacher, perhaps one who has more experience than you. Another challenge coaches face is working with colleagues who have a different philosophy about teaching or a negative attitude about some of their students or the families of those students. You will find that not every teacher is eager to work with you in your coaching role. At these times, it helps to keep in mind that coaching is not about you, and it is not about your colleagues.

Bottom line, coaching is about the students.

Sure, the coach works directly with teachers to help them implement effective instruction, but the only reason coaches care about making that happen is because coaching ultimately benefits students. We have found that keeping students' needs at the heart of your coaching can help you during those inevitable moments of discomfort or awkwardness to refocus onto that essential purpose of SFC—coaching is about the kids.

Professional relationship is another key phrase in our definition of SFC. Coaching cannot occur outside of some kind of professional relationship. When you work with other teachers as a coach, you may have the opportunity to work with someone who is, or who may become, a personal friend. More often, you may be working with a peer colleague (or administrator/supervisor) you barely know. At times—we hope they are rare—you may even find yourself working with a person with whom you have a tense, uncomfortable relationship. When these awkward, uncomfortable moments happen, take a deep breath and remember that coaching is about the students and not about making friends or having a good time with a fellow teacher. All of us who have taken on a coaching role sometimes need to find a way to get past our own personal discomfort and resolve to complete the hard work despite differences. In Chapter 4, we discuss communication and relationship-building skills and provide specific suggestions and strategies for how to start and maintain professional relationships and deal with those inevitable challenging moments.

Coaching must be based on a relationship that is, at minimum, cooperative. This is a key point: You cannot provide coaching services to someone who does not want to cooperate with you. Coaching is simply not possible in those situations. If working with a coach is not a voluntary process, then it becomes something more like supervision than coaching. Ideally, by engaging in effective SFC coaching with a colleague, you can help change a minimally cooperative relationship into one that is at some point fully collaborative, in which you and your colleague are equally involved; equally trusting; equally respectful of each other's skills, knowledge, and experience; and equally committed to helping students. The powerful outcomes of collaboration are realized by first engaging in a cooperative process, with participants mutually engaged and mutually focused on helping students. We often talk about starting with a small spark of cooperation that can ultimately build into a roaring bonfire of collaboration. In Chapters 6 and 7, you will learn about the SFC Collaborative Problem-Solving Process that has been specifically developed to help build a collaborative professional relationship while also addressing students' needs and building skills and confidence in teachers.

When the SFC definition refers to *mutually engaged,* we are underscoring the fact that the SFC process is not directive or top-down, with the coach trying to fix the teacher or make teachers do anything. In fact, we often remind our SFC coaches of this reality: Coaches have no power and no authority. That statement is often met with both concern and relief. What we mean by this phrase is that coaches are no more powerful than their peer colleagues; they are teachers, not administrators, who are working in a different role. Instead of providing direct services to students, coaches partner with teachers to assist them with providing the best possible instruction and support to every student.

REFLECTION

There are three roles in which SFC coaches should engage: Facilitator, Collaborative Problem-Solver, and Teacher/Learner. When you think about each role, what do you picture yourself doing as an SFC coach? Write these ideas down and make any adjustments as you learn more about each role.

The Facilitator Role for SFC Coaches

SFC coaches are engaged in the Facilitator role when they

- Support effective, skillful teachers to continue to be successful

- Spend time building the all-important professional relationships that can get the coaching process started

- Help lead their school, district, or agency toward a commitment to the success of all students by supporting the successful implementation of systems of support, such as leadership teams

It is a legitimate use of some of an SFC coach's time to assist busy teachers with logistics (e.g., finding a missing workbook to accompany a lesson, tracking down assessment materials, helping with data entry or analysis, following up on a parent's request, locating an online patch for a software glitch). These efforts can be enormously valuable to a busy and hard-working teacher. Because coaching is an indirect service delivery model based on a collaborative professional relationship, the Facilitator role also covers the time a coach devotes to developing those relationships as well as working with administrators/supervisors and colleagues to help define the role of the coach.

Effective schools often use leadership teams to help harness the collective knowledge and wisdom embedded within their communities (Louis et al., 2010). Shared decision making about things such as school schedules, PDL, and resource allocation—both human and material—can have a positive impact on the outcomes of achievement and the overall feeling of trust within school climates (Montgomery et al., 2013). An SFC coach, in their role as Facilitator, can and should spend time supporting the successful implementation of systems of support, including leadership teams.

As vital as these tasks of the Facilitator role are, it is important that a coach not spend too much time in this role. Too much time spent doing these kinds of helpful tasks, as appreciated as they are, can turn the coach into an assistant or quasi-administrator and minimize the impact of coaching for teachers and, therefore, students. When engaged in the Facilitator role, the coach is not directly involved in providing PDL, which is the coach's primary purpose. We discuss the Facilitator role more fully in Chapter 3. There are two other valuable ways SFC coaches spend their time providing differentiated, sustained PDL.

The Collaborative Problem-Solver Role for SFC Coaches

The role in which we hope that SFC coaches will spend most of their time is the Collaborative Problem-Solver role in which an SFC coach employs the systematic, structured process called *SFC Collaborative Problem Solving* to work with teachers to address problems in the classroom that may be keeping students from making adequate gains. In this process, the coach leads the teacher—or a group of teachers—through a step-by-step process to carefully examine the issues related to the identified problem, collect and analyze relevant information to focus their efforts, develop goals, and come up with a targeted action plan (TAP). The TAP is then implemented by the teacher(s), with the coach providing support and guidance as needed. The effects of the TAP are evaluated, and next steps are determined.

The function of a coach in SFC Collaborative Problem Solving is to manage the process effectively and efficiently, but creating the TAP is a truly collaborative effort. Chapters 6 and 7 in this book describe the process in detail, and other chapters provide guidance on carrying out the process effectively and efficiently (see Chapters 8 and 9). We hope that the Collaborative Problem-Solver role will be the primary focus of SFC coaches' efforts because we have learned that there are three powerful and important outcomes of engaging in the SFC Collaborative Problem-Solving process:

1. It is an effective way to provide targeted and sustained PDL support to teachers.

2. It has the possibility of actually solving classroom-based problems that can result in improved outcomes for students (which is always our goal).

3. Participating in this process—when conducted effectively and efficiently—is the best way to build essential professional collaborative relationships.

The Teacher/Learner Role for SFC Coaches

The third role for SFC coaches is to provide more traditional PDL support to their teacher colleagues by sharing effective, proven strategies and supporting their successful implementation in the classroom. We have labeled this role Teacher/ Learner because we have found that the outcomes of coaching are significantly enhanced by presenting and maintaining the role of the SFC coach as a true peer colleague of teachers. Just the notion that coaches are there to provide PDL to their colleagues can imply so much that is incorrect—the coach is somehow smarter or more skilled than the other teachers, the coach has some mystical wisdom to bestow on the colleagues who are "just" classroom teachers, or the coach does in fact have some level of power and authority beyond that of teacher. The coaching role can imply a top-down, one-sided, expert/novice relationship that does not feel very equal or collaborative.

Certainly, taking on the role of the coach does not confer any kind of special power, nor does it come with a magic wand to solve every classroom problem—as much as we sometimes wish it did. The best and most effective coaches know that along with effectively providing differentiated, sustained PDL support as needed to their colleagues—teaching them better ways to help students—they must also remain grounded in their role as learners. Coaches have a responsibility to keep themselves well informed about the findings from high-quality, well-designed research and resulting best practice strategies. (Chapter 11 of this book is an overview of the research that a coach should know about effective instruction). Subsequently, coaches have a responsibility to help bring those ideas and strategies into full and successful implementation in their colleagues' classrooms.

The Teacher/Learner role comprises all those activities that involve planning and directly providing differentiated, sustained, and appropriately targeted PDL opportunities for teachers. This can include having the coach identify an article, book, or blog that is relevant to classroom instruction and organizing a study group or using a professional learning community (PLC) format for teachers to examine and learn from those materials. Presenting workshops or seminars focused on an issue or concern for which a group of teachers would like to have more information and resources (e.g., supporting struggling readers in content classes, learning to identify dyslexia and providing supports for students with dyslexia across the grades, offering resources to support and extend learning with a new math or science curriculum) would fall under the Teacher/Learner role. Such workshops or seminars could also be designed to target an area of concern that has been identified by the administrator/supervisor from examining assessment scores or other data sources. Coaches are also engaged in the Teacher/Learner role when they participate—alone or with one or more colleagues—in their own PDL, such as by reading current research on instructional best practices or attending webinars, workshops, or conferences. It is a professional responsibility of a coach to keep themselves well-informed and up to date on the information they are expected to share with their colleagues.

The Teacher/Learner role also includes those times when teachers request a coach to visit their classrooms, observe them teaching a lesson, and provide feedback. If you think this sounds like the peer coaching process that Showers and Joyce studied extensively and found to be ineffective, then you would be correct because it is definitely like that process of observing and providing feedback. The key difference here is the teachers requested that the coach observe them and provide constructive feedback. Coaches should always be open and prepared to offer this kind of valuable service. We discuss this process in more detail and provide some ideas for how to do this work in Chapter 10.

Other Roles for SFC Coaches

As we continue to note, we, like you, work in the real world. We are highly aware that no coach ever spends all their time engaged only in these three roles in school settings. Coaches—whether following the SFC model or not—are frequently asked to engage in other tasks that include administrative and managerial activities. Coaches may need to attend meetings; review or evaluate instructional materials; communicate with others via mail, e-mail, texts, or telephone; order and manage curriculum materials; and spend time completing forms, paperwork, and reports. Some coaches may also provide supervision to a paraprofessional or instructional assistant, student teacher, or volunteer. They may be asked to monitor students on the playground, in bus loading areas, in hallways, or in the cafeteria or auditorium. At times, a coach may need to serve as a substitute for a classroom teacher. Some coaches are also involved in directly teaching students on a regular schedule.

From time to time, every coach will need to perform some of these and numerous other additional tasks. This is part of the reality of working in a school setting. Engaging in these tasks—especially those that involve engaging with students—can be beneficial if they help teachers view the coach as one of them. We consider all these tasks to be outside of the coaching role, however, so any amount of time spent doing these tasks takes away from the limited time available for actual coaching. For optimal outcomes, keep your focus on the tasks involved in the roles of Facilitator, Collaborative Problem-Solver, and Teacher/Learner.

It is common that coaches are also asked to take on a role that borders on supervising teachers. Based on the research conducted on consultation and peer coaching, we strongly suggest that coaches never engage in supervision or contribute in any way to the formal evaluation of teachers. It is important for the success of coaching that coaches be aligned with teachers rather than administrators. Teachers must trust that coaches are their peers and their partners in helping students succeed. If teachers believe or even suspect that a coach is evaluating the quality of their teaching, and perhaps sharing that information with the principal, then those teachers will be much less likely to want to work with the coach. We understand that different field-based settings may take a different stance than we do; however, we must stress our firsthand experiences in multiple settings across the country. Circumstances in which a coach is seen as an evaluator almost always lead to a lack of trust and a strained professional relationship. We have learned, however, when an SFC coach is able to commit to a well-defined set of responsibilities, relationships with teachers flourish, trust is established, and the coach is readily available to provide differentiated, sustained PDL.

Unfortunately, many coaches are required to provide coaching as a top-down process in which coaches lead (sometimes unwilling) teachers to adopt a new set of practices to use in their classrooms, frequently using a coaching cycle (coaches observe a lesson after a preconference, followed by a postobservation conference) "repeated several times as the teacher advances toward mastery" (Gulamhussein, 2013, p. 37). This coaching cycle was adopted with little-to-no modification from the identical three-step process of clinical supervision used in teacher evaluations since the late 1970s (Littrell et al., 1979). The widely used coaching cycle is a reason many teachers feel that coaches are supervising or evaluating them, rather than providing valuable and relevant support. Teachers feel they are being supervised because they are being coached using a supervisory process. Again, SFC coaches can certainly use a coaching cycle process in the Teacher/Learner role if the teacher requests it. In Chapter 2, "Getting Started as an SFC Coach," we discuss more ideas about how to separate coaching from supervision. Chapter 5, "Managing Time," provides a tool for you to use to help monitor how you are spending your time across the three roles of SFC, including all the other tasks coaches are asked to do. Armed with that information, you can help focus your work appropriately: To engage in efforts that support teacher development to enhance student learning.

CHARACTERISTICS OF A GOOD COACH

Having read about what instructional coaching is and its purpose, we should spend a bit of time discussing an important question: "Who makes a good coach?"

REFLECTION

Before proceeding, write down your response to the question, "Who makes a good coach?" Include skills and knowledge that you believe a coach should possess.

Effective instructional coaching requires many skills and a wide breadth of knowledge. Skills such as communication, time management, problem solving, and goal setting; knowledge of educational research and how to translate it to educational practice; and how to design and implement effective instruction and PDL opportunities can be learned. Our hope is that this book will help you strengthen some of your skills and knowledge in these specific areas.

In addition, most people who become instructional coaches should also bring a certain level of teaching experience to the table. Research has not identified a minimum (or maximum) number of years' experience that a teacher should have before considering taking on a coaching role. Common sense would suggest that having some level of teaching experience would be valuable for a prospective instructional coach, both to build up your self-confidence and expand your professional toolkit of strategies and experiences. A coach should be someone who becomes better at their professional craft over the years; we all hope that our 10th year of teaching is better than our first year of teaching.

Other aspects of being a coach are less tangible, however, and may include skills that would be considered more like innate personality traits and a working style that are less amenable to change. These may be characteristics that anyone who is considering taking on the role of instructional coach needs to possess before receiving training. These characteristics could include, but are not limited to, being comfortable and enjoying working collaboratively with other adults, possessing empathy, being resourceful and resilient, persevering through challenges, and being self-aware. The ability to forgive easily—both yourself and others—is helpful. And having a good sense of humor is always a plus.

GOALS FOR STUDENT-FOCUSED COACHING

This book is designed to help you develop or deepen your skills as a coach so that you may work confidently and effectively to build professional relationships with colleagues and help them work successfully with every student. As you engage in these challenging and important efforts, we encourage you to stay focused on four broad goals that are aligned with our definition of the SFC model.

Goal 1: Enhance Student Learning

Although coaching can be a powerful way to provide effective PDL support to teachers, the SFC model always focuses on the needs of students. SFC coaches work to help teachers, parents, and everyone in the system use the best possible strategies and support to help every student successfully achieve their academic, behavioral, and social-emotional potential. That is the number one goal of our work. (*Note:* Throughout this book, we use the term *family engagement* [Mapp, 2016] to describe the involvement of family or families that include any adult caregiver [e.g., biological parents, foster parents, grandparents, siblings] who takes care of children.)

Goal 2: Maximize Every Teacher's Knowledge and Skills

SFC coaches understand that the purpose of coaching is to provide PDL support to their teacher colleagues. SFC coaches know that coaching can be provided through three different roles: Facilitator, Collaborative Problem-Solver, and Teacher/Learner. Each coaching encounter is unique. The SFC coach uses the three SFC roles as appropriate to respond to the unique needs of each colleague at that moment and helps their colleague provide the most effective instruction and support to their students and those with whom they will work in the future.

Goal 3: Learn From Each Other

The SFC model of coaching is based on a process that requires at least minimal cooperation and hopefully becomes a truly collaborative partnership. SFC coaches are responsible for sharing what they know and continuing to learn with their colleagues to help teachers provide the best possible instructional support to all their students and strive to achieve Goal 1: enhance student learning. We want our teacher colleagues to learn from us, but SFC coaches know that the most effective coaching is not a process that moves only in one direction. The most successful SFC coaches accept the fact that they do not know everything (no one ever does) and do not see themselves as responsible for fixing every classroom problem. Successful SFC coaches are always open to learning from and alongside their colleagues. The focus of SFC is not the coach or the teacher. The focus is how we can help students and become even better at our own important work.

Goal 4: Prevent Future Problems

A coach can do far more than simply help a teacher improve a single student's learning. A coach can help build teachers' understanding, knowledge, skills, competence, and confidence so they will be better prepared to handle similar concerns in the future. At the school level, a coach can also help identify and address broader concerns such as a group of teachers who may need PDL in a specific area, students from one grade level who are showing academic concerns that could have been addressed in previous grades, or gaps in curriculum materials that should be considered to reduce and/or prevent problems.

THE ESSENTIAL PARTNER TO SFC COACHES: THE ADMINISTRATOR

We would be remiss in ending this chapter describing the work of the SFC coach without discussing the role of the administrator/supervisor, who is the essential partner to successful coaching. The role of an instructional coach is implemented in schools in different ways, some more successful than others. It sometimes seems like trying to establish the role of an onsite PDL specialist can be compared with building an airplane while it is in flight. Coaches cannot work alone—the very nature of their job requires collaboration with peer colleagues and support from their administrator/supervisor, often a principal. It is essential for administrators/supervisors who work with coaches to take the time to learn as much as possible about this exciting and challenging role. Chapter 12, "Working With Administrative Partners," is devoted to this essential partnership.

COACHING IN THE REAL WORLD

We want to assure you once again that we work in real-world settings and understand that you do too. Schools are complex and challenging environments. Most teachers and administrators/supervisors are aware of students who come to school with little preparation for learning, live in highly stressful situations at home, or have negative attitudes about their own abilities to be successful. These realities are sometimes made worse by inadequate instructional materials, lack of support for high-quality PDL efforts, philosophical differences about how students should be taught, and more.

We want to begin our work together by acknowledging these realities with these wise words, "It goes without saying that there never was, isn't now, and never will be enough time, money or trained personnel to do the hard work that schools have undertaken" (Kroth & Edge, 2007, p. vii). At first glance, this might sound like a statement of surrender—the job of teaching students is a lost cause without enough time, money, or help. Yet, the message of Kroth and Edge that we take to heart is this: We simply cannot use the lack of these resources as excuses, or we will become too discouraged to keep on trying to meet the needs of all of our students. We accept these realities and proceed with our work despite them. We cannot give up. Our job is critically important: To maximize every teacher's knowledge and skills to enhance student learning.

CONCLUSION

The role of the Student-Focused coach can be challenging, but it can also be an effective way to help provide teachers with the guidance and support they need and deserve to meet the needs of every student in their classes. The SFC model was developed from an extensive research base and has been successfully used in school settings for many years. Using the three roles of SFC coaches—Facilitator, Collaborative Problem-Solver, and Teacher/Learner—allows us to provide differentiated and effective coaching to every colleague. Adhering to this model can help ensure success for coaches in every school setting, and the remaining chapters provide a range of tools and strategies to help make coaching a success.

Before proceeding to the next chapter, complete the form in Appendix 1.1 to assess your current understanding of the SFC model. Also, revisit your responses to the questions at the start of this chapter and make any adjustments based on new knowledge or insights gleaned, and take time to make any changes or updates to the application exercise.

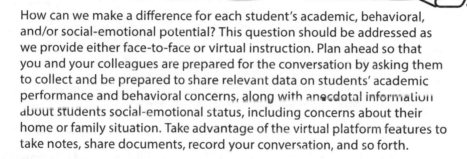

VIRTUAL COACHING TIP

How can we make a difference for each student's academic, behavioral, and/or social-emotional potential? This question should be addressed as we provide either face-to-face or virtual instruction. Plan ahead so that you and your colleagues are prepared for the conversation by asking them to collect and be prepared to share relevant data on students' academic performance and behavioral concerns, along with anecdotal information about students social-emotional status, including concerns about their home or family situation. Take advantage of the virtual platform features to take notes, share documents, record your conversation, and so forth.

REFERENCES

American Institutes for Research. (2004). *Conceptual overview: Coaching in the professional development impact study* [Unpublished manuscript].

Chetty, R., Friedman, J. N., & Rockoff, J. E. (2014). Measuring the impacts of teachers II: Teacher value-added and student outcomes in adulthood. *The American Economic Review, 104*(9), 2633–2679.

Costa, A. L., & Garmston, R. J. (1993). Reflections on cognitive coaching. *Educational Leadership, 51*(2), 57–61.

Denton, C. A., & Hasbrouck, J. (2009). A description of instructional coaching and its relationship to consultation. *Journal of Educational and Psychological Consultation, 19*(2), 150–190.

Deussen, T., Coskie, T., Robinson, L., & Autio, E. (2007). *"Coach" can mean many things: Five categories of literacy coaches in Reading First* (Issues & Answers Report, REL2007-No.005). U.S. Department of Education, Institute of Sciences, National Center for Education Evaluation and Regional Assistance, Regional Laboratory Northwest Projects.

Erchel, W. P., & Sheridan, S. M. (2014). The state of scientific research in school consultation. In W. P. Erchel & S. M. Sheridan (Eds.), *Handbook of research in school consultation* (pp. 3–17). Routledge.

Fullan, M. (2007). Change the terms for teacher learning. *National Staff Development Council, 28*(3), 35–36.

Fullan, M., & Hargreaves, A. (2016). *Call to action: Bringing the profession back in.* Learning Forward.

Great Schools Partnership. (2014). *Glossary of education reform*. Author.

Gulamhussein, A. (2013, July-August). The core of professional development. *American School Board Journal, 36–37.*

Guskey, T. R. (2003, April 21–25). *The characteristics of effective professional development: A synthesis of lists* [Paper presentation]. The 84th Annual Meeting of the American Educational Research Association, Chicago, IL, United States.

Hasbrouck, J. E. (1991, April). *Solving problems through responsive consultation: A strategy that works* [Paper presentation]! The meeting of the Council for Exceptional Children, Atlanta, GA, United States.

Hasbrouck, J. E., & Garrison, M. (1990, October). *Responsive consultation for solving classroom-based concerns* [Paper presentation]. The meeting of the Council for Learning Disabilities, Austin, TX, United States.

Hughes, J. N., Hasbrouck, J. E., Serdahl, E., Heidgerken, A., & McHaney, L. (2001). Responsive systems consultation: A preliminary evaluation of implementation and outcomes. *Journal of Educational and Psychological Consultation, 12,* 179–201.

Idol, L., Paolucci-Whitcomb, P., & Nevin, A. (1995). The collaborative consultation model. *Journal of Educational and Psychological Consultation, 6*(4), 329–346.

Ingvarson, L., Meiers, M., & Beavis, A. (2005). Factors affecting the impact of professional development programs on teachers' knowledge, practice, student outcomes and efficacy. *Education Policy Analysis Archives, 13,* 1–26.

Jackson, C. K. (2016). *What do test scores miss? The importance of teacher effects on non-test score outcomes* (No. w22226). National Bureau of Economic Research.

Kampwirth, T. J., & Powers, K. M. (2016). *Collaborative consultation in the schools: Effective practices for students with learning and behavior problems* (5th ed.). Pearson.

Kraft, M., Blazar, D., & Hogan, D. (2018). The effect of teacher coaching on instruction and achievement: A meta-analysis of the causal evidence. *Review of Educational Research, 88*(4), 547–588.

Kroth, R. L., & Edge, D. (2007). *Communicating with parents and families of exceptional children.* Love Publishing.

Littrell, J. M., Lee-Borden, N., & Lorenz, J. A. (1979). A developmental framework for counseling supervision. *Counselor Education and Supervision, 19,* 119–136.

Louis, K. S., Leithwood, K., Wahlstrom, K. L., & Anderson, S. E. (2010). *Investigating the links to improved student learning: Final report of research findings.* University of Minnesota, Center for Applied Research and Educational Improvement.

Mapp, K. L. (2016). *Working with families and caregivers: Family engagement as a core element of effective practice.* Retrieved from http://www.teachingworks.org/images/files/2016_AACTE_Karen_Mapp.pdf

Martin, L., Kragler, D., Quatroche, K., & Bauserman, K. (2014). *Handbook of professional development in education: Successful models and practices, prek–12.* Guilford Press.

Montgomery, P., Ilk, M., & Moats, L. (2013). *A principal's primer for raising reading achievement.* Sopris West Educational Services.

Rowe, K. (2003). *The importance of teacher quality as a key determinant of students' experiences and outcomes of schooling.* Retrieved from http://research.acer.edu.au/research_conference_2003/3

Scott, S. E., Cortina, K. S., & Carlisle, J. F. (2012). Understanding coach-based professional development in Reading First: How do coaches spend their time and how do teachers perceive coaches' work? *Literacy Research and Instruction, 51,* 68–85. doi:10.1080/19388071.2011.569845

Sheridan, S. M., & Cowan, R. J. (2004). *Consultation with school personnel.* Department of Educational Psychology, University of Nebraska-Lincoln.

Showers, B., & Joyce, B. (1996). The evolution of peer coaching. *Educational Leadership, 53,* 12–16.

U.S. Agency for International Development. (2014, February). *The power of coaching: Improving early grade reading instruction in developing countries.* Author.

Self-Assessment Checklist for SFC Coaches

Name: _____

Date: _____

Please self-assess on the following statements by marking an X in the appropriate box.

1 = not at all   2 = somewhat   3 = quite a bit   4 = fully

		1	2	3	4
1	I understand the PURPOSE of instructional coaching and can accurately DESCRIBE it to others.				
2	I understand the Student-Focused Coaching (SFC) MODEL and can accurately DESCRIBE it to others.				
3	I understand the three ROLES in which SFC coaches engage—Facilitator, Collaborative Problem-Solver, Teacher/Learner.				
4	I understand my ROLE as an SFC coach and recognize the limitations of the role. I can accurately and concisely DESCRIBE my role as an SFC coach to others.				
5	I ENGAGE in all three ROLES in of SFC coaching: Facilitator, Collaborative Problem-Solver, Teacher/Learner as appropriate.				
6	I understand and work to achieve the four GOALS of SFC coaching: 1) enhance student learning, 2) maximize every teacher's skill and knowledge, 3) learn from each other, and 4) prevent future problems.				
7	I work to establish and maintain an effective PARTNERSHIP with my principal(s) and/or supervisor(s).				
8	I have strategies for ENROLLING colleagues into the coaching process.				
9	I make regular CONTACT with ALL my colleagues (using facilitator questions).				
10	I understand and use specific strategies to help establish and maintain trusting PROFESSIONAL RELATIONSHIPS with all types of colleagues.				
11	I can effectively DIFFERENTIATE coaching based on the needs/desires of my colleagues.				
12	I can plan and deliver effective professional development and learning SERVICES in multiple formats (one to one, small group, large group).				
13	I respect and protect the CONFIDENTIALITY of the coaching/colleague relationship.				
14	I have good verbal and nonverbal COMMUNICATION SKILLS. I can USE these skills proficiently in situations that are tense, high stakes, and/or unclear.				
15	I can skillfully make respectful, ASSERTIVE REQUESTS of colleagues ("Solution Sandwich").				
16	I understand and can use the SYSTEMATIC PROBLEM-SOLVING STRATEGY for collaborative planning effectively and efficiently.				

17	I understand and can effectively use the systematic TEAM PROBLEM-SOLVING strategy.				
18	I can accurately document and effectively manage my professional TIME as an SFC coach.				
19	I can assist a building/department to FOCUS on coaching/professional development efforts using multiple sources of data.				
20	I continue to extend and deepen my own professional KNOWLEDGE BASE.				

NOTES/COMMENTS:

Student-Focused Coaching by Jan Hasbrouck and Daryl Michel.

2

Getting Started as an SFC Coach

Before reading this chapter, consider the following questions. Jot down some notes on your current understanding, and then at the end of the chapter, we will revisit these questions to assess the knowledge and insight you gained during your reading.

- From your perspective, how is coaching similar to or different from supervising?

- How would you develop trusting relationships with colleagues and campus administrators/supervisors? How will you maintain the confidentiality of those seeking your support?

- As a coach, how will you clearly and unambiguously articulate one or more of your responsibilities to your colleagues?

- What is your plan for working with all colleagues, including those who are reluctant and resistant to those who are open and eager?

APPLICATION EXERCISES

As you develop your role as a coach you will need to 1) identify and communicate to your colleagues the knowledge or skills you have to offer, 2) determine strategies to use when communicating with colleagues who might be either resistant or eager to work with you, and 3) develop trusting relationships with colleagues and administrators/supervisors.

Create a personal coaching vision statement (i.e., what will you say when someone asks what you do) using your definition of coaching and the roles and responsibilities that you listed in the introductory chapter. Here are a few things to think about:

- Your personal coaching vision statement should be specific, concise, and succinct. For example, "I work collaboratively with colleagues by modeling or coteaching lessons; delivering differentiated, sustained PDL; observing classroom instruction and providing feedback; and using data to guide instructional planning. By collaboratively working with colleagues, I help to develop teacher knowledge that affects student learning."

- You should be able to describe what each responsibility means. For example, "I will plan and deliver differentiated, sustained PDL for colleagues and administrators/supervisors." This means that I will

  - Focus on campus or individual colleague's goals

- Use strategies such as modeling or coteaching a lesson, leading book or article studies, or fostering teacher collaboration during grade-level, department, or faculty meetings
- Guide teachers in digging deeper into one skill or concept over a period of time (e.g., learning about academic vocabulary during five consecutive weekly meetings)

INTRODUCTION

You are recognized as a person in your school or district who knows a lot about effective instruction. You have skills to engage collaboratively and positively with your colleagues. You may have assisted in a curriculum-selection process or served as a mentor to student teachers or a first-year classroom teacher. Perhaps you are a certified reading or math specialist. Now, your administrator/supervisor has tapped you for this new role—instructional coach. That sounds exciting, but how do you get started? This chapter is designed to help you with that process.

FOUNDATIONAL KNOWLEDGE FOR SFC COACHES

Coaches provide many services to their schools in instruction and leadership roles. Coaches do all the things listed next, along with a lot of other varied tasks (Dole, 2004; International Literacy Association, 2015; Lefevere-Davis et al., 2003; U.S. Agency for International Development, 2014):

- Observe teachers and provide feedback.
- Visit teachers' classrooms and model lessons.
- Review curriculum materials and make suggestions for adoption or for supplementing instructional resources.
- Participate as a member of the PLC and leadership team.
- Organize and facilitate teacher study groups to explore relevant topics of interest.
- Provide workshops to introduce teachers to new strategies and provide follow-up support for PDL.
- Help teachers with the organization and management of their programs in literacy, math, or other areas.
- Advise administrators/supervisors on how research applies to program policy decisions.
- Meet families who have concerns about their children.
- Conduct assessments and use the results to make instructional recommendations.

As discussed in Chapter 1, we have organized all the possible coaching tasks that an SFC coach might do into the three roles, including 1) Facilitator: supporting effective and skillful teachers to continue their success, building professional relationships, and helping to facilitate systems of support; 2) Collaborative Problem-Solver: using a strategic and structured process to work with teachers to address problems and concerns that arise in their classrooms; and

3) Teacher/Learner: sharing effective, proven strategies, methods, and techniques with groups of teachers through various PDL processes.

The decision regarding which role to use at any given moment is guided by the needs of the various participants at that time, determined through regular contacts with each teacher once your coaching work has begun, as well as data collected at the larger systems level. We walk you through the process of getting started as a coach and provide some strategies to make this process smooth and easy. Entry is the first step in this process.

Entry

The professional literature on coaching and consultation usually devotes some attention to the topic of *entry*, generally defined as how to get started in coaching or consulting in a school or district. *Entry* is usually defined as a process as opposed to an event. You cannot just stand up at a faculty meeting and announce, "I'm your new instructional coach and here's what I can do for you," and expect all the other teachers to flock to your door to seek your assistance with their classroom challenges. It is also important for your fellow teachers to not expect you to be walking the halls, politely asking whether they need anything and generally helping out wherever you can.

What Will You Do as an SFC Coach?

Clearly defining the role of instructional coach for yourself is the first and essential step to take in this ongoing entry process. In Chapter 1, we defined *coaching* broadly as a cooperative, ideally collaborative, professional relationship with colleagues mutually engaged in efforts that help maximize every teacher's skills and knowledge to enhance student learning. We also identified four goals for SFC coaches: 1) enhance student learning, 2) maximize every teacher's skill and knowledge, 3) learn from each other, and 4) prevent future problems. A coach who is new to the SFC model should spend some time thinking about this definition and list of goals, as well as any other guidelines available to define the role, such as a job description for your position or any district or state guidelines for the role of instructional coach.

You eventually want to be able to clearly articulate what you think the role of an SFC coach should be and how you plan to provide coaching services to your colleagues. You must be able to describe to your colleagues and administrators/supervisors

- The rationale for this role

- The coaching process

- The tasks you will be doing as a coach and the services you can provide

- How you will be spending your time during the school day

- How you can be contacted by a teacher who may want to work with you

You will also want to spend some time thinking about the kinds of tasks you will not be undertaking because coaches are often seen as the person who can address every student-related concern. Although most coaches wish they could solve each of those problems as they arise, it is unlikely that your time will allow for that.

What Will Your Colleagues Do?

It will also be helpful to have a clear understanding of what role your colleagues will play when they seek out your assistance as a coach. This will, in turn, help you to be clear about the coaching process as your role is introduced to them. For example, if you clarify coaching as a professional, cooperative process focused on helping students improve their learning, then your colleagues will better understand that meeting with you is not just a chance to vent or complain about challenging situations or share frustrations about other teachers or administrators. Coaching is not the correct venue for expressing dissatisfaction with a curriculum or lamenting the lack of in-service training to help address new challenges in the classrooms. Although such concerns may be relevant—and may indeed be discussed briefly (and professionally) as part of coaching—the focus must be on the students' learning needs. The entire coaching process should be driven as much as possible by objective data rather than the beliefs, frustrations, or assumptions of the participants.

Some of these issues will begin to come into sharper focus as you work through the remaining chapters of this book, which will help you to define and articulate how you want to work as an SFC coach to best serve the needs of students.

Defining Your Role With Your Administrator/Supervisor

Of course, you will not be able to define your role completely by yourself. As much as this may sound appealing (we all like to create and define our own jobs), it is critical to involve your administrator/supervisor early on in this process. It is entirely possible that your administrator/supervisor will ask you to take the lead in defining your role. Having an instructional coach in their building is new territory for most administrators/supervisors as well. If someone walks into a school building and announces to the administrator/supervisor that they are the new counselor, second-grade teacher, physical education coach, or seventh-grade science teacher, an administrator/supervisor generally knows what to expect from that person. When it comes time to evaluate this new staff member, the administrator/supervisor likely has guidance from experience and training and · can accurately and fairly judge whether that person is performing adequately in the assigned job. This might not be true when the new staff member is an instructional coach.

SFC coaches will also have to be supervised and evaluated. If an administrator/supervisor has never worked with or been an instructional coach before, then how will they be able to make these important decisions about a coach's performance? This will not be a serious problem in most cases. We know of at least one case, however, in which this issue was cause for some concern. A teacher who had previously held a more traditional role in a school, and had consistently received positive annual evaluations, was then moved into a new role as an instructional coach (with no specialized training, unfortunately). At the end of the year, the administrator believed this teacher's performance in her new role had been inadequate. The teacher was then given a negative evaluation and terminated. This is obviously an extreme case, and it would have been avoidable by engaging in a process such as the one we are describing here—to thoughtfully develop and share a clear description of the role of an SFC coach with your administrator/supervisor and hold ongoing discussions about the role and expectations for performance.

We developed an Evaluation Checklist for SFC Coaches that you and your administrator/supervisor may find useful. A copy is included in Appendix 2.1.

It is wise for a new instructional coach to take the lead in including the administrator/supervisor in the process of defining the role of coach. Ask your administrator/supervisor about some of the issues previously raised:

- What is your rationale for this new role?

- What is your understanding of the coaching process?

- How would you describe the process of coaching?

- Have you had previous experiences supervising an instructional coach? If so, what were those experiences like?

- What tasks do you envision that I will do as a coach, and how would you like to see me spending my time during the school day?

Some of these questions are complex and will not be completely addressed at a single meeting, and your role will continue to develop and evolve over time. As it does, remember to make time for another professional discussion with your administrator/supervisor about your role and how well they see you fulfilling it. Treat such meetings as professional discussions, not as time to advocate for more resources or lament about having too little time to do your work. As much as possible, bring any available relevant data to this meeting and treat it as a problem-solving activity (we provide a tool for tracking how you are spending your time in Chapter 5). Bringing this kind of data to meetings with your administrator/supervisor will help keep the conversation focused on your role. Keep these discussions focused, professional, and nondefensive. Use your best communication skills (see Chapter 4) and take detailed notes.

Coaching Versus Supervision

As you and your administrator/supervisor work to develop a clear definition of your role, one area that must be addressed directly is that although coaching often mirrors the process of supervision, it must be understood to be something completely different. As an instructional coach, your role is clearly different from the role of a more traditional teacher. The coaching process can begin to look a lot like the process of supervision, however, especially in the SFC Teacher/Learner role. Coaches sometimes observe a teacher conducting a lesson and then provide feedback to them about the quality of the instruction that was provided. On the surface, this looks much like the traditional process used in the formal evaluation of the teacher's classroom performance. It is critical for a coach (and the coach's administrator/supervisor and colleagues) to understand the subtle, yet significant, differences between coaching and supervision.

Although the processes of supervision and coaching do, in fact, appear at times to be nearly identical, there are at least three key differences. One difference is their purpose. A primary purpose of supervision is to provide information so a supervisor can make evaluative judgments: Is this teacher performing in a professionally competent manner? Should this teacher continue in the job or be reprimanded, possibly suspended, or terminated? Of course, an effective administrator/supervisor also works with teachers to help them improve their professional skills, but the key point is formal evaluation. Coaching, in contrast to supervision, is never about making evaluative decisions about professional competence. Coaching is providing targeted and supportive PDL that is always focused on improving the outcomes for students, not judging or evaluating teachers.

A second difference between coaching and supervision is the requirement to be cooperative, which evaluations do not require. A coach must be invited to observe a lesson and then provide feedback to a teacher. If a teacher is not willing to cooperate and engage with a coach, then coaching cannot occur—period. Obviously, this is not the case when an administrator/supervisor arrives to observe a teacher. Although a teacher may have some control and input about when to be supervised, the option of not allowing the administrator/supervisor to watch a lesson being taught does not exist. Being certain that all participants are fully aware of these essential differences can help you avoid problems in the future.

A third way that supervision differs from coaching takes us into the legal arena. In most, if not all, states, administrators/supervisors who make decisions regarding the hiring or termination of employees must have specific training and certification. Administrators/supervisors who deal with human resources issues need to have essential knowledge of legal requirements in the area of personnel law as it pertains to their school district and state. They are required to have specific licenses or certification to legally conduct this work. Coaches, in most cases, do not have this training or certification. Even if you do have valid and current administrator/supervisor certification, that is not relevant when you are engaged in the role of coach. For your own legal protection and that of other teachers and administrators/supervisors, be sure there is a hard and fast line between supervision and coaching.

Some coaches do have duties and responsibilities that require them to work with teachers in a way that mirrors supervision. We consider that coaches in these situations are providing coaching plus supervision. We maintain that the coaching role itself should be defined as a voluntary peer-to-peer process that stays completely away from any part of the formal evaluation process. Once again, good, clear, and open communication will help reduce the chance of challenging situations.

REFLECTION

What strategies can be implemented to ensure that coaching and supervision are not seen as synonymous terms?

The Cornerstones of Coaching: Trust and Confidentiality

The issue of confidentiality is one thing that will inevitably arise as a concern to instructional coaches. SFC coaches have opportunities to spend significant amounts of time in their colleagues' classrooms. They will observe what is happening in classrooms and hear teachers share concerns and frustrations. It is essential for your administrator/supervisor and your teacher colleagues to understand that your role as a coach precludes you from sharing any information—good or bad, positive or negative—about a teacher's performance that you may learn while providing coaching without the clearly stated permission of the teacher.

What follows is an example of how a coach can model the essential importance of confidentiality at all times by asking a teacher's permission to share some work they successfully completed.

Coach: Thanks for thinking through and helping to outline the intervention plan for Eric.

Teacher: You bet.

Coach: The scaffolding of skills is so important, and I think the interventionist will appreciate seeing and using this plan to organize explicit lessons.

Teacher: I agree. It's important that the interventionist who works with Eric understands the concepts that I'm teaching during Tier 1 instruction so that she can deliver targeted Tier 3 lessons with him.

Coach: Yes, it's really helpful to align our instruction to ensure we are meeting individual student needs.

Teacher: Yes, that makes so much sense.

Coach: I have meetings scheduled with a few teachers later this week to outline intervention plans. Would you mind if I typed up a summary of our conversation to share with these teachers along with the plan we created? I really think it would be helpful for other teachers.

Teacher: Sure, that's fine with me. I'm all for sharing tips with others.

Trust and confidentiality are cornerstones of coaching. As we have discussed, coaching can occur only within a cooperative professional relationship. As in all human interactions, a professional relationship must be built on trust and mutual respect. A coach perceived by teachers as a spy for the administrator or a gossip who talks about one teacher to another will soon be unable to provide coaching services at all.

Few, if any, teachers will want to open their classrooms and allow themselves to be observed if they do not believe the coach will maintain a sense of respect and privacy and a commitment to keeping all communications confidential, including information teachers may share with you about any of their students' families. Keeping the coaching process fully and completely confidential will also help maintain that strong boundary between coaching and supervision. We think of the work of an SFC coach as occurring within a protective bubble of confidentiality. Of course, behavior that is clearly abusive must be immediately reported in accordance with your school, district, or state regulations. We hope you never have any such experience in your coaching work, but it is far better to have at least considered the possibility in advance if an event should ever occur.

Keeping your coaching work fully confidential may seem easy to do, but keeping such a promise can be challenging in the real world of schools. Sometimes coaches are assigned to schools where they have previously worked in a different role. In such cases, the coaches are likely to have formed various kinds of relationships with others at the school—professional as well as personal. Perhaps one or more of the teachers is a close friend of the coach or maybe the coach and the administrator/supervisor have formed a friendship that extends beyond the school day. Yet, there may be a couple of teachers with whom the coach long ago got off on the wrong foot, and those relationships may have never improved. In either situation, the coach has a real challenge—restructuring some of these personal relationships into different professional relationships. There is certainly no reason to give up a friendship with a colleague just to take on the role of instructional coach, but it may mean that the content of some of the conversations will have to change. Although a couple of teachers or administrator buddies can vent frustrations and share experiences to each other about fellow teachers, a coach cannot do this because of professional ethics and to ensure that all colleagues with whom the coach works will be treated equally and professionally.

Enhancing student learning is another issue we must consider while we are discussing confidentiality. A coach is in a school to help every student get the best possible instruction and make the most progress as possible by providing PDL support to teachers. Instructional coaches working in school settings are considered mandated reporters. This term is used in the United States and many parts of the world to describe those who have regular contact with vulnerable people such as children and youth and are legally required to report to the proper authorities if neglect or abuse is observed or even suspected. Most of us are confident that we would recognize and have no hesitation reporting physical abuse. The question facing coaches is: What might rise to the threshold for reporting in terms of academic neglect or abuse? Or emotional abuse? What if, in your role as coach, you observe a teacher who is providing inadequate instruction to students? What if you consistently witness poor instruction? Or, no instruction? What if a teacher calls a student a derogatory name or rolls their eyes when a student asks a question? Should it be reported? If so, to whom? These are challenging questions with no clear answers. In taking on the role of SFC coach, it is important for you to have at least thought about these issues and, ideally, to have discussed such possibilities—and the steps to take in response to such observations—in advance with an administrator/supervisor.

REFLECTION

How will you demonstrate to colleagues that you can be trusted to keep conversations confidential?

Rules of Professional Ethics

Heron et al. (1996) suggested that professionals who work as consultants in schools develop a clear ethical framework to guide their decisions and behavior. The challenging professional environment of conflicting laws, regulations, and procedures and the often high emotions raised by complex issues, such as student academic success, make this a top priority for instructional coaches. This is compounded by the previously discussed axiom that there never was, never will be, and is not now enough time, money, or trained personnel to do the important work we undertake (Kroth & Edge, 2007). Some topics to consider when developing your own personal ethical framework include recognizing your professional limitations, needs, and strengths; confining practice to your own competence and limits of trying and preparation; ensuring that recommendations you offer as a coach have a solid empirical basis whenever possible; and keeping abreast of new PDL.

Heron and colleagues (1996) also discussed how personal values may at times contribute to unethical professional behavior. They cited an example that may be relevant to your work as a coach. What if coaches who are philosophically biased against direct instruction in phonics use their influence to coerce a colleague to reject phonics instruction for a student? Heron et al. contended that coaches must be sure to keep their values out of the coaching process and rely instead on data and well-validated research findings to guide their recommendations. They also suggested a set of questions a coach may use in a professional self-analysis that will lead to ethical professional behavior.

- *Will my actions produce the maximum benefit for all concerned?* Know the limits of your own training and experience, along with the reasonable time limits for meeting goals. Know when it is appropriate to request assistance from others or remove yourself from a situation in which you may be unable to offer appropriate services.

- *Will my actions communicate how I want others to behave toward me and other profes sional colleagues, families, and students?* Coaches must model appropriate, respectful, considerate, and professional behavior while engaging in coaching-related activities.

- *Does my daily professional practice adhere to local, state, or national standards for ethical behavior, laws, and policies?* (See Corey et al., 2014, for further guidance in professional ethics related to coaching.) As part of the series of conversations you will hopefully have with your administrator/supervisor to define your role, spend a few moments discussing issues related to professional ethics, as well as the procedures that must be followed about confidentiality.

Taking the time to thoroughly discuss and define your role with your administrator/supervisor is important, and the payoff for getting this right is enormous. We also recognize that not all administrators/supervisors are going to be willing partners in this effort. Some people are just easier to talk with than others. (Chapter 4 gives you some strategies and tools to help you deal with challenging conversations around your role as a coach.) We do recommend that you and your administrator/supervisor make time for conversations at least three times each year—the beginning, middle, and end of each year—to make plans and share expectations, adjust and recalibrate as needed, and debrief about how things went. Of course, on top of these three meetings, we hope all coaches and their administrator/supervisor have a lot of other conversations along the way.

Here is an example of a coach sharing her personal limitations with her administrator/supervisor.

Coach:	It is my understanding that the district purchased a new math curriculum that kindergarten teachers will implement next year. Is this true?
Administrator/supervisor:	Yes, we were told about this during our meeting last week.
Coach:	Will I have a role in supporting this new curriculum?

Administrator/supervisor:	Yes, we'll likely need you to attend the initial training and then provide support for teachers.
Coach:	This makes me nervous. I was a middle school teacher for 15 years and don't have any experience with kindergarten students. I've been the instructional coach at this elementary school for 2 years now, but I'm just not knowledgeable about kindergarten curriculum.
Administrator/supervisor:	Well, the kindergarten teachers will be new to this curriculum too, so you'll be learning the curriculum together.
Coach:	This makes me even more nervous. Not only am I unfamiliar with kindergarten curriculum, but I'm also unable to support them with this new curriculum.
Administrator/supervisor:	What do you propose that we do?
Coach:	I don't have a problem attending the training with the teachers; however, I do think it's important that the kindergarten team knows that I'm participating as a learner just like they are. I do want them to know that I'll do whatever I can to provide support when they start implementing this curriculum. Specifically, we can practice strategies when we meet, and I can go into classrooms to observe student behaviors to see how they are responding. A benefit of this will be that I can use the learner side of my SFC Teacher/Learner role.
Administrator/supervisor:	How about we set a time to talk with the kindergarten teachers and work together to set expectations for participating in and providing support when implementing this new curriculum?
Coach:	I'm already feeling less stressed. Thank you so much for this support. I want to reiterate that I'm here to do whatever I can to support our kindergarteners, but I also know my background knowledge and limits.

Introduction to Your Colleagues

You have now had an opportunity to think about your role as a coach and hopefully have a discussion (or perhaps a series of discussions) with your administrator/supervisor about defining your role. The next step is to share this clear role definition with your teacher colleagues. Your administrator/supervisor is the person who should take the lead. This introduction can happen at a meeting of the entire faculty, by e-mail, or perhaps both. Having the administrator/supervisor stand up in front of all the teachers and clearly state the purpose of your role as a coach, what tasks you will be doing and what you will not be doing in the role, what the expectations are for colleagues who work with the coach, and how to get in touch with you to begin the process.

Your administrator/supervisor brings the power and authority to this step. For example, in Chapter 12, in which we describe the optimal coach and administrator/supervisor partnership, we make a case for having your administrator/supervisor mandate that teachers share their most current student performance and assessment data with you, including students' grades. This introduction by your administrator/supervisor can play a big role in jump-starting a successful coaching process. We also hope that your administrator/supervisor fully embraces the concept of confidentiality in the coaching process and describes how that works to the teachers at this step.

Enrolling Colleagues in the Coaching Process

You have developed a clear vision of your role, and your administrator/supervisor and colleagues have heard about what great things you can do as an SFC coach. You might now be wondering if any of your colleagues are actually going to want to work with you in this role. We urge you not to panic or spend too much time worrying about this. Trust us on this one. There is a scenario that plays out for almost all instructional coaches. In the beginning, only a few teachers seek out their services. Then, usually around the middle of the year or so, the concern is the opposite. "I'm swamped with requests for my time! Help! Too many teachers want coaching! What should I do?" We offer suggestions for that second concern later in this book. For now, let's help you drum up some business.

We greatly admire the work of Dr. Jim Knight who has been identifying best practices for instructional coaching with his colleagues at the University of Kansas and the Instructional Coaching Group for many years. We have adapted his process for enrolling colleagues to help you take the next steps as a coach (Knight, 2007). We suggest using the following nine ideas to help encourage teachers to engage with you in your coaching role. Each suggestion is discussed in more detail in coming chapters.

1. *Be introduced by your administrator/supervisor.* As previously discussed, this is an important first step so your teacher colleagues have a clear understanding of your role and how to get in touch with you to start the process. Because the role is introduced by the administrator/supervisor, it comes with some authority.

2. *Hold regular, planned one-to-one conversations with every teacher (part of the Facilitator role).* SFC coaching requires that a professional relationship be established. The best way to establish (and maintain) relationships—professional or otherwise—is to communicate. We suggest that coaches ask some version of the following questions, which we call the Facilitator Questions:

   • What is working well for you?

   • Are all of your students making progress? Let's take a look at your data. (This data could include attendance records, any office referrals, grades, recent assessment results, and samples of classwork. We hope your administrator/supervisor has mandated that all teachers share this kind of information with you. If that has not happened, then you can simply ask for permission to look at the data together.)

- Do you have any questions or suggestions for me?

We discuss communication more extensively in Chapter 4.

3. *Start small; work with the most willing colleagues (Facilitator role)*. Do not worry if early on only one or two teachers express an interest in working with you. This is very common, and your caseload will increase over time. You probably want some experience under your belt before the really challenging cases come. You may find that novice teachers are the most open to having some guidance and support. Seek them out. It is not cheating to start with the teachers who are the most eager and open to work with you.

4. *Initiate informal conversations (Facilitator role)*. If no one calls, sends you an e-mail or text, or fills out your referral forms, then you may have to go to them. Look for opportunities to make yourself available to your colleagues. Spend time in faculty rooms when others are taking breaks or having lunch. Stop by their classrooms before school or during prep periods; just start chatting and asking a few general questions. These kinds of informal and unscheduled contacts may lead to a request for some advice and can ultimately move toward becoming a more formal coaching opportunity.

5. *Don't separate roles (Facilitator role)*. Try to keep your role in the school as similar to that of your colleagues as possible. Due to the nature of the coaching role, coaches have to engage in activities that sometimes make them look more like an administrator than a teacher. Coaches move from classroom to classroom; their schedules may be much more under their own control than the schedules of most teachers. This kind of flexibility and variety can make some of your colleagues a bit envious. Seek ways to stay professionally aligned with other teachers to defuse any possible resentment that might arise.

6. *Advertise and market your services (Facilitator role)*. Make sure everyone hears about the role you will be playing and how you see yourself working with them to help improve their students' reading outcomes and achievements. We all know that teachers are busy people. Our experience has been that simply having your administrator/supervisor make the initial announcement about this new role as one item in a full agenda for an after-school faculty meeting will probably not get everyone's attention. Follow the initial announcement or introduction with more information.

7. *Continue advertising and give credit to others (Facilitator role)*. As you begin working with other teachers and problems begin to be solved and concerns successfully addressed, it might be helpful to let others know about these accomplishments. Remember the issues of confidentiality, however. You may only spread the word about a successful coaching outcome if the teacher you worked with agrees to have their experiences shared publicly. Some teachers will be reluctant to let others know they sought assistance from a coach, even if the results were positive. This reluctance usually diminishes as time passes and your role as the coach becomes a more commonplace component of daily school life.

8. *Organize small- or large-group presentations (Teacher/Learner role)*. Survey the teachers about what topics they might like to learn more about. Look at your school

data to identify areas of academic need and design a workshop to address the need. Begin a book or article study group. Ask your administrator/supervisor what topics to address in a workshop format. (How to design and provide effective workshops is discussed in detail in Chapter 10.) This is also a great opportunity to build a sense of collaboration with teachers. If there are one or more teachers who have expertise in some area, then see if they might be willing to coplan and copresent with you to foster the collaborative nature of coaching. Teachers will be more likely to seek out your services once they see that you have some valuable professional expertise.

9. *Obtain referrals from administrators/supervisors.* Due to the bubble of confidentiality within which we hope all SFC coaches get to do their work, it is not acceptable for your administrator/supervisor to tell you directly or even suggest that you should provide coaching to a specific teacher without that teacher's permission. Knowing about an administrator/supervisor's concern about the quality of the work of one of your colleagues puts you inside the evaluation process and makes you privy to personnel information that ethically and legally should be known only by an administrator/supervisor. Yet, an administrators/supervisor can directly suggest to your teacher colleagues that they should consider seeking out your services. Again, because coaching must be seen as an optional service for teachers that they can engage in if they are willing to show a minimal level of cooperation, an administrator/supervisor must not mandate that a teacher work with a coach. If a teacher chooses to follow the administrator/supervisor's suggestion, then that teacher is free to share with you (or not) that the administrator/supervisor suggested that the coach be contacted. It is the teacher's right to confidentiality that we are working to honor and protect. If a teacher chooses to disclose information regarding the suggestion or referral, then that is within their rights.

Which Role to Use

As we mentioned earlier, the decision regarding which of the three SFC coaching roles to use at any given moment is guided by the needs of the teacher you are working with at that time. These needs are determined through regular contacts with each teacher once your coaching work has begun as well as data collected at the larger systems level.

If things are going well for a teacher and their students are making progress, then the Facilitator and Teacher/Learner roles would be most appropriate. Look for opportunities to encourage teachers and find ways to support their work. Even the most skilled teachers need support and encouragement at times (see Chapter 3). Perhaps a teacher is doing something successfully in their classroom that you should learn more about and then find a way to help that teacher share it with others (see Chapter 9). The Teacher/Learner role would also be appropriate to consider if you find that several teachers seem to share the same concern—you could think about designing some kind of group PDL activity. When a teacher does share a concern about a student or group of students, or you identify a concern while you are collaboratively examining their student data, you can move into Collaborative Problem-Solver mode (see Chapters 6, 7, and 8). An SFC coach should always try to be flexible and responsive to the needs of any professional situation, which may require engaging in more than one role simultaneously.

This may be the most strategic and efficient way to help with concerns that are being raised by more than one individual teacher. For example, if several of your colleagues feel the need to incorporate more active engagement into their instructional programs but are unsure what materials or strategies to use, or if several teachers have found that their students are having difficulty reading and understanding their assignments in content areas (e.g., social studies, science, health), then suggest putting together an after-school workshop on evidence-based suggestions for active engagement strategies or helping students develop content-area reading strategies. Coaches can design and deliver these kinds of PDL activities themselves or perhaps work with the administrator or district to bring in a consultant or trainer to address a specific topic. To foster collaboration, always consider working with other teachers who have effectively incorporated these ideas in their own classrooms.

Regularly visiting with your administrator and other school leaders and doing a collaborative analysis of student performance data is another way to determine whether PDL support is needed. Are there identifiable patterns of weakness or low performance in students that should be a strategic focus of PDL efforts? (We share tools to review Student Perception Data or Student Assessment Data in Chapter 10.) You could regularly send out questionnaires to teachers to learn about possible topics of interest or support needed. Appendices 2.2 and 2.3 include sample questionnaires. The Teacher Priority Questionnaire focuses on the implementation of the explicit instruction elements that are described in detail in Chapter 11. This questionnaire asks teachers to rate their current level of implementation. The second example focuses on literacy instruction (i.e., reading, writing, spelling). We include a literacy example because it is taught directly or indirectly in every grade level and subject; however, this can be adapted and used in any content area. Teachers are asked to rate their current level of implementation for the explicit instruction elements and specific elements of effective literacy instruction. We recommend that you distribute and collect the Teacher Priority Questionnaire first. You want to empower teachers and ensure that they understand that you are in your SFC coach role to serve them and their needs. Additional questionnaires/surveys for teachers are included in Chapter 10, in which we discuss the Teacher/Learner role and providing optimal PDL.

Doing a Reset on the Coaching Role   If you have already been in a coaching role for a while and are learning about the SFC model for the first time, then you may be thinking that you wish you could do a reset on how the coaching role was introduced and used in your setting. Maybe your coaching has been too much like supervision. Perhaps it was more top-down than the SFC model. Your coaching might not have been conducted with a full commitment to confidentiality or set up to be as fully collaborative as SFC. You might be wondering if it is even possible to do a full reset of a coaching implementation. Yes, it definitely is possible. Start with a new role definition. State clearly and directly to your administrator/supervisor and colleagues, "I appreciate you being on this journey with me. I have learned a lot about the coaching role since I started and would like to adjust the way I've been doing coaching, starting with a new definition of coaching and a new description of my role." Of course, this would all be presented in your own words and with the involvement and support of your administrator/supervisor.

Different Levels of Readiness for Working With a Coach

Teachers, just like students—or just like all human beings for that matter—approach new opportunities with varying levels of readiness. It may seem logical to categorize colleagues as either ready and willing to work with you in your coaching role or resistant to that idea. In our work, however, we have found this to be a bit more complicated. We have identified patterns in the level of readiness of our colleagues that we have divided into four categories or types. We do this only so we can make some specific suggestions and provide some guidance to you when you encounter a teacher colleague who you believe might fit into one of these categories. Of course, every teacher is an individual and must be respectfully treated as such.

REFLECTION

Did your own level of readiness for possibly working with a coach change from when you were a novice or beginning teacher to the present day? As you read this next section, can you see some of your current or former colleagues in any of these levels of readiness?

Type 1: Eager and Open   In most schools there will be some teachers who are both eager to begin working with you as soon as they hear you describe your role as an instructional coach and are open to trying new techniques or strategies in their classrooms. The most eager and open of your colleagues are sometimes those novice teachers in their first few years in the classroom. When most of us think back on our experiences as beginning teachers, we likely remember how overwhelmed and isolated we sometimes felt. Novice teachers can benefit greatly from the support of a coach. Many new teachers are quite skilled and have been well prepared by their college coursework. They may need only some general guidance and encouragement. Others may be confused about important issues such as how to organize their classrooms to provide whole-group and small-group instruction to a wide range of students, effectively use the school's curriculum for their assigned grade levels and content areas, provide the extra instruction needed by some of their lower performing students, or administer or interpret the results of diagnostic assessments and other concerns.

Yet, you may be surprised to learn that some of the most veteran and the most skillful teachers in a building fit into this first category. Maybe that is why they are so skilled: They continue to actively look for new and better ways of providing effective instruction to their students. If working with a coach will make them a better teacher, then they are eager to do that.

Finding these Type 1 teachers and doing anything even slightly related to coaching is a wonderful way to start the process. Working with these teachers is where you can practice your Facilitator, Collaborative Problem-Solver, and Teacher/Learner skills. You might consider collaborating with these teachers in workshops or trainings to help demonstrate that you do not see yourself as the only knowledgeable or skilled educator around. If one of these Type 1 teachers has a particular expertise that could be shared with others, then offer to watch their classrooms so they can work with other teachers to share that knowledge or skill. These teachers can also provide that important validation of the value of your work to other colleagues (Step 6 of the Enrolling Colleagues in the Coaching Process steps). Once you have successfully worked together, consider asking them to provide a testimonial to other teachers about the coaching process.

Type 2: Eager but Resistant   Another group of teachers who may be eager to use your services can be quite different to work with as a coach. There are some teachers who believe that any classroom problem they have has little or nothing to do with their own actions but rather is caused by "a student who won't do the work," "the family," "those primary grade teachers who just are not getting students ready for fourth grade," "the inadequate materials we were given to teach from," and so forth—you get the picture. Although these teachers are often enthusiastic about the chance to work with a coach (eager), you may find that in reality they really do not want suggestions about things they may need to do different in their classroom (resistant). Some teachers in this category may appear to want to learn new ways of doing things, but then you never seem to see any changes in their classrooms. This passive-aggressive response can be extremely frustrating.

When you work with a teacher who appears to fit into this category, our best advice to you is to monitor your time. Remember, as a coach, you have no power or authority to make a teacher do anything. Coaching must have at least a spark of cooperation. Spend your precious and limited coaching time with teachers who are open to learning and developing their professional skills, but remember to keep the door open for possible future work. Keep visiting these teachers on your regular teacher visitation schedule to ask the three Facilitator Questions, invite them to any workshops or book study groups you have, and engage in informal conversations about their class when the opportunities arise. Do not continue to spend time working with those teachers who are not ready to make changes, however.

Type 3: Reluctant but Not Resistant   We found that there are (at least) two other types of teachers, and neither group will be likely to beat a path to your door the day you put out your "open for business" sign. Type 3 teachers are reluctant but not resistant and are frequently those veteran teachers who are experienced and often successful and have gotten along just fine without coaching services in the past. They may be feeling justifiably confident about how they are teaching and may see no immediate need to seek out your services. This may cause us to see them as reluctant at this initial stage to work with the coach. When you visit teachers who you believe might fit within the Type 3 category to check in and ask the three Facilitator Questions, they may respond cordially but perhaps not especially warmly, "Thank you, but I'm fine right now." Colleagues in this category are not saying that they do not ever see value in working with you, just not yet. Again, like our Type 2 colleagues, keep the door open with these teachers. We have found that Type 3 colleagues are often just waiting to figure out what value you bring to the table. They are especially influenced by the testimonials of other teachers who have had a positive experience working with you, so do not forget to encourage teachers to share their success stories with others.

Type 4: Reluctant and Resistant   This final group is comprised of those teachers who are often reluctant to try any new program or service, not just coaching. There may be some among this group who could definitely use some help in improving their instructional practices but are highly resistant to making changes, or they could simply feel anxious about having another adult in the classroom watching them teach. This group can be challenging for a coach to reach. It may help to try to view the situation from the teachers' point of view. You might begin by honestly asking yourself, "What may be keeping these teachers from working with the coach? What are the benefits and costs of working with the coach (from these teachers' perspectives)?"

Type 4 teachers may not be fully aware of the benefits of coaching, such as improved student outcomes, increased competence and confidence in their ability to provide effective instruction to all students, more favorable evaluations by the administrator/supervisor, feeling respected and valued as a professional educator, and/or the social satisfaction of being part of a group that is working toward a common goal (Hasbrouck & Denton, 2010). Maybe you need to continue to advertise your services as we discussed in the enrolling steps. Understand, however, that some of these teachers may have very legitimate concerns that override the possible benefits of coaching, including how much time coaching might take, the real difficulty of changing teaching practices that may have been in place for years, a fear of failure in successfully implementing a new practice, fear of public embarrassment or humiliation, worry that their personal experience and knowledge are not valued or respected, fear of their jobs being threatened if the administrator/supervisor believes they are not competent, a reluctance to let go of current philosophies about how a classroom should be run, and/or a perception that the coach has a hidden agenda (Hasbrouck & Denton, 2010).

Working with Type 4 teachers can be a wonderful opportunity for some honest self-reflection. In these situations, SFC coaches should ask themselves, "What can I do to assure my colleagues that they will not be humiliated and that I respect them, their time, and their experience? That I will never share information from our coaching conversations or observations in their classrooms without their permission? What can I do to help make them feel more like members of a team with a shared goal of helping every student be successful?" We want the work of every SFC coach to play a role in reducing the isolation and lack of support that too many of our teacher colleagues feel (Joyce & Showers, 1982). Keep using the same enrolling activities we suggested for our Type 2 and Type 3 colleagues. Maybe one day one of these teachers will surprise you and show an interest in working with you in your coaching role.

CONCLUSION

The process of defining and beginning a new role within the kind of system you will find in a school building or school district is not a single event. It happens over time because the role of a coach evolves as the participants engage in the process. Given this, you may want to consider seeking input from your colleagues as time passes. Informal chats about how they feel about your coaching or more formal data collection, such as a survey or questionnaire, may provide you and your administrator/supervisor with valuable information about ways to improve the delivery of coaching services. Open and honest dialogue among all participants greatly facilitates the development of this new professional role.

Before proceeding to the next chapter, revisit your responses to the questions at the start of this chapter and make any adjustments based on new knowledge or insights gleaned. Also, take time to make any changes or updates to the application exercise.

VIRTUAL COACHING TIP

Evaluating the effectiveness of the coaching role overall, or any of the separate SFC roles of Facilitator, Collaborative Problem-Solver, or Teacher/Learner, could be conducted virtually. Take advantage of the virtual platform features by using a poll feature. Pose one or more of the following questions, and record responses in the chat:

- What do you see that is working well at our school (district, agency)?
- What evidence do you have to show that this is working and affecting student learning?
- Is there some part of your professional practice you'd like to improve?
- What is one thing you could do to make this improvement?
- How can I support you in achieving your next step?

REFERENCES

Corey, G., Corey, M. S., Corey, C., & Callanan, P. (2014). *Issues and ethics in the helping professions* (9th ed.). Cengage.

Dole, J. (2004). The changing role of the reading specialist in school reform. *The Reading Teacher, 57*(5), 462–471.

Hasbrouck, J., & Denton, C. (2010). The reading coach 2: More tools and strategies for student-focused coaches. Sopris West Educational Services.

Heron, T. E., Martz, S. A., & Margolis, H. (1996). Ethical and legal issues in consultation. *Remedial and Special Education, 17*(6), 377–385.

International Literacy Association. (2015). *The multiple roles of school-based specialized literacy professionals* [Research brief]. Author.

Joyce, B., & Showers, B. (1982). The coaching of teaching. *Educational Leadership, 40*(1), 4–10.

Knight, J. (2007). *Instructional coaching: A partnership approach to improving instruction.* Corwin.

Kroth, R. L., & Edge, D. (2007). *Communicating with parents and families of exceptional children.* Love Publishing.

Lefevere-Davis, S., Wilson, C., Moore, E., Kent, A., & Hopkins, S. (2003). Teacher study groups: A strategic approach to promoting student literacy development. *The Reading Teacher, 56*(8), 728–784.

U.S. Agency for International Development. (2014, February). *The power of coaching: Improving early grade reading instruction in developing countries: Final report.* Retrieved from https://www.globalreadingnetwork.net

Evaluation Checklist for SFC Coaches

Competency Focused on the Facilitator, Collaborative Problem-Solver, and Teacher/Learner roles	Rating Exceptional (E) Satisfactory (S) Improvement needed (I)	Comments/questions Based on evidence and specific to each competency
Organizes and delivers personalized and sustained professional development and learning activities for various stakeholder groups		
Guides and supports stakeholders in the collection and analysis of data to guide instructional decisions that improve student outcomes		
Observes teachers' lessons and provides modeling, demonstration, and feedback for instructional improvement at the teachers' request		
Helps teachers with the organizing and managing instructional programs		
Works collaboratively with colleagues to support student needs and an equitable learning environment		
Assists various stakeholders with planning and implementing with fidelity the delivery of instructional and intervention programs		
Identifies and addresses schoolwide concerns		
Participates in professional learning activities or meetings to learn from each other and explore relevant topics of interest		
Expands knowledge base and shares effective, proven strategies with stakeholder groups		
Understands or is knowledgeable about local, state, and federal rules, regulations, and policies		
Leverages digital integration to enhance learning		
Advises administrators on effective instructional practices based on research		
Maintains the confidentiality of all participants in the coaching process		

Coach signature/date: _____   Supervisor signature/date: _____

Teacher Priority Questionnaire

Directions: This questionnaire includes a compilation of explicit instruction elements (Archer & Hughes, 2011; Hasbrouck & Denton, 2005; Rosenshine, 2012). Please circle the appropriate number to rate your current level of implementation for each element as High Priority, Medium Priority, or Low Priority. For example, if you believe you always "sequence skills logically" when teaching a lesson, then you would circle the number 1 under the Low Priority heading. If there is an element that you do not teach, then circle Not Applicable (N/A).

Explicit instruction element	High priority	Medium priority	Low priority	Not applicable
Determining critical content	3	2	1	N/A
Sequencing skills logically	3	2	1	N/A
Reviewing previously learned material and building on prior knowledge	3	2	1	N/A
Stating the lesson's goal and making relevant connections	3	2	1	N/A
Presenting material in small steps	3	2	1	N/A
Thinking aloud and providing step-by-step demonstrations	3	2	1	N/A
Using unambiguous language to explain or model	3	2	1	N/A
Providing examples and nonexamples	3	2	1	N/A
Providing guided and supported practice	3	2	1	N/A
Asking questions and requiring frequent responses	3	2	1	N/A
Monitoring student performance	3	2	1	N/A
Providing immediate affirmative and corrective feedback	3	2	1	N/A
Preparing students for successful independent practice	3	2	1	N/A
Providing immediate, distributed, and cumulative practice opportunities	3	2	1	N/A
Teacher name:				
Grade level:				

Sources: Archer & Hughes, 2011; Hasbrouck & Denton, 2005; Rosenshine, 2012.

Teacher Priority Questionnaire

Directions: This questionnaire includes areas of literacy (i.e., reading, writing, spelling). Please circle the appropriate number to rate your current level of implementation for each element as High Priority, Medium Priority, or Low Priority. For example, if you believe you are always "implementing research-based reading, writing, and spelling programs and resources" when teaching a lesson, then you would circle the number 1 under the Low Priority heading for this element. If there is an area that you do not teach, then circle Not Applicable (N/A).

Areas of literacy	High priority	Medium priority	Low priority	Not applicable
Teaching phonemic awareness	3	2	1	N/A
Teaching phonics	3	2	1	N/A
Teaching fluency	3	2	1	N/A
Teaching vocabulary	3	2	1	N/A
Teaching comprehension	3	2	1	N/A
Teaching writing	3	2	1	N/A
Teaching spelling	3	2	1	N/A
Organizing and managing small-group instruction	3	2	1	N/A
Monitoring student progress in reading, writing, and spelling	3	2	1	N/A
Implementing research-based reading, writing, and spelling programs and resources	3	2	1	N/A
Teacher name:				
Grade level:				

3

The Facilitator Role

Before reading this chapter, consider the following questions. Jot down some notes on your current understanding, and then at the end of the chapter, we will revisit these questions to assess the knowledge and insight you gained during your reading.

- How will you initiate formal/informal conversations to build professional relationships with the most eager and open teacher to the most reluctant and resistant teacher?

- What does a coaching system of support look like/sound like at your setting?

- When posing the three Facilitator Questions outlined in Chapter 2 and discussed further in this chapter, what valid, reliable data do you believe will be most beneficial for supporting student progress?

- In what way(s) will you stay professionally aligned with the teachers whom you support versus being seen as an administrator?

APPLICATION EXERCISES

The Facilitator role focuses on supporting effective and skillful teachers to continue their success, building professional relationships, and helping to facilitate systems of support. To fulfill this role, you must be able to effectively communicate with and inform colleagues that you have something to offer. In part, this means advertising and marketing your services. Create a recruitment campaign that highlights your position of being mutually engaged in efforts that help maximize every teacher's skill and knowledge to enhance student learning. When complete, schedule a time to present this campaign to colleagues.

INTRODUCTION

We presented information in Chapter 2 about getting off to a good start with the SFC role. We suggested some ways that we have found helpful to formally introduce a new coach to their colleagues and pointed out that several aspects of the Facilitator role play an important part in that process. This entire chapter is devoted to supporting your understanding of this essential role for SFC coaches.

THE FACILITATOR ROLE FOR SFC COACHES

SFC coaches are engaged in the Facilitator role when they

- Support effective and skillful teachers to continue to be successful

- Spend time building the all-important professional relationships that can get the coaching process started

- Help lead their school, district, or agency toward a commitment to the success of all students by aiding other school professionals in the implementation of systems of support, such as leadership teams

Let's take each of these components of the Facilitator role and explain them in more detail.

Supporting Effective and Skillful Teachers to Continue to Be Successful

An important part of the SFC model is that SFC coaches work to help maximize teachers' knowledge and skills, regardless of their current level of expertise or need for support. There is a role for coaches to play with even the most effective and skillful teachers because the overarching of our work is always on increasing the success of every student in every classroom.

Unfortunately, many people mistakenly believe that the role of an instructional coach is primarily to find teachers who have weak skills or are more challenging and then somehow fix them. We have certainly heard this expressed by many of our colleagues, either openly and directly to us or in more private and subtle ways. There is a major problem with having your colleagues believe this might be your role. What does that mean when you show up at the doorway of their classroom? "Uh, oh. The new coach must think I'm one of those poor teachers and they need to fix me. Yikes!" Of course, nothing could be further from the truth. How do we counteract this widely held (mis)belief? One way is to make certain that you, your administrator/supervisor, and all your colleagues have been clearly informed of and embrace the definition of SFC: A cooperative, ideally collaborative, professional relationship with colleagues mutually engaged in efforts that help maximize every teacher's knowledge and skills to enhance student learning. There is nothing in this definition that implies that the job of the coach is to fix teachers. Making sure that you continuously structure your daily work around this definition, embracing and modeling the concepts of collaborative, professional relationships, mutual engagement, and enhancing student learning should go a long way in helping to dispel the idea that you are seeking out struggling teachers to fix. We specifically mention this in the description of the Facilitator role (and labeled it "facilitator," not "fixer") to underscore our strongly held belief that every teacher can benefit from working with a skillful coach and deserves that opportunity. Therefore, be sure you are spending some time in your coaching facilitating the work of your most effective and skillful colleagues.

What might this look like? Strategically engaging these skilled colleagues in your work as a Collaborative Problem-Solver and Teacher/Learner can support their work. Every teacher, even the most successful and experienced, will face challenges on occasion, and receiving support from an SFC coach can facilitate their work. Following is an example of using the Facilitator role (and incorporating the Collaborative Problem-Solver and Teacher/Learner roles) from Jan's own coaching experience.

At the very start of her coaching work, Jan was approached by one of the third-grade teachers on the staff of the school in which she worked. This teacher, who we will call Diane, was a highly experienced veteran with many years of teaching under her belt. She was also revered by the staff as a top-notch colleague who cared deeply about all her students. Many teachers reading this may have had the great pleasure of working alongside a teacher such as Diane and feeling inspired and even awestruck. You may also have watched these outstanding teachers be "rewarded" by having the most challenging students assigned to their classrooms. This was exactly what had happened to this teacher.

A new third-grade student came to the school just after Thanksgiving. He had an individualized education program (IEP) for emotional and behavioral disorders (E/BD) and would receive services from the school's special education staff. He needed to have a "home" classroom and teacher, however, and Diane was the obvious choice. As soon as Diane learned that she would be receiving this new student, she proactively reached out to Jan to get some support. Jan was surprised ("Really? Diane needs help?"), but she was also honored that such a skilled teacher would consider her to be helpful. Jan clarified that her professional expertise was primarily with students with academic learning issues, not students with E/BD, but she would certainly do her best to help support her and this student in any way she could.

Together they read through the student's cumulative folder and special education file. They met with the special education teacher to set up a way to communicate between the classrooms to be sure that both teachers would be providing a consistent message to the student. Jan called the student's previous classroom and special education teachers to see if they had some suggestions about strategies and supports that had previously worked with this student, and she shared this information with Diane. Jan also connected her with some PL opportunities (the Teacher/Learner role), and they collaborated on a plan to be proactive for any possible challenging behaviors that this new student might display (Collaborative Problem-Solver). So, while in the Facilitator role to support this already skillful teacher, Jan also incorporated aspects of the other two SFC roles.

REFLECTION

How do you see a coach working to help maximize teachers' knowledge and skills, regardless of their current level of expertise or need for support?

Building Professional Relationships

Spending time building professional relationships is the second component of the Facilitator role. It is impossible to provide coaching without a connection that is, at minimum, cooperative. Being available to support your busy colleagues can go a long way to get this started. This can include little things such as helping them track down a missing workbook to accompany a lesson, preparing assessment materials, helping with data entry or analysis, following up on a family's request, or locating an online patch for a software glitch, all of which can be so appreciated and important.

In addition to providing general helpful support to teachers, regularly check-ing in with every colleague also helps build professional relationships. The fre-quency of these contacts would obviously depend on the size of the coaches' potential caseload and whether they work full or part time, but they should occur regularly and as consistently as possible. When we are directly engaged in train-ing and supervising novice SFC coaches, we actually require them to schedule visits with every teacher for face-to-face conversations, either live or virtually, on a regular basis and direct each coach-in-training to track their contacts with every teacher. (To maintain the strict requirements of confidentiality to which we adhere, the log they kept was coded so that the names of teachers were unknown to the supervisors.)

There was an important reason for this requirement: To encourage beginning coaches to break out of their comfort zones of only approaching or working with teachers with whom they are comfortable or have already formed an amenable working relationship. Wanting to spend time with the colleagues with whom we feel most comfortable is completely understandable. As professionals, however, we are responsible for working with everyone, just like teachers are responsible for working with every student. The coaches we trained told us that documenting that they are, in fact, at least making contact with all of their colleagues does help them expand the number of colleagues to work with and feel more comfortable reaching out to start these professional relationships. Obviously, we will not be directly supervising you, but we do strongly recommend that you set up a way to document your own contacts with your colleagues so that you can hold yourself accountable for having regular and ongoing connections with every teacher. We promise, it will get easier and more natural as time goes by.

We also suggest that during these visits you are always ready to ask a person-alized version of the Facilitator Questions:

1. *What is working well for you?* (This question helps to start off the conversation with a positive tone and can function as a kind of ice-breaker or general con-versation starter.)

2. *Are all your students making progress? Let's take a look at your data* (e.g., attendance records, office referrals, grades, recent assessment results including progress monitoring results, samples of classwork). As we previously mentioned, it is optimal if your administrator/supervisor mandates that all teachers share this kind of information with you during your classroom visits. Such a mandate takes away the potential burden of having to encourage a teacher to share this information if they feel uncomfortable or reluctant. Making all coaching deci-sions based on collaboratively analyzed data and documented evidence goes a long way to help keep the coaching student focused and ensure that your coaching efforts are successful. If such a mandate to share data has not been made, then you can simply ask for permission to look at the data together and hope each teacher will be willing. If this proves to be a concern, then revisiting the idea of a mandate can be discussed with your administrator/supervisor in the future as you continue to define your role.

3. *Do you have any questions or suggestions for me?* We want to wrap up our conver-sation with teacher colleagues on a note that expresses our intent to provide coaching in a collaborative and functional manner. "Is the way I'm providing coaching working for you and your students? Are there things I could be

doing differently? Are there supports or services you need me to provide?" As SFC coaches, we need to always be open to suggestions for change and improvement. The teacher's response to this final Facilitator Question could possibly open the door for some future PDL support for this teacher or others. "I've heard my department is adopting a new curriculum. Will there be training provided?" "Are you still doing book studies? That last one was so helpful."

Remember to personalize these three Facilitator Questions. It would likely feel awkward to you and your colleague if you simply robotically read off the questions from a clipboard, cell phone, or computer. Understand the reason for each question and use the words you are most comfortable with to 1) start the conversation positively, 2) check on student progress, ideally by collaboratively analyzing current student data, and 3) wrap up the conversation in a warm, engaging way that keeps the door open for further collaboration.

Aside from regularly visiting each of your colleagues and using some form of the Facilitator Questions, keeping your role in the school similar to your colleagues is another important way that SFC coaches can work to build professional relationships. Actively find ways to participate in the duties and tasks that most teachers undertake, perhaps serving on committees, monitoring hallways, bringing snacks to the faculty meetings, attending open house or curriculum nights at your school, or participating in family–teacher association meetings. Teachers will be far more open to working with you if they see you as one of them rather than as some kind of quasi-administrator.

Openly advertising your services is another way you can successfully develop collaborative professional relationships with your colleagues. Create one-page flyers (attention-grabbing graphics, catchy slogans, easy-to-read at a glance) to put in teachers' mailboxes, post around the school in staff-only spaces (e.g., over the faculty room microwave), send out via e-mail, or put up on the school's web site. Besides reminding teachers about what an instructional coach is and the kinds of tasks and services a coach can provide, such printed information should also state your schedule and when, where, and how a teacher can reach you so you can start helping to enhance student learning.

We need to keep reminding our busy and often stressed colleagues that we are there to support their work. Besides the regular visits to ask the Facilitator Questions and any initial advertising you might choose to do, another way to develop professional relations is to ask a colleague with whom you have successfully engaged in a coaching activity to share their story with others. This can have a positive impact on your work. Remember Jan's story about working with Diane who had reached out for Jan's support when she got a new, challenging student assigned to her classroom? Things went quite well for that student, and Diane gave a lot of credit to Jan. Jan was just getting started in her coaching role in that school and was still working to make contact with many of the other teachers. She thought having Diane share this story with the general faculty could help with this effort. Diane said she was happy to do this, so Diane asked for some time on the agenda at a faculty meeting and spent about 5 minutes sharing how she had reached out to Jan for some coaching support and had found the process to be beneficial. Likely because Diane was so revered by the other teachers, this short testimonial went a long way in helping establish Jan's credibility in the school and dramatically increased the number of teachers who were now eager and open to receiving coaching services.

Be sure to stress the collaborative nature of the process whenever a teacher is open to sharing a coaching success story. As tempting as it may seem to be viewed as the instructional guru with a magic bag of tricks to solve all possible academic problems, such an image is likely to set you up for a fall. It is better to emphasize the shared process of coaching and credit the efforts of the teacher who did the actual work with the student. Reducing the expert aura will result in a greater sense of confidence and trust among your colleagues, which is essential for building the cooperative and collaborative professional relationships needed to provide effective coaching.

REFLECTION

In what way(s) do you see a coach spending time to build professional relationships with colleagues?

Implementing Successful Systems of Support

Helping to facilitate systems of support, including leadership teams, is the third component of the Facilitator role. This aspect of the work of SFC coaches encourages us to take a broader, macro view of our work. We need to expand our work beyond one teacher at a time to achieve the highest purpose of SFC—helping maximize every teacher's knowledge and skills to enhance student learning. If the numerous structures and systems in a school are working optimally, then they help ensure optimal outcomes. Faculty members should have support to collaborate effectively, using appropriate data to strategically measure progress and performance. Great things can occur when schools have structures in place to maximize learning by wisely using instructional time and materials and their human resources.

In Chapter 11, we present a framework for school success called SAILS, which stands for Standards, Assessment, Instruction and intervention, Leadership, and a Sustained commitment for success (Hasbrouck & Denton, 2005). The SAILS model was developed as a framework for school success and was based on a broad empirical base often referred to as *effective schools research*. That chapter discusses the importance of having a system in place for school improvement and success.

Sharing a belief that no one person has all the answers is one important aspect of school success. Schools in which a shared decision-making process is a part of the fabric fare far better than those in which top-down decisions are the norm. Higher achieving schools provide all stakeholders with greater influence on decisions compared with lower achieving schools. The higher performance of these schools might be due to the greater access they have to collective knowledge and wisdom embedded within their communities (Louis et al., 2010).

Effective schools often use leadership teams to help harness the collective knowledge and wisdom embedded within their communities. Building leadership teams are an avenue for shared decision making to become a reality. Shared decision making about things such as school schedules, PDL, and resource allocation—both human and material—can have a positive impact on the outcomes of achievement and the overall feeling of trust within school climates (Montgomery et al., 2013). Teachers become invested and empowered when leadership of a school is a shared responsibility. They not only care about their own classroom but also the entire school. SFC coaches can and should use some of their time within the Facilitator role to help the administration analyze the function of the various systems and structures in a school and help ensure that all are functioning well to facilitate student outcomes.

And one last word of caution here. We have sometimes seen the Facilitator role become the main way that SFC coaches are providing services to their colleagues. As vital as these tasks of the Facilitator role are, it is important that a coach not spend too much time in this role. It is a legitimate use of some of an SFC coach's time to assist busy teachers with logistics and being available to help. These efforts can be enormously valuable to busy and hard-working teachers. But, too much time spent doing these kinds of tasks, as appreciated as they are, can turn the coach into an assistant or quasi-administrator and minimize the impact of coaching for teachers and, therefore, students. The coach is not directly involved in providing PDL when engaged in the Facilitator role, which is the coach's primary purpose. There are two other valuable roles in which SFC coaches spend their time to provide high-impact, differentiated, sustained PDL that we discuss in detail in upcoming chapters: Collaborative Problem-Solver and Teacher/Learner. We provide some suggestions for tracking and analyzing how you are spending your time across the three roles of the SFC coach in Chapter 5.

REFLECTION

What role(s) do you see a coach playing with facilitating structures or systems of support?

CONCLUSION

SFC coaches spend some of their time supporting effective and skillful teachers, helping build professional relationships, and supporting the successful implementation of systems of support while engaging in the Facilitator role. It is essential that coaches are not seen as only working with struggling teachers. Coaching can only happen within an established professional relationship. Schools can only succeed when the myriad of systems and structures that support their work are organized and functioning optimally. Within the Facilitator role, the SFC coach thoughtfully and strategically spends time laying the crucial foundation for all these things, with the understanding that most of their time and effort should be spent in the other two SFC roles that more directly support student and teacher success.

Before proceeding to the next chapter, revisit your responses to the questions at the start of this chapter and make any adjustments based on new knowledge or insights gleaned. Also, take time to make any changes or updates to the application exercise.

VIRTUAL COACHING TIP

Supporting effective and skillful teachers to continue their success, building professional relationships, and helping to facilitate systems of support can be accomplished in face-to-face and virtual settings. Consider hosting informal events where colleagues can share success stories, engage in conversation around a specific topic, or simply learn more about each other. Many virtual platforms include features such as breakout groups or chat, shared documents or slides, virtual sticky notes, or ability to share screens. Facilitating these voluntary virtual events could be geared toward a specific group of teachers or anyone who is interested. Plan ahead so that you have adequate time to advertise and market the event. Also consider scheduling one-to-one conversations or informal conversations using a virtual platform. Both can address individual needs and/or build or strengthen relationships. Who knows, you might even get a reluctant and/or resistance colleague to take part.

REFERENCES

Hasbrouck, J., & Denton, C. (2005). *The reading coach: A how-to manual for success.* Sopris West Educational Services.

Louis, K. S., Dretzke, B., & Wahlstrom, K. (2010, September). How does leadership affect student achievement? Results from a national U.S. survey. *School Effectiveness and School Improvement, 21*(3), 315–336.

Montgomery, P., Ilk, M., & Moats, L. (2013). *A principal's primer for raising reading achievement.* Voyager/Sopris West Educational Services.

4

Communication for Collaboration

Before reading this chapter, consider the following questions. Jot down some notes on your current understanding, and then at the end of the chapter, we will revisit these questions to assess the knowledge and insight you gained during your reading.

- How would you define *communication?*

- Using your definition for communication, describe a time when you experienced effective communication. What happened? Would you say that any of your coaching conversations align with this experience? Justify your reasoning.

- Using your definition for communication, describe a time when you experienced ineffective communication. What happened? Would you say that any of your coaching conversations align with this experience? Justify your reasoning.

APPLICATION EXERCISE

Audio- or video-record a 5- to 10-minute coaching conversation with at least one colleague. Replay the recording and listen/watch for verbal and nonverbal responses you used. What observations did you make? What conclusions can you draw? Make sure to seek permission from your colleague before recording.

INTRODUCTION

Let's take a moment to revisit our definition of SFC from Chapter 1: A cooperative, ideally collaborative, professional relationship with colleagues mutually engaged in efforts that help maximize every teacher's knowledge and skills to enhance student learning. Chapter 2 provided an overview of the roles of an SFC coach, along with a discussion of some critical issues related to working as a coach in a school setting, and Chapter 3 took a detailed look at the Facilitator role. Chapters 4 and 5 focus on two essential tools for helping an experienced teacher become a coach who works effectively with colleagues across all the three SFC roles—collaborative communication skills and time management.

THE ART OF COMMUNICATION

Coaching is an important and challenging job. Skillful coaching requires the mastery of many important skills, along with a substantial professional knowledge base. Most knowledgeable educators agree that foundational skills for a coach include the ability to listen, understand, empathize, and effectively share information with colleagues. Collectively, these abilities are the art of communication.

Interpersonal exchanges are governed by specific cultural influences and expectations. It is imperative for coaches to be aware of the need to establish and maintain sensitive and responsible cross-cultural interactions when attempting to engage in formal communication with colleagues from a different cultural or linguistic background (Le Roux, 2002). This book addresses communication processes used in the majority culture in North America, with acknowledgement that variations on some of our recommendations might need to be made for working with those from culturally and linguistically diverse backgrounds.

A Relationship Skill

It may seem strange to see a section on communication in a book for coaches. Clearly, someone who has been asked to take on the role of coach is a person who has already shown some level of mastery of communication. Communicating is a part of daily life. It is vital for establishing and maintaining relationships. We all learned how to talk, listen, respond, and converse with others long ago and have many years of practice under our belts. You may even have taken a course in communication skills somewhere along the way and are now familiar with various concepts of communication, such as active listening, paraphrasing, summarizing, and open- or close-ended questions.

A Professional Skill

Although most of us do, in fact, have perfectly adequate communication skills for daily life, the work of a coach frequently requires the use of strategic and well-practiced communication skills to help you first establish a professional relationship with a colleague and later facilitate communication with someone who may be feeling deeply frustrated, angry, anxious, suspicious, irritated, confused, or embarrassed. If you coach long enough, then you will definitely face difficult circumstances like these. We developed this section of the book to assist you with these inevitable challenging conversations.

Here is an important rule of communication: The more tense, high stakes, and confusing the situation, the more skillful and formal you need to be in your communication. This is true in professional situations as well as personal ones. A skillful and formal manner of communication uses the same basic skills of listening and responding as we use in the everyday conversations we have, but it must be ramped up to become more focused and intentional. You need to have previously rehearsed your advanced communication skills to be prepared for those unavoidable tense and high-stakes situations. Having simply attended a 3-hour workshop on effective communication a few years ago will not help you much when you are faced with a frustrated and apprehensive colleague. It is certainly helpful to be aware of foundational communication skills, but that is just the first step. It is essential that you spend time learning the skills more deeply and give yourself time to practice them by rehearsing some challenging situations that might arise.

REFLECTION

What, if any, sustained PDL have you taken part in to develop your communication skills? Based on your response, which communication skills do you believe you need to further develop, or which communication skills could you model for others?

Nonverbal Communication Techniques

We will start our overview of communication skills by discussing how to present yourself in formal communication both psychologically and physically. Egan and Reese (2019) reminded us that high-stakes, tense, or confusing interpersonal transactions require an "intensity of presence" (p. 100) along with an "empathetic presence" (p. 98). If you are perceived as being deeply attentive and compassionate during such interactions, then you subliminally transmit positive messages about the importance of the other person and how much you value what they are saying to you. A disengaged or insensitive presence promotes distrust and hesitancy. The way you orient yourself physically during formal communications can contribute to this sense of engagement and trust.

The SOLER Technique   We have adapted the acronym SOLER (Sit squarely, maintain an Open posture, Lean forward, maintain Eye contact, be as Relaxed as possible) from Egan and Reese (2019) to describe the microskills used to attend to the person with whom you are communicating:

- *S: Sit squarely in front of the other person.* If possible, arrange to sit so there is not a desk between you. A teacher may feel more comfortable seated behind their desk, however, when you are meeting with them in their classroom. Try not to twist in your seat as you chat. Facing another person directly is associated with a nonverbal message of engagement and availability.

- *O: Maintain an open posture.* Avoid crossing your arms or legs or allowing an angry or anxious expression to be revealed on your face. Consider how your face can represent openness. The position of your eyebrows can communicate emotions including shock, surprise, insecurity, or distrust. Of course, simply crossing your legs or narrowing your eyebrows does not prevent you from fully attending to a personal interaction. What is important, however, is how your posture and gestures are interpreted by those you are coaching.

- *L: Lean forward slightly as you speak and listen.* Egan and Reese (2019) noted that, "in North-American culture, a slight inclination toward a person is often seen as saying, 'I'm with you, I'm interested in you and in what you have to say'" (p. 101); whereas, leaning backward can imply lack of engagement even boredom. Be sure that a forward lean is slight, however. An aggressive or exaggerated forward lean can be perceived as threatening.

- *E: Maintain eye contact.* People engaged in deep, meaningful conversations almost appear to have locked their eyes on each other. It is important to find the right intensity for eye contact in a professional conversation. It is not negative to glance away occasionally (e.g., taking a look at your notes or the folder of information you brought along), but make sure your eye contact suggests real interest and involvement. The amount and intensity of eye contact has definite cultural implications. If you are coaching or consulting with members of culturally or linguistically diverse groups, then you will need to adapt this and some of the other recommendations regarding the use of communication skills (Le Roux, 2002).

- *R: Throughout the process, try to be as relaxed as possible.* Bolton (1979) called this *relaxed alertness,* suggesting that you are not only relaxed and comfortable but also caring and attentive. If you can communicate a sense of calm, then you can greatly influence the mood and direction of the conversation. This ability to stay relaxed while fully engaged in intense and, at times, emotionally challenging professional conversations comes only from practice and rehearsal.

As you begin to use the SOLER technique, you should also try to adjust or censor reactions you may have during a conversation. If you feel yourself beginning to tense up or feel angry or threatened, perhaps scowling, crossing your arms, or leaning away from the other person, use that moment as an opportunity to identify where those negative reactions are coming from and think about positive ways to deal with those challenges so you can keep the communication moving forward.

REFLECTION

What, if anything, have you noticed about your nonverbal communication techniques? Based on your response, which communication techniques do you need to improve, or which do you believe are your strengths?

Not Just Listening: Active, Deep, and Authentic Listening

The act of listening is the most important single skill involved in communication. Skillful communicators do not only hear the words being spoken; they work hard to understand the meaning of what is being said, interpreting the stated words and the unstated nonverbal communication. For example, think about this quote (attributed to many different people, including Richard Nixon, Robert McCloskey, and Alan Greenspan): "I know you believe you understand what you think I said, but I am not sure you realize that what you heard is not what I meant." A goal for a skillful coach should be to hear and understand the meaning behind and between the spoken words.

Before we delve into active, deep, and authentic listening, two other levels of listening need to be considered (Starr, 2003, 2016). Cosmetic listeners are not really listening to you. It may look like they are listening, but their mind is somewhere else. "What did you say?" "Can you repeat that?" "I'm so sorry. I got distracted." are common phrases from cosmetic listeners. This is not an appropriate level of listening for an instructional coach. Conversational listening is where we spend a good amount of time in daily life—listening, talking, thinking, listening, talking, thinking. This type of listening is necessary, especially when building relationships. In such communications, two (or more) people are engaged in a conversation in which both have a part. Active listening is being highly intentional. You make every effort to listen and stay focused: Take mental notes, respond with appropriate sounds ("uh-huh") or gestures (e.g., nodding head), and seek to understand with asking additional questions, paraphrasing, or summarizing. Monitor your coaching conversations and plan for 70% listening and 30% speaking as a measure (Growth Coaching International, 2020). Deep listeners not only share the active listening behaviors but are also aware of what they see and notice. Deep listeners spend more time focused on the other person than on themselves. What does the other person's body language suggest? Do they seem ready to engage in a coaching conversation? Do they seem responsive and open to what is happening in the conversation? The coach should spend about 90% of their time listening and 10% speaking when deep listening (Growth Coaching International, 2020).

Stone et al. (2010) pointed out that "the heart of good listening is authenticity" (p. 168). Using the right posture and listening techniques are certainly important, but they will only take you so far. Are you, as the listener, genuinely and sincerely curious about what the other person is saying? Do you truly care about their feelings? Can you try to listen without being fearful or defensive? Listening is most powerful and effective when it is active, deep, and authentic.

Active, deep, and authentic listeners are dynamic and engaged. Being a successful listener requires a certain attitude or mindset about the communication process. An active, deep, and authentic listener must be and do the things in the following list (which are also great attributes for a successful SFC coach). An active, deep, and authentic listener must

- Have empathy
- Postpone interpretation
- Suspend judgment
- Stay attentive to the speaker
- Have patience
- Be present
- Pose questions
- Utilize minimal encouragers

Several types of verbal responses are typically recommended as part of active, deep, and authentic listening, including reflecting, paraphrasing, asking questions, summarizing, avoiding jargon, and avoiding unnecessary interruptions.

REFLECTION

Before proceeding, write down your description for reflecting, paraphrasing, asking questions, summarizing, avoiding jargon, and avoiding unnecessary interruptions.

Reflecting   One recommended verbal response is *reflecting*, which can be defined as a response that focuses on the speaker's feelings (or affect) by providing feedback about what the speaker appears to be experiencing. The listener offers a guess, or hunch, based on cues obtained from the speaker's presentation, both verbal and nonverbal. A reflective response is nonjudgmental and concise. For example, if a teacher is relating in great detail about the various ways they have attempted to help one of their students improve reading fluency with little or no effect, then a coach might reflect, "Wow, you've really worked hard trying to help Lenny. Seeing no improvement in his fluency must have made you feel very frustrated." You are not commenting on the quality or appropriateness of the interventions the teacher has tried. You are only acknowledging that they have worked hard and are probably feeling a bit discouraged.

Skillful reflecting can help verify and validate a speaker's emotional state and help the speaker become more aware of the feelings a situation is generating. This can be a big step in establishing trust; it's good for a teacher to be thinking, "That coach really hears what I'm trying to say—my coach gets it." Once feelings have been heard, the person sharing may be more ready to move past the emotional reactions and on to a thoughtful process to tackle the problem.

Paraphrasing   Another skill in active, deep, and authentic listening is paraphrasing, a succinct response that restates the essence of the speaker's content in the listener's own words. Paraphrasing can convey that you are carefully attending to what is being said and are seriously attempting to understand. Paraphrasing conveys attention and understanding because to paraphrase skillfully requires a listener to pay close attention and make a sincere attempt at understanding. You cannot fake a paraphrase; it takes real concentration.

A skillful paraphrase is condensed and concise, a statement of the essential facts and ideas of the speaker's message rather than the feelings. A paraphrase should help cut through the clutter of presented details and highlight the fundamentals. It is critical to avoid parroting (an exact repetition of the speaker's own words), which usually inhibits, rather than encourages, continued conversations. An example of a good paraphrase follows:

Teacher: I know that we are supposed to be collaborating and working together, but I'm just not sure I can work with Regina's special education teacher. He only has an alternative certification, and he's already told me he has no experience working with kids with problems such as Regina's.

Coach: Okay. I think I see. You're uneasy about having to work with Regina's special education teacher because you are concerned about the quality of his professional preparation and his lack of experience.

Asking Questions   It is often necessary to ask questions during active, deep, and authentic listening, and there are skillful and effective ways to do this. In a later section on interviewing, we tell you in detail how to obtain information strategically and efficiently to develop appropriate intervention plans. Here we mention a few questioning procedures to support active, deep, and authentic listening in more general conversations.

Questions that are designed to check the perceptions of the listener help ensure that we have correctly understood the intended message of the speaker and helps avoid assuming too much, which can reduce defensiveness and possible conflicts. Perception checking has three steps: 1) describing the behavior you noticed, 2) providing two possible interpretations of the behavior, and

3) requesting clarification. Here are two examples of perception checking obtained from the Conflict Resolution Education in Teacher Education (CRETE) web site http://www.creducation.net.

Example 1:

1. Describing the behavior: "When you walked out of the room without saying 'goodbye' . . ."

2. Two possible interpretations of the behavior: "I didn't know if you were mad at me or if you were in a hurry and were distracted."

3. Request clarification: "What was up?"

Example 2:

1. Describing the behavior: "You haven't checked in for a few days . . ."

2. Two possible interpretations of the behavior: "I'm not sure if you are upset with me or if you've just been busy."

3. Request clarification: "What's going on?"

Clarifying questions can also be used by listeners to determine if the message being sent by the speaker is being correctly interpreted. A clarifying question may follow a paraphrase: "Did I get that right?" Some questions can be used to seek elaboration, "Can you tell me a bit more about the types of things you've already tried with this student?" This is an example of a closed-ended question, asked to obtain specific information. This type of question attempts to elicit a limited response. An open-ended question can be used to begin a conversation or start the flow of shared information without direction or an agenda. An open-ended question could be, "Please tell me your concerns about Kelly's grades this semester." We try to avoid using leading questions in active, deep, and authentic listening because they can subtly prompt the respondent to answer in a particular way. Leading questions imply there is only one correct answer. They are considered undesirable because they can result in the speaker providing false or slanted information or feeling like they are being judged by the listener.

Summarizing   As a conversation continues, there will be moments when it is important to summarize the important bits of information that have been offered to that point. Summarizing is a method of tying together the most relevant ideas at key moments in the conversation. Summaries can be especially important when information has been shared in a rather fragmented manner, which is common when emotions are running high. A summary should be a fairly brief statement of the important themes, issues, or feelings that have been expressed. The listener can use the summary to share some tentative conclusions and receive feedback to make sure the conclusions are accurate. A well-constructed summary can help the speaker see an integrated version of the concerns and issues that have been shared. In the formal problem-solving process that we discuss in Chapter 6, summarizing is a way to bring closure to one phase of the process and make the transition to the next phase. Summarizing helps move the process forward in a productive manner.

Avoiding Jargon and Slang   It is important for the coach to avoid using jargon or professional terminology that may not be familiar to the speaker during active, deep, and authentic listening. Using unfamiliar jargon can make the listener feel disrespected or demeaned. And using unfamiliar terms certainly does not facilitate accurate and clear communication.

In the same vein, avoid using slang as well. This can be an issue especially for younger, novice coaches who may have developed a relaxed manner of communication among their peers and find themselves using informal slang phrases such as, "So, I hoped that, you know, we could, like, find some time to get together?" "I kinda wanted to ask you some questions." "I was talking with her mom and she goes, 'I don't want to talk now,' so I go, 'Well, we need to talk sometime,' and she goes . . ." If you feel you may be using these kinds of informal slang terms in your speech, then record yourself or ask a trusted colleague to give you some honest feedback.

Building and maintaining collaborative relationships, with a primary goal of helping to address students' needs, is a major purpose of professional conversations for SFC coaches. Using words that are unknown, unclear, or possibly intimidating or irritating to the speaker could serve to make the speaker feel uncomfortable, unimportant, irrelevant, or incompetent. A coach should strive to use language that is clear, concise, and unambiguous, so monitor your own language choices and be sure to encourage the speaker to stop you at any time you may unconsciously use an unfamiliar or unclear term or phrase. A coach can encourage such behavior through modeling. For example, if a speaker uses a word or term that is unclear, then use that as an opportunity to stop the conversation and ask, "I need to ask, what do you mean when you say your student's family is just wacky? Can you clarify what you mean by 'wacky'?" This indicates that you are both listening carefully and truly care to understand what is being shared.

Avoiding Unnecessary Interruptions   An active, deep, and authentic listener also knows that it is important to interrupt as infrequently as possible with questions or reactions. This, of course, needs to be balanced with the responsibility to efficiently and effectively manage the time being invested. This responsibility may at times require the coach to interrupt the speaker. When a speaker is beginning to ramble, speaking about things that are not relevant or helpful, repeating information already shared, or is unsure how to terminate the conversation, a coach can interrupt in a purposeful way, perhaps by reflecting the speaker's feelings, paraphrasing, asking questions, or summarizing strategically: "Let me interrupt here. I think I have a good idea at this point about what your concerns are, and I'm watching the time. You mentioned that you needed to be back in your classroom by 2:45 p.m., and we're getting close to that time. Let's see if I can summarize your concerns correctly."

Use Minimal Encouragers (Verbal and Nonverbal)

It can be helpful to use what communication experts call *minimal encouragers,* neutral verbal and nonverbal indications that acknowledge you are following what is being said, while someone is talking. These have also been referred to as the *grunts and groans* of conversation. The most common of the verbal minimal encouragers are probably "Uh, huh" or "Mm-hmm," which both imply, "Please continue—I'm listening, and I understand what you are saying." Most people have their own favorite sets of minimal encouragers, such as "I see," "Oh?" "Really?" "Right," or "Go on." Nodding while maintaining a neutral or serious facial expression is probably the most common of the nonverbal encouragers.

Good communicators also must have the patience to wait through pauses and silences. It is often human nature to want to fill those pauses, so some listeners may talk too much in those moments. Silence can be necessary to allow the speaker to collect thoughts, reflect, or sort out options about what to say and how to say it. And, as an active, deep and authentic listener, you can use these periods of silence to assess your SOLER position and reflect about what words have been stated or what is not being stated in words.

REFLECTION

Refer to your description for reflecting, paraphrasing, asking questions, summarizing, avoiding jargon, and avoiding unnecessary interruptions. How do your descriptions relate to or differ from our descriptions?

MAKING REQUESTS: USING THE "SOLUTION SANDWICH"

Sometimes coaches will face situations in which they feel as if they have reached a roadblock or some kind of dead end in their interactions with someone. Recall that in the SFC model, we acknowledge, for better or for worse, that coaches have no special powers and no more authority than their teacher colleagues. No one can force anyone to do things the way we think they should, but as coaches we know how to establish professional relationships and perhaps influence change. We can consider making a request for change in those dead-end, road-blocked situations. Those requests require us to be respectfully assertive which can be an act of bravery for some of us. We recommend using a structured process that we have found can support individuals to be assertive enough to make respectful and clear requests when necessary. We call this process the "Solution Sandwich," which we adapted from the work of Dr. Laurel Mellin at Emotional Brain Training.

This strategy uses the image of a sandwich (two slices of hearty, nutritious bread placed around a piece of meat—or a tasty vegetarian or vegan option) to serve as a prompt for the steps of the process. A request is made after an initial statement of genuine empathy or appreciation for the person from whom you are making the request and another empathetic statement of gratitude or appreciation is made again immediately after the request. The wording for the first slice of bread would include phrases such as "I understand . . . ," "I appreciate . . . ," or "I care that . . ." The actual request, or the meat, is stated in three parts: "I feel . . . ," "I need . . . ," and "Would you please . . ." Immediately after stating the request, a second slice of bread is offered again, using words such as "I understand . . . ," "I appreciate . . . ," or "I care that . . ."

Be sure to pick a time to deliver the request when it is reasonable to expect a positive outcome to maximize the odds that your request will be well received and to minimize the odds that making this request will cause any kind of negative response. Ask yourself, "Is this a good time for me to be making this request? Does this appear to be a good time for the person from whom I'll be making the request?" Do not deliver the sandwich if you are feeling angry, afraid, stressed, or tired. Pick a time that you believe is as optimal as possible for the other person—likely not in a hallway on a Monday morning with students all around you, right before a faculty meeting, or after a negative interaction with the person from whom you will be making the request. There can never be a perfect time, but there are times that are less than optimal, so it is important to be strategic and empathetic when planning these requests.

We would recommend using the following steps for the Solution Sandwich procedure:

1. Get calm.

2. Write out the "sandwich." Rehearse.

3. Ask yourself, "Is it reasonable to expect a positive outcome for me if I make this request now?" If not, wait.

4. Get calm. Feel honest empathy. If you do not feel empathy, then do not deliver the sandwich. (Return to Step 1, perhaps on another day.)

5. Express empathy purely (first slice of bread). Do not mix this with the request.

6. Express an honest feeling (not a thought), "I'm sad," "I'm afraid," "I'm worried," "I'm angry," and so forth.

7. Express an honest need, "I need . . ."

8. State your request, "Would you please . . ."

9. Feel and express honest empathy to close (second slice of bread).

Of course, this process has no guarantee of success. It is quite possible that your request will be declined or refused. If you feel that this request is important, or perhaps not having your request accepted really is not even an option, then you can increase the strength of the request by using stronger words across three different levels. A Level 1 request is what we have shared here already, "I need . . . ," "I feel . . . ," or "Would you please . . ." A Level 2 request is a bit more insistent, "I really feel . . . ," I really need . . . ," or "Would you please . . ." A Level 3 request is usually more of an ultimatum because you are stating a consequence of not accepting the request, "I really feel . . . ," "I really need . . . ," or "Would you please . . . , and "If you don't, (state a consequence)."

Here is an example from an SFC coach working in a real school in which using a Solution Sandwich might be considered. The coach told us, "I've been experiencing some conflict with the other instructional coach on campus. I don't want to step on her toes, but she has been telling the teachers to do things I feel are unprofessional and borderline unethical."

Here is what she came up with as possible wording for the bread and the meat for a sandwich/request:

Slice 1:	"I want you to know that I value having you as a colleague and know how hard your job can be at times."
The meat/request:	"I feel sad and worried because at times I've heard you ask other teachers to do things that make me uncomfortable. I need to have a conversation with you about this sometime. Would you please consider making time to discuss this with me?"
Slice 2:	"I do understand how busy you are, and I would greatly appreciate it if you'd consider this request."

This is a request for a meeting, a first step in the process of discussing the coach's concern with her colleague. If the coach feels good about this draft of a request (Step 2 in the process), then she can continue by rehearsing, picking a reasonable time, and delivering the request following the nine steps of the Solution Sandwich process.

REFLECTION

Think about a personal or professional roadblock that you have experienced. Write down a script using the Solution Sandwich process should you face this same roadblock a second time.

LEARNING TO BE A SKILLFUL COMMUNICATOR: PRACTICE MAKES PERFECT

Most of the time you will not be using communication skills in such a formal manner as we have described here. As a coach, you will frequently hold conversations with colleagues without thinking twice about how you are sitting or standing or whether you should summarize or paraphrase what was just said. There will be circumstances, however, when you are faced with a communication challenge in which someone has strong emotions or passionate beliefs about a topic that needs to be addressed. When these situations arise, be sure you have practiced all these critically important communication skills and are so comfortable and confident that using them feels effortless. You stop listening when you need to stop and think about what to say next or how to respond to what a colleague or parent just said.

In our training sessions with coaches over the years, we have found that the best way to become a skillful communicator is through role playing, ideally in a group of three participants. Find a couple of willing colleagues (perhaps other coaches from your district) who also want to improve their professional communication skills. To begin, each person who is participating should independently reread this chapter. Then, get together to identify, define, and discuss the components of skillful communication—active, deep, and authentic listening; SOLER; and reflecting feelings, paraphrasing, asking questions, summarizing, avoiding jargon, avoiding unnecessary interruptions, and using nonverbal communication skills. Use the Communication Skills Practice Form (see Appendix 4.1) to guide a review and discussion of the communication skills you will be practicing.

After studying the information on the form, set aside 45 minutes to 1 hour so the three of you can meet for a role-playing practice. During this practice session, each person takes one turn in each of the three different roles—Coach, Colleague, and Observer. The Coach and Colleague engage in a dialogue, discussing an emotionally charged situation presented by the Colleague. The Observer monitors this conversation and notes the Coach's use of key communication skills. Following the role play, the Observer also guides all participants through a structured debrief of the exercise.

Each participant should come to the practice session with a scenario relevant to situations that an SFC coach may encounter and be ready to perform in a role-play as the person in the scenario who is seeking support or assistance from the

Coach. The person seeking help could be a family member who is seriously concerned about the instruction their child is receiving, a teacher who is angry at the administrator about the lack of support for using a certain commercial program, or a teacher who is overwhelmed by a student who is struggling academically and/or engaging in challenging behaviors.

It is ideal if the person in the Colleague role has personally experienced the situation or one similar to it and is able to share some details while playing out that role. The scenario is not shared in advance with the Coach or the Observer. All details of the situation are shared only through role playing, as the Coach asks questions of the Colleague and responds using the other communication skills. Remember, the scenario should have enough details (real or imagined) to enable a conversation of about 10 minutes between the Coach and the Colleague. After those 10 minutes, the Observer notifies the participants that time is up so the coach can wrap up and practice bringing closure to the dialogue. The Observer then leads the Coach and the Colleague through a structured, three-way debriefing that should last about 5 minutes. After debriefing, everyone switches roles, and the process begins again with a new scenario.

This type of practice works best if everyone participating makes a serious effort to stay in character. The value of the practice opportunity will be seriously diminished if the Colleague, Coach, or Observer interrupts the conversation to make a comment such as, "I feel so silly" or "Wow, you sure are reminding me of a parent I worked with a few years ago!"

Role Playing the Colleague

You will have the chance to show off your latent theatrical talents when you take on the role of the Colleague! Remember, the purpose of this session is primarily to provide the person who is role playing the coach an opportunity to practice using good communication skills in a potentially challenging situation. The Colleague should display emotions such as anger, frustration, aggravation, discouragement, pessimism, helplessness, and confusion as honestly and realistically as possible. Try not to be too over the top, however, so the Coach is presented with an impossible situation.

Role Playing the Coach

When you role-play the Coach, you simply need to practice your best communication skills by listening and responding appropriately as the Colleague shares concerns. The Colleague needs to feel as if they have been heard. This is not the time to try to figure out how to solve any problem or concern being presented to you. As you role-play, think of this initial dialogue with a colleague as an information-gathering opportunity as well as a chance to build a professional, collegial relationship. Later, in Chapter 6, we talk about engaging in a collaborative, systematic problem-solving process, and, in Chapter 7, we discuss how to gather information to solve problems. We want to discourage coaches from getting in the habit of simply hearing a problem or concern and then offering a solution on the spot. As we learn in future chapters, this is both ineffective and can be damaging to the collaborative process. For now, your task is simply to listen actively, deeply, and authentically and respond appropriately. Do *not* offer or suggest a solution.

Being the Observer

The Observer has three important responsibilities: 1) monitoring the time during the practice session, 2) observing and taking notes about the coach's communication skills, and 3) facilitating the debriefing session by following the script at the bottom of the Communication Skills Practice Form. During the conversation, the Observer takes detailed notes about the communication skills the Coach is using on the Communication Skills Practice Form. The more specific and concrete you can make your notes, the more helpful they will be for the other participants. The value of this exercise depends on the Observer honestly sharing critiques (not criticism) about the Coach's use of communication skills. This is a learning exercise. It is hard, if not impossible, to improve our skills if we do not get accurate feedback. After about 10 minutes, the observer lets the Coach know that time is up so the Coach can wrap up the conversation appropriately.

Getting Started

Before beginning, prepare three copies of the Communication Skills Practice Form, one for each round of practice. Have each person select the role they will play for the first round of the practice. The Observer labels the form with the names of the people playing each role.

First 10 Minutes   The Coach begins the role-playing with introductions. ("Hi. I'm Natalie, the coach here at Whitaker Middle School. I was told you wanted to see me. I have about 10 minutes to visit with you right now. Is this a convenient time?") Follow this with an open-ended question to give the person playing the Colleague role a chance to provide you with background information ("So, tell me what's going on?"). From there, ask additional closed- or open-ended questions to obtain additional information and encourage the Colleague to provide clarification or elaboration. Spend 10 minutes or so responding to the answers, as appropriate, reflecting affect, paraphrasing, summarizing, and using your best active, deep, and authentic listening techniques. Remember to also practice your SOLER posture and use some minimal encouragers.

When the Observer signals that time is up, or the dialogue has come to a natural end, the Coach brings closure to the conversation, perhaps by summarizing what has been shared and making suggestions about what might happen next, but not offering a solution. ("Thank you for taking the time to let me know about this situation. I think that I may be able to be helpful as we identify some possible next steps to take.") Appropriate, hypothetical "next steps" might be another meeting, a classroom observation, or sharing some materials.

Next 5 Minutes   When the Coach has wrapped up the session, the Observer immediately leads the participants through a structured, three-step debriefing process that usually lasts about 5 minutes:

> *Step 1:* The Observer starts by asking the colleague, "How well did you feel the Coach listened and responded to your concerns? What communication skill(s) did the Coach use most effectively in communicating with you? What suggestions do you have for the Coach?"

> *Step 2:* The Observer honestly and accurately shares observations made from the notes taken during the role play. The Observer asks any relevant questions

of the Coach, then offers comments about what the Coach did well and makes constructive suggestions for ways the Coach may improve next time.

Step 3: The Coach shares their impressions about the conversation.

Step 4: Everyone can freely share their opinions about what might possibly be a real-world solution to the concern presented by the Colleague and ask questions of the Colleague.

After the first debriefing is complete, the roles are switched for a new scenario until all participants have played all three roles.

You can plan a similar practice session for the Solution Sandwich process. Form groups of three participants. Have each person write out a Level 1 request. Practice making a respectfully assertive request and give each other feedback and support.

Rehearse Your Communication Skills for Those Challenging Conversations

Even skillful, experienced professional communicators feel the need to keep their skills well practiced. If you know that a potentially difficult conversation with a teacher, administrator/supervisor, or family member has been scheduled, then it is quite appropriate and even highly encouraged to rehearse the situation ahead of time. Ask a friend, spouse, partner, or peer to spend a few minutes role playing with you. Or, run some possible dialogues in your head and try out responses. Do not let these rehearsals take you so far that you have memorized questions and/ or answers. That could get in the way of careful listening. Instead, use rehearsal times to assure yourself that you will be able to handle strong emotions or other communication challenges.

REFLECTION

Revisit the Solution Sandwich you wrote during the previous Reflection, and find two colleagues who will practice the colleague, coach, and observer roles with you. After you practice, write down what you noticed about your behaviors and the behaviors of others. What did you learn about yourself or your colleagues?

Postponing Conversations   Good, productive communication cannot occur when one or more parties are angry or upset. It is simply not physiologically impossible. Problems cannot be solved when participants are so frustrated that their purpose for meeting with you is simply to express rage or vent anger. It is always perfectly appropriate for you to end any conversation in which you feel threatened or unsafe or in any situation where it appears that a participant wants only to express aggravation. In such a situation, the professional response is to reschedule the session. If you feel you are in physical danger, then remove yourself immediately from the situation or move to an area where others may be available to provide assistance. For instance, "Mrs. Kingston, I can see you are still angry about what has been happening with Joshua's teachers. I can certainly understand this. And I want you to know that I am sincerely interested in working with you to solve this problem to your satisfaction, but I don't believe we can make any progress right now when you are clearly so upset. Perhaps you could accompany me to the office where we can see if an administrator may be able to hear your concerns."

CONCLUSION

Learning how to communicate skillfully and purposefully will greatly enhance your ability to provide excellent coaching services to enhance student learning, maximize every teacher's skill and knowledge, learn from each other, and prevent future challenges.

Before proceeding to the next chapter, revisit your responses to the questions at the start of this chapter and make any adjustments based on new knowledge or insights gleaned. Also, take time to make any changes or updates to the application exercise.

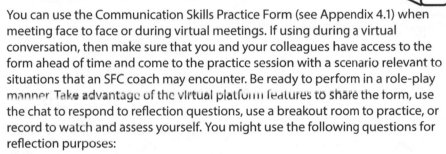

VIRTUAL COACHING TIP

You can use the Communication Skills Practice Form (see Appendix 4.1) when meeting face to face or during virtual meetings. If using during a virtual conversation, then make sure that you and your colleagues have access to the form ahead of time and come to the practice session with a scenario relevant to situations that an SFC coach may encounter. Be ready to perform in a role-play manner. Take advantage of the virtual platform features to share the form, use the chat to respond to reflection questions, use a breakout room to practice, or record to watch and assess yourself. You might use the following questions for reflection purposes:

- What did you notice about your verbal responses (e.g., questions you posed, how you paraphrased)? What would you like to do better during future conversations?

- What did you notice about your nonverbal cues? What did you notice about the teacher's nonverbal cues? What might this tell you?

REFERENCES

Bolton, R. (1979). *People skills: How to assert yourself, listen to others, and resolve conflicts.* Simon & Schuster.

Egan, G., & Reese, R. J. (2019). *The skilled helper: A problem-management and opportunity-development approach to helping* (11th ed.). Cengage.

Growth Coaching International. (2020). *Introduction to leadership coaching.* Author.

Knight, J. (2016). *Better conversations: Coaching ourselves and each other to be more credible, caring, and connected.* Corwin.

Le Roux, J. (2002). Effective educators are culturally competent communicators. *Intercultural Education, 13*(1), 37–48.

Starr, J. (2003). *The coaching manual: The definitive guide to the process, principles, and skills of personal coaching.* Pearson.

Starr, J. (2016). *The coaching manual: The definitive guide to the process, principles and skills of personal coaching* (4th ed.). FT Press.

Stone, D., Patton, B., & Heen, S. (2010). *Difficult conversations: How to discuss what matters most.* Penguin.

Communication Skills Practice Form

Coach:_____ Colleague:_____ Observer:_____

	Comments
SOLER: sit squarely, open posture, lean forward, eye contact, relaxed	
Active, deep, and authentic listening: expresses empathy, postpones interpretation, suspends judgment, stays attentive to speaker, demonstrates patience	
Reflecting feelings/affect: nonjudgmental, concise, acknowledging	
Paraphrasing succinct response: restate essential facts and ideas	
Asking questions: check perceptions, clarify, seek elaboration, closed and open, avoid leading	
Summarizing brief statement of important themes, issues, or feelings; share tentative conclusions and receive feedback	
Avoid jargon and slang: clear, concise, unambiguous	
Interruptions only as necessary; examples include rambling, irrelevance, repetition	
Minimal encouragers: neutral, nonverbal, and verbal	
Do not offer solutions/recommendations	

Debrief (lead by Observer)

1. Colleague: How well did you feel the Coach listened and responded to your concerns? What communication skill(s) did the Coach use most effectively in communicating with you? What, if any, suggestions do you have for the Coach?

2. Observer: Share your notes from the observation and ask any relevant questions. Next, comment about what the Coach did well. Offer any constructive suggestions for improvement.

3. Coach: Share your impressions about the conversation.

4. Discuss possible solutions if desired and time allows.

5

Managing Time

Before reading this chapter, consider the following questions. Jot down some notes on your current understanding, and then at the end of the chapter, we will revisit these questions to assess the knowledge and insight you gained during your reading.

- From what you have learned in previous chapters, approximately how many hours per week do you think you spend in each SFC role: Facilitator, Collaborative Problem-Solver, Teacher/Learner?

- Who, if anyone, dictates your daily schedule? Which schedule activities specifically focus on affecting student needs?

- In what way(s) do you formally and informally communicate your availability for coaching?

APPLICATION EXERCISE

Using an 8-hour workday as a guide, write down what you do during an average week as a coach. When finished, analyze your findings. What do you do most? What do you do least? In what way(s), if at all, do your findings align with the responsibilities listed in your job description?

INTRODUCTION

One challenge that professionals can expect to face as they make the transition from their previous position to that of a coach is having a schedule that is generally far more open ended than a traditional teacher. Coaches often have a certain degree of flexibility to set their own schedules, deciding when to do things such as visit a teacher's classroom, schedule an assessment of a student, or meet with a family. This can be a great perk of becoming a coach, and this flexibility can feel quite liberating after years of having your schedule dictated almost entirely by external considerations (e.g., the start of the school day, bus schedules, lunch, recesses) and managed by the ringing of bells or buzzers. The problem that inevitably begins to arise is when your schedule as a coach starts to fill and overfill. How do you get everything done in a reasonable number of hours?

General Time Management Issues to Consider

The notion that effective time management is a professional balancing act is one of the first things to consider as you begin to deal with scheduling. It is something you will need to master if you want to be considered a skillful, qualified, and capable coach. Unfortunately, the reality of time management is that it does not get you any additional time. Good time management skills simply help you displace less critical tasks with more important ones.

Considering the reality that some time issues are under our control, and others are not, is a realistic place to start thinking about professional time management. We must accept those aspects of a schedule that cannot be changed—externally generated time problems—such as mandatory meetings and other teachers' schedules. What we can control are internally generated time problems, including procrastination, disorganization, task-hopping, and allowing ourselves to become overcommitted.

USING A SYSTEMATIC PROBLEM-SOLVING PROCESS

Skillful time management is not magic. As you know, there are only so many minutes in an hour and so many hours in a day. You cannot create more time. Recall how Kroth and Edge (2007) reminded us that no matter how hard we try, there is never enough time to accomplish all of the important work we have to do. What you can do, however, is use the time that is under your control as efficiently as possible. To accomplish this, consider using the four-phase, systematic problem-solving process that is described next (and discussed in greater detail in Chapters 6 and 7).

Phase 1: Problem presentation and analysis

Phase 2: Data analysis and intervention development

Phase 3: Implementation

Phase 4: Evaluation

Phase 1: Problem Presentation and Analysis

To start developing an effective time management system, start with a baseline description of your current time management processes. How are you currently spending your professional time? This baseline data can point you toward the time-related concerns that you need to address. To determine where you are now with time management, ask yourself whether you are spending some of your valuable professional time 1) engaging in nonessential work, 2) attending unnecessary meetings, 3) dealing with general disorganization in your paperwork or materials, 4) spending too much time with one individual or group, or 5) participating in activities that are not related to your professional performance goals, such as responding to non–work-related e-mails or reading news briefs.

To address these issues, begin by collecting data and using it to improve your own time management system. Collecting time data can be as simple as keeping a journal or informal log that you summarize at the end of the day or week to help identify problematic areas. We have also developed a more formal system for tracking and analyzing time called the Time Tracking Tool for SFC Coaches (3T-SFC; Hasbrouck, 2016) based on previous research studies (Franz et al., 2008; Hasbrouck et al., 2003; Hasbrouck et al., 1999; Tindal et al., 1992). The 3T-SFC (see Appendices 5.1 and 5.2) is an instrument for monitoring the time an SFC coach spends in professional activities, both directly and indirectly related to the core tasks of Facilitator, Collaborative Problem-Solver, and Teacher/Learner. The 3T-SFC can be used for at least three different and important purposes:

1. *Accountability:* How is time being spent by the coach? Is enough time being allowed to cover essential services? Are activities not directly related to coaching taking a significant amount of time?

2. *Program planning and evaluation:* Is the coach spending their time as productively as possible to accomplish targeted goals?

3. *Self-monitoring:* Does the coach have an effective personal management system to monitor their time?

Using the 3T-SFC begins by becoming familiar with the definitions of codes that have been assigned to various coaching tasks, which are organized into two sets of tasks: 1) those directly related to the three SFC roles and 2) other tasks in which coaches are frequently asked to participate, including teaching, management or administration, supervision or monitoring, and breaks and transitions between tasks. Time is tracked in 15-minute blocks on a recording form (see Appendix 5.2). For busy coaches, it is common that several activities may occur within a single block of 15 minutes or activities may run over from one block of time to another. We suggest that coaches use their best judgment to estimate how the majority of time was spent within each time block and use that task code for each time block.

In previous field tests of this time tracking tool, we have found that tracking your time for 6 days spread across a 2-week period is likely to give you the best overall picture of how you are spending your time as an SFC coach (e.g., Tuesday, Thursday, and Friday one week, then Monday, Wednesday, and Friday the following week). Describe your activity in brief notes on the recording form as soon as possible when each activity ends to increase the accuracy of your coding. The final step in the process is to download the 3T-SFC Summary Form (available with the book's online materials) and enter all the data you have collected for each separate day, which translates the daily data into an easy-to-interpret bar graph. Use the summary report for self-reflection, task analysis, or supervision feedback.

REFLECTION

Become familiar with the 3T-SFC code and follow the instructions for tracking your time for 6 days, spread over a 2-week period. Enter your data using the Chapter 5 appendices and 3T-SFC Summary Form (available with the book's online materials). See the About the Online Materials page at the front of the book for directions on how to access the digital version of these appendices and the summary form.

Phase 2: Data Analysis and Intervention Development

The second phase in a systematic problem-solving process involves analyzing the data you have collected and developing a plan for making any desired changes in the way you are currently managing your time. An analysis of your data helps you develop a problem formulation; in this case, a clear idea of any time-related problems you want to address. If your time management appears to be out of control, then you may need to make a list of all your problem areas and prioritize them to see which ones you want to tackle first.

After getting a handle on the real time-related concerns, the next step is to set some goals: How do you want to distribute your time across professional activities? What are your professional priorities? What do you want to achieve at the end of each week? Of course, involving your administrator/supervisor in setting time management goals is a good idea. We provide strategies on how to engage administrators/supervisors in the process later in this chapter.

Identifying one to three realistic goals may be appropriate. If you are currently spending close to 2 hours daily managing paperwork and materials, then setting a goal to reduce this to no more than 15 minutes a day is probably unrealistic, at least right away. It may be appropriate to set some interim goals that are more immediately achievable. Make your goals as concrete as possible. Specify what you will achieve in a specific time period: "My goal in 4 weeks is to be spending no more than 50 minutes on average each day on my paper and materials management." Finally, decide how to determine whether you have achieved your goals in the allotted amount of time. For example, you may decide that after 4 weeks or so you will once again spend a few days using a log or journal (or the 3T-SFC) to give you a new set of data about how you are doing now in managing your time.

To develop your time management intervention plan, take a thoughtful look at your goals and ask yourself what you must change in your daily or weekly routine to achieve them. Do you need to spend a few hours organizing your filing system? Is there a way to regulate the amount of time you spend reading and responding to e-mails or other messages? Should you consider getting rid of some of the books and materials you have cluttering your office? Can you delegate some of the paperwork that is taking much of your time? Perhaps there is a more efficient organizational system that could be implemented? To help you brainstorm ideas for tackling the things you want to change, it may be worthwhile to read some time management books or visit web sites that provide ideas on how to get organized. You can also attend time management workshops or webinars or simply ask your most organized friends and colleagues to share their favorite ideas and strategies.

Once you have a set of good ideas, narrow the list to approaches that will work for you. It will be a waste of time (which you certainly want to avoid!) and a big frustration if you try to use someone else's best tactic that just does not suit your own individual style. Perhaps your tech-savvy friend told you excitedly how the key to her amazing productivity was a time-management app on her phone. But using an app might not be the answer for you if one of your problems is spending too much time checking your phone anyway!

After selecting a few approaches to try, write them down. It may also help to develop a time line for implementation: What tasks will you undertake first? What will need to be accomplished by the end of Week 1? Week 2?

REFLECTION

Revisit the 3T-SFC data that you collected during the previous Reflection and analyze your findings. Based on your analysis, write down one to three goals that you would like to work toward achieving.

Phase 3: Implementation

Implementation is the next phase in this problem-solving process. Because you put your plan into writing, and perhaps even developed a time line, you now have a tool to help determine whether you are fully implementing your plan and making progress toward your overall goals. During the implementation of this plan, you will want to make some interim decisions about how the plan is working and determine whether to make some modifications along the way. If you have decided to tackle your organizational challenges by using a new computerized system to rearrange all of your files and then learn that the software you need is not compatible with your computer's operating system, then you will have to adjust either your plan or your time line.

REFLECTION

Revisit the one to three goals you wrote down during the previous Reflection. How will you stay focused on your time management goals?

Phase 4: Evaluation

Collect and analyze new data at the end of the period identified for improving your time management to assess how you are now spending your time. These findings will help you decide your next steps. If all or some of your goals have been met, then you may want to set new ones—perhaps returning to the longer list of goals you developed from the first round of data gathering. If your goals were not met but you are making steady progress, then you may want to stick with your plan awhile longer. If you are still far from making the changes you had hoped for, then consider reviewing the list of ideas you generated in Phase 2 and rewriting or modifying your goals.

REFLECTION

You set one to three time management goals and implemented your plan. What worked? What did not work? What are your next steps?

USING TIME MANAGEMENT STRATEGIES TO DEFINE YOUR ROLE AS A COACH

There is clearly some work involved in becoming an efficient time manager. It is quite possible that your current time management strategies only need fine tuning as you begin your new role as an SFC coach without using the four-phase problem-solving process. The ongoing process of defining their role, however, is one area in which coaches often find a need for this more formal course of action.

We presented entry into a new system as an ongoing process in Chapter 2. We also mentioned that even if the amount of work you begin doing as a coach is rather small at first, your workload is likely to grow. As this starts to happen, we strongly advise you to return to this time management problem-solving strategy. It can generate concrete data to use when holding professional discussions with your supervisor about how you are—and how you should be—spending your time.

As your role develops and expands, and the full benefits of having a coach in the building becomes more obvious, your administrator/supervisor is likely to begin thinking of even more tasks that you could do. If this happens, you may readily agree that all the new tasks are important and could definitely help improve students' outcomes in your school. It is also likely that at this same time more teachers have learned what a valuable resource a coach can be in helping them work with their students. You may begin to feel overwhelmed at some point and sense that you simply cannot stretch out your time any further and continue to perform in a professional manner.

To address this concern, we would not advise you to simply stop by an administrator's office and shout, "You've got to help me! I just have too much work to do!" This is especially ineffective if you just happen to stop by the office when the administrator/supervisor is also feeling buried by their own workload demands. We suggest a better approach, one that is much more likely to make a real difference in getting your administrator/supervisor to pay attention to your concerns.

Make an appointment with your administrator/supervisor. Pick a time of day when things in the office tend to have calmed down a bit. Bring along some current time management data you have collected over the past week to document exactly how much time you are spending on various tasks. For this kind of high-stakes discussion about time management in a professional setting—which could have an impact on your job description—we strongly suggest you use a formal data collection system such as the 3T-SFC for monitoring time, rather than a journal or log. Early versions of the 3T-SFC have been validated as an accurate data collection system and provide an easily interpreted graph of the ratio of time to tasks. You may also want to conduct a rehearsal of this conversation, perhaps using the communication skills practice activity discussed in Chapter 4. Consider also preparing and practicing a Solution Sandwich to make a request of your administrator/supervisor.

Begin your discussion by acknowledging that you have heard your administrator's/supervisor's requests for you to take on additional tasks and that you agree that these tasks are important and valuable. Using your newly honed professional communication skills, the discussion could go something like this:

"Thank you for making time to meet with me. I know how busy you are. I read your e-mail outlining your ideas for new responsibilities you'd like to have me take on as part of my work as the SFC coach in this building. I certainly agree with you that all the tasks you listed are very valuable and are ones that really do need to be done. I'm also flattered and pleased that you believe that I would be able to do these important jobs for our school. I actually feel confident that I could do them well, in collaboration with you and my teacher colleagues, and I would sincerely like to add these tasks to my role. I know you understand how busy I already am because of our frequent conversations. In fact, I've collected some data over the past 2 weeks to document how I am currently spending my time. (Show the graphed results of your personal time survey.) Given that you are my administrator/supervisor, I'd really appreciate your guidance and input about what tasks I should stop doing, or cut back on, so that I'll have sufficient time to add these new responsibilities to my workload. Perhaps there are some suggestions you could offer about how I could be doing my work more efficiently."

This kind of calm, rational, data-based professional discussion can be enlightening to both you and your administrator/supervisor. It can be the beginning of an important discussion about what a coach should be expected to do and what resources can be used to help get all the important tasks accomplished. *Note:* It may also be useful to encourage your administrator/supervisor to read this book—or at least Chapter 12 "Working With Administrative Partners." That final chapter is a synopsis of the entire book, with emphasis on the importance of having the administrator/supervisor and coach work collaboratively to define—and redefine—the coach's role and responsibilities.

CONCLUSION

There are many new skills to learn when becoming an instructional coach. For some of us, one of those new skills might be formal time management. Using systematic strategies to help us track, organize, and effectively manage our limited time can be helpful in accomplishing professional goals. Using data from tracking coaching activities can also play a helpful role when having discussions with your administrator/supervisor about your role as a coach. All around, time management is a valuable tool to add to your growing coaching toolkit.

Before proceeding to the next chapter, revisit your responses to the questions at the start of this chapter and make any adjustments based on new knowledge or insights gleaned. Also, take time to make any changes or updates to the application exercise.

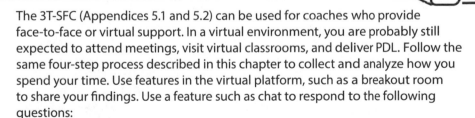

VIRTUAL COACHING TIP

The 3T-SFC (Appendices 5.1 and 5.2) can be used for coaches who provide face-to-face or virtual support. In a virtual environment, you are probably still expected to attend meetings, visit virtual classrooms, and deliver PDL. Follow the same four-step process described in this chapter to collect and analyze how you spend your time. Use features in the virtual platform, such as a breakout room to share your findings. Use a feature such as chat to respond to the following questions:

- After reviewing your findings, what became clearer to you?
- What is working for you?
- What adjustments, if any, might you make?

REFERENCES

Franz, D. P., Vannest, K. J., Parker, R. I., Hasbrouck, J. E., Dyer, N., & Davis, J. L. (2008). Time use by special educators and how it is valued. *Journal of School Leadership, 18,* 551–576.

Hasbrouck, J. (2016). *3T-SFC: Time tracking tool for student-focused coaches.* JH Educational Services.

Hasbrouck, J. E., Parker, R. I., & Denton, C. A. (2003). *3T-SR: Teacher time-tracking in special programs for reading teachers & specialists.* Department of Educational Psychology, Texas A&M University.

Hasbrouck, J. E., Parker, R. I., & Tindal, G. (1999). Perceptions of usefulness of case-related activities: Implications for training. *Journal of Educational and Psychological Consultation, 10*(1), 83–90.

Kroth, R., & Edge, D. (2007). *Communicating with parents and families of exceptional children.* Love Publishing.

Tindal, G., Parker, R., & Hasbrouck, J. E. (1992). The construct validity of stages and activities in the consultation process. *Journal of Educational and Psychological Consultation, 3,* 99–1118.

3T-SFC
Time Tracking Tool for Student-Focused Coaches
CODING MANUAL DIRECTIONS

Begin by reading through the following code definitions so you can be consistent in your record keeping. You will be coding your activities in 15-minute blocks. Several different activities may occur within a single time block, or activities run over from one block of time to another. Use your best judgment to estimate how the majority of time was spent within each time block and use that code.

Collecting data for 6 days across a 2-week period may give you the best summary of how you are spending your time. To do this, make six copies of the 3T-SFC Recording Form (see Appendix 5.2). Describe your activity and make brief notes on the Recording Form as soon as possible when each activity ends. Do not worry about coding each activity until you have more time.

The final step in the process is to enter all the data you have collected on the Excel 3T-SFC Summary Form for each separate day; this Excel form is available with the book's online materials (see About the Online Materials in the front matter for directions on how to access). Enter your data into each Day tab (e.g., Day 1, Day 2) of the Excel file. Then return to the Total Time tab to see a summary of how your time is spent. Use the summary report for self-reflection, task analysis, or supervision feedback.

SECTIONS 1–5: TASKS DIRECTLY RELATED TO THE SFC COACHING ROLE	
1. Relationship-building, role definition, and facilitation Facilitator role for SFC coaches	a. Visiting classrooms, checking in with colleagues, including using SFC Facilitator Questions (see Chapters 2 and 3)
	b. Helping with logistics (includes short-term, brief efforts such as locating materials, making a contact with a parent, or making photocopies)
	c. Meeting with administrator(s) directly related to coaching role (includes defining and redefining the coaching role, planning for tasks, discussing obligations or responsibilities, or reporting on coaching activities)
	d. Other activities related to establishing, explaining, defining, and redefining the coaching role with colleagues and others
2. Collaborative problem solving Collaborative Problem-Solver role for SFC coaches	a. Meetings or discussions with colleagues(s) related to Phase 1, 2, or 4 of SFC collaborative problem-solving activities (including planning, organizing, or participating in team problem solving, data analysis, or child/student study meetings)
	b. Collecting data for problem solving (observations, interviews, assessments, record reviews)
	c. Analyzing or preparing data specifically collected for problem-solving efforts
	d. Providing support prior to or during Phase 3 (includes discussing students' progress, modifying a plan, addressing implementation questions, locating materials related to the plan, or creating data forms)

3. Receiving professional development/learning (PDL) Teacher/Learner role for SFC coaches	a. Receiving PDL related to coaching role, including content-specific skills and knowledge (includes time spent participating in webinars, listening to professional podcasts, attending professional conferences, or attending meetings during which the primary purpose is to provide training and support to coaches)
	b. Reading, watching, and listening to sources of professional information related to coaching roles and/or content specific skills and knowledge
4. Providing PDL Teacher/Learner role for SFC coaches	a. Assessing PDL needs of colleagues or the school system (using needs assessments, assessment results, or other data sources)
	b. Planning and preparing PDL to be delivered (workshop, training, literature circle, book study group, or webinar)
	c. Providing PDL to two or more colleagues, paraprofessionals, volunteers, and/or families (includes meetings in which the coach facilitates discussion of effective instruction, student needs, assessment data, workshops, or study groups)
	d. Observing teachers' instruction and providing feedback (includes one-to-one work with a teacher in which feedback is provided for the general purpose of improvement of instruction or intervention, the fidelity of implementation of a specific program or material, or classroom organization and management)
	e. Modeling or demonstrating (includes one-to-one work with a teacher coplanning lessons, modeling/demonstrating teaching strategies or methods; it can also include coteaching or side-by-side teaching)
	f. Providing other one-to-one PDL (includes PDL not directly related to an observation, including discussing strategies, techniques, or methods related to instruction or intervention; behavior management; classroom organization; providing PDL to administrator)
	g. Evaluating PDL
5. Student assessment Related to Facilitator and Collaborative Problem-Solver roles for SFC coaches	a. Conducting assessments of students
	b. Managing or facilitating teachers' assessment of students (includes scheduling assessments, providing training on using specific assessments, obtaining or making copies of tests, or answering questions related to assessment)
	c. Managing student assessment data (includes collecting data from teachers, providing data entry, preparing visual displays, organizing data for reporting)

APPENDIX 5.1

SECTIONS 6–10: TASKS OUTSIDE THE SFC COACHING ROLE	
6. Teaching Outside SFC role and responsibilities	a. Preparing, planning, or providing instruction or intervention directly to students on a consistent schedule b. Temporary or short-term teaching (includes substituting or covering a class for a colleague so they can observe another teacher) *Note:* This section does not include coplanning, modeling, or demonstrating a strategy or technique for a teacher; see Section 4.
7. Management or administration Outside SFC role and responsibilities	a. Attending meetings other than those previously described (includes grade level, professional learning community, department, job-alike, schoolwide, or district staff meetings) b. Reviewing or evaluating instructional materials c. Communications (reading or sending mail or e-mail or making telephone calls related to professional work) d. Completing or managing required forms or paperwork; writing required reports e. Other general managerial or administrative tasks (budgeting, ordering) *Note:* This section does not include meetings related to relationship building, role definition, collaborative problem solving, or professional development; see Sections 1–4.
8. Supervision or monitoring Outside SFC role and responsibilities	a. Formally evaluating teachers' quality of instruction or fidelity of implementation of an instructional program *Note:* This does not include providing professional development/learning for the teacher but reporting to some outside entity; see Section 4 for PDL activities. b. Formally evaluating or supervising others (paraprofessionals, student teachers, or volunteers) c. Monitoring students (hallways, bus loading/unloading, cafeteria, or playground) d. Other supervisory or monitoring activities
9. Break or transition	a. Meal or refreshment break (includes time reading personal mail or e-mail and making telephone calls) b. Traveling to or from coaching sites, meetings, or PDL trainings (does not include commuting time to/from work at start or end of the day) *Note:* If professional tasks are completed during breaks or transitions, then code the time as the task rather than as a break or transition.
10. Other	Other tasks not previously described

3T-SFC
Time Tracking Tool for Student-Focused Coaches
RECORDING FORM

Use this form to collect data throughout the day on how you are using your time. Describe your activity and make brief notes on the Recording Form as soon as possible when each activity ends.

Do not worry about coding each activity until you have more time.

We recommend printing six copies of this form and using them to track your time for 6 days across a 2-week period. For example, the first week you could track your time on Monday, Wednesday, and Friday; the second week you could track your time on Monday, Tuesday, and Thursday.

At the end of your 2 weeks, use the codes listed after this form to label your time spent.

3T-SFC RECORDING FORM

Date: _____   Coach: _____   Site(s): _____

(1) RELATIONSHIP BUILDING, ROLE DEFINITION, AND FACILITATION	(2) COLLABORATIVE PROBLEM SOLVING	(3) RECEIVING PROFESSIONAL DEVELOPMENT/LEARNING (PDL)	(4) PROVIDING PDL	(5) STUDENT ASSESSMENT
1a Visit classroom 1b Logistics 1c Meet with administrator(s) 1d Other	2a Phase 1, 2, 4 2b Collect data 2c Analyze data 2d Phase 3 support	3a Receive PDL 3b Gather information about PDL	4a Assess for PDL 4b Plan and prepare 4c Provide PDL 2+ 4d Observe teachers 4e Model 4f Provide other PDL 4g Evaluate PDL	5a Collect data 5b Facilitate 5c Manage
(6) TEACHING	(7) MANAGEMENT OR ADMINISTRATION	(8) SUPERVISION OR MONITORING	(9) BREAK OR TRANSITION	(10) OTHER
6a Teach scheduled 6b Teaching temporary	7a Attend meetings 7b Review materials 7c Communications 7d Paperwork 7e Other administrative task	8a Evaluate teachers 8b Supervise others 8c Monitor students 8d Other	9a Meal/refreshment break 9b Travel	

TIME	CODE (S)	ACTIVITY DESCRIPTION
7:00		
7:15		
7:30		
7:45		
8:00		
8:15		
8:30		
8:45		
9:00		
9:15		
9:30		
9:45		
10:00		
10:15		
10:30		
10:45		
11:00		
11:15		
11:30		
11:45		
12:00		
12:15		
12:30		
12:45		

TIME	CODE (S)	ACTIVITY DESCRIPTION
1:00		
1:15		
1:30		
1:45		
2:00		
2:15		
2:30		
2:45		
3:00		
3:15		
3:30		
3:45		
4:00		
4:15		
4:30		
4:45		
5:00		

Evening:

NOTES AND COMMENTS:

Student-Focused Coaching by Jan Hasbrouck and Daryl Michel.

6

The Collaborative Problem-Solver Role and the SFC Collaborative Problem-Solving Process

Before reading this chapter, consider the following questions. Jot down some notes on your current understanding, and then at the end of the chapter, we will revisit these questions to assess the knowledge and insight you gained during your reading.

- When meeting with a teacher to discuss an academic or behavioral concern, what action(s) do you take as the coach to make sure that you clearly understand the teacher's need(s)?

- How would you describe your approach in helping a teacher set one or more goals?

- In what way(s) do you provide targeted support to help a teacher achieve a goal?

APPLICATION EXERCISE

In this chapter, you will learn about the SFC Collaborative Problem-Solving Process. We encourage you to select a teacher and practice as you learn and read about each phase. Take time to reflect after each practice session. How did I use the SFC Collaborative Problem-Solving Process to guide the conversation? What did I do during the conversation? What did the teacher do? If I practiced with another teacher, what would I do similarly or differently?

INTRODUCTION

Chapter 2 introduced the three roles of an SFC coach: Facilitator, Collaborative Problem-Solver, and Teacher/Learner. This chapter presents the role of Collaborative Problem-Solver, and the next two chapters provide you with tools and strategies to incorporate this role into your work as an instructional coach. Over the many years that the SFC model has been developed and implemented, we found that having SFC coaches engage in the Collaborative Problem-Solver role is the most effective and powerful way for them to spend their time. The support coaches provide in the role has the highest impact on achieving the goals of enhancing student learning, maximizing every teacher's knowledge and skills, learning from each other, and preventing future problems. Skillfully incorporating a structured, collaborative, and systematic problem-solving process into your set of coaching tools provides you with an effective, research-validated way to work with colleagues to tackle a range of problems—from relatively simple concerns to extremely complex problems involving academic, behavioral, and social-emotional issues that often extend beyond the walls of a classroom into the school, home, and community.

The structured process we have developed for use in the SFC Collaborative Problem-Solver role has evolved over many years. It was initially developed to help novice coaches feel confident as they collaborated with colleagues to address concerns they had never before encountered. The step-by-step structure of the process served to remind coaches that their role was to collaboratively support their colleagues and their students, not to solve problems on their own.

One reason collaborative problem solving is the most effective way to provide PDL to our colleagues (Denton et al., 2003) is because we start the process with a concern identified and targeted by the teachers themselves, rather than an outside agenda that suggests a teacher should be making changes identified by the coach. Collaborative problem solving helps us find a way to work with even the most reluctant teachers. Implemented correctly, it lays a foundation for a trusting, respectful professional relationship between the coach and teacher colleagues, which has been identified from research in education, business, psychology, philosophy of science, and cultural anthropology as essential for effective coaching outcomes (Knight, 2011a). Because coaching relies on the existence of this kind of collaborative relationship, investing time in a process that leads to this outcome is a wise choice for a coach (Hasbrouck & Denton, 2010; Knight, 2011b). Going through the structured process together allows a coach to provide valuable PDL to colleagues within the context of their own classrooms, which adds great value to the new information, skills, or strategies being shared. This format is deeply personalized, sustained, and sufficiently intensive to maximize the learning outcomes for the teacher and have a higher likelihood of positive impact on student outcomes.

The SFC Collaborative Problem-Solving Process often involves a coach working with one teacher who has a concern about one student. The process can work equally well in other situations. You can also use the SFC Collaborative Problem-Solving Process to work with a teacher who has a concern about a group of students, including a concern about a group of students who are not making progress or a content-area class (e.g., science, social studies) in which some students are struggling with the reading and writing requirements of the course. Yet, another way to use collaborative problem solving includes having a coach work with family members and a teacher together, sometimes referred to as *conjoint consultation* (Hughes et al., 2001). The direct participation of family members in a strategic problem-solving process can be powerful, especially for concerns that involve behavioral or social-emotional concerns.

A generic process for problem solving has long existed (see D'Zurilla & Goldfried, 1971; Gick, 1986; Hayes, 1989; Krulik & Rudnik, 1984; VanGundy, 1987; Voss et al., 1983) and has been used across many disciplines, including business, mathematics, chemistry, engineering, and social sciences. In this generic model, four steps or phases are typically identified:

1. Identify the problem to be solved

2. Develop a solution

3. Implement the solution

4. Evaluate the effectiveness of the implemented solution

What occurs in each phase of the problem-solving process seems self-explanatory. The first phase involves accurately identifying what the problem actually entails. Once a clear and precise definition of the concern has been developed, the second phase is to design a plan to solve the problem. The plan then needs to be implemented, and, finally, an evaluation should be conducted to determine the degree to which the problem has been solved. Simple, right?

Well, yes, at times it is, in fact, simple. Although a four-phase process to tackle problems sounds rather straightforward, things quickly get more challenging in the real world because the problems are often quite complex. This is certainly true when we think about the kinds of challenges facing instructional coaches. Academic and behavioral issues are frequently multifaceted and intertwined, and a coach must consider all the contributing variables to fully analyze most of these concerns. These can include the quality and nature of instruction; curriculum materials being used; skill and experience of the teacher; classroom environment and organization; any disabilities or learning challenges a student may have; the effect of an academic problem on the student's behavior, motivation, and self-esteem; and more. Just knowing about a four-phase problem solving process is certainly not sufficient.

Remember, the key purpose of coaching is to provide effective PDL so that students can achieve to their highest potential. Simply offering a teacher a quick answer to a concern is rarely the best way to accomplish this in a way that has lasting impact. Your understanding of the actual problem might not be completely accurate, so your suggestion might not end up solving the problem. The solution you offer to the teacher might be something that could be successful in your own classroom but might not match your colleague's way of managing the classroom or providing instruction. The teacher might not fully understand how to effectively implement your suggestion and uses it incorrectly or incompletely. They may end up feeling like you were not helpful. There are many pitfalls to trying to quickly solve problems. Engaging in the SFC Collaborative Problem-Solving Process can take care of all these concerns.

While using this process, it is critical to clearly explain to your colleagues that you plan to provide coaching support and services to them primarily using a sometimes-lengthy collaborative process. Many teachers assume that you will simply listen to their descriptions of problems and then immediately provide a prescription, or solution for solving them. Remember the idea of coaches having a special power and magic wand discussed in Chapter 1? Many teachers seem to believe that coaches come with these amazing tools and abilities. "I will tell you my problem, you do your 'coaching magic' and voilà—problem solved!" Although there may be some occasions where you can quickly and appropriately give advice or suggest a plan of action to a teacher without going through the full process described in this chapter, in most cases, you will find that you are much more successful if you follow some version of the more detailed Collaborative Problem-Solving Process rather than magically coming up with a solution. Because providing coaching via a problem-solving process is not intuitive to most teachers or other school-based colleagues, it is best to start the process with a discussion of how you will be proceeding. Consider walking them through diagrams of the SFC Collaborative Problem-Solving Process (see Figures 6.1 and 6.2) or the SFC Collaborative Problem-Solving Process Checklist (see Figure 6.3) and assure them that you will help them come up with a solution to their concern as quickly and efficiently as possible.

SFC COLLABORATIVE PROBLEM-SOLVING PROCESS

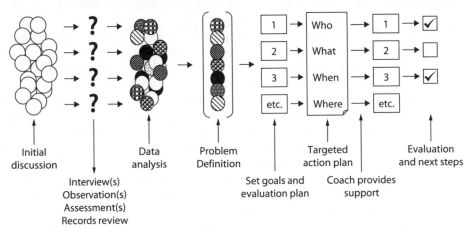

Figure 6.1.   SFC Collaborative Problem-Solving Process.

SFC COLLABORATIVE PROBLEM-SOLVING PROCESS
FOUR PHASES

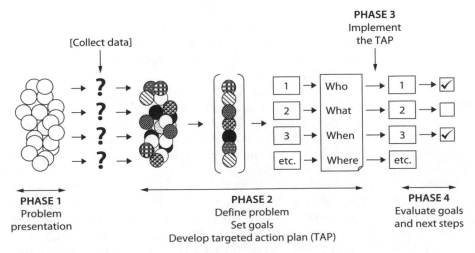

Figure 6.2.   SFC Collaborative Problem-Solving Process: Four phases.

Phase 1: **Problem presentation** (15- to 20-minute meeting)	Notes
• Hear presented problem (description, context, history; current understanding of the concern)	
• Data collection plan (interviews, observations, assessments, records review as needed)	
• Learn about your colleague (beliefs, background, experience, teaching "style," philosophy)	

COLLECT DATA

Phase 2: **Define the problem, set goals, develop targeted action plan (TAP)** (one or more meetings; perhaps 1 hour total)	Notes
• Share and discuss collected data (stop the meeting if more data is needed)	
• Develop problem definition	
• Set goals	
• Create an evaluation plan (for Phase 4)	
• Develop the TAP (for Phase 3)	
• Determine how the SFC Coach will support the TAP implementation	

Phase 3: **Implement the TAP** (perhaps several weeks or months)	Notes
• Teacher takes the lead; SFC Coach provides support	

Phase 4: **Evaluate goals and next steps** (30- to 45-minute meeting)	Notes
Evaluate each goal separately	
Goal achieved:	
• End the TAP immediately or phase it out over time	
• Develop new goals and new TAP	
Goal not achieved:	
• Adjust the goal	
• Eliminate the goal	
• Adjust or modify the TAP	
• Continue the TAP for now	
Next steps?	

Figure 6.3. SFC Collaborative Problem-Solving Process Checklist.

It is important to emphasize the collaborative nature of the work throughout the process. The Collaborative Problem-Solver role is the centerpiece of the SFC model because it is the most effective way to provide PDL to our colleagues and achieve the four goals of SFC: 1) enhance student learning, 2) maximize every teacher's knowledge and skills, 3) learn from each other, and 4) prevent future problems. But engaging in problem solving can only achieve these goals if the process is fully collaborative. That does not mean that you and the teacher will always contribute exactly 50-50 at each stage of the process. For example, as the SFC coach, you have

100% of the responsibility for managing the process. A highly experienced, veteran teacher may have more ideas and resources to contribute to a possible solution and may have more skill in carrying out the eventual plan in the classroom than a novice teacher. Be sure to invite and include your colleague's participation in every step. "What are your thoughts?" "What would you like to try?" "How should we get this done?" "What would you think about . . .?" Your language and authentic desire to engage in collaboration is key to making this process successful.

REFLECTION

Before proceeding, think about a problem-solving process you have implemented with a teacher when coaching or a problem-solving process with which you are familiar. What are the steps? What evidence exists to demonstrate that the process is collaborative? In what way(s) does the process enhance student learning?

SFC COLLABORATIVE PROBLEM-SOLVING PROCESS

Before we discuss the Collaborative Problem-Solving Process in detail, please note that the student's family should be contacted whenever a teacher involves a coach in a student's academic, behavioral, or social-emotional concern. A child's family should be involved whenever there is a concern about their child's performance at school. Some schools or districts may have a specific, formal policy about obtaining permission before even considering the development of an individual remedial or intervention plan for a student. Be sure you know what the policies and procedures are regarding family notification before you begin using the processes described in this chapter.

As we previously described, problem solving traditionally moves from problem to solution using a four-phase process. The problem-solving process that was developed explicitly for SFC coaches also involves four phases. We have adapted and customized each phase to match coaches' specific problem-solving needs in school settings. (We suggest you have copies of the SFC Collaborative Problem-Solving Process Overview and Phases [Figures 6.1 and 6.2] and the SFC Collaborative Problem-Solving Process Checklist [Figure 6.3] available to review as we describe the process.)

Our SFC Collaborative Problem-Solving Process for coaching proceeds through these four phases:

1. Problem presentation

2. Define the problem, set goals, develop a TAP

3. Implement the TAP

4. Evaluate goals and next steps

The first phase of the SFC Collaborative Problem-Solving Process begins when a teacher (or administrator/supervisor, specialist, or other colleague) seeks your assistance as a coach. This may occur during a scheduled meeting, perhaps after school or during a shared planning period, or maybe during one of the regular check-in visits where you will ask the three Facilitator Questions from Chapter 3: "What is working well for you?" "Are all your students making progress?" and "Do you have any questions or suggestions for me?"

Once you have heard a general overview of your colleague's concerns and determine that engaging in collaborative problem solving would be the best way to address the concern, you should schedule about 15–20 minutes for the official first phase of the process. Remember to clearly explain how the process will unfold across all four phases. (*Note:* This chapter provides an overview of the SFC Collaborative Problem-Solving Process. More specific, procedural details are provided in Chapter 8: "Gathering Information for Problem Solving" and Chapter 9: "Developing, Supporting, and Evaluating Effective Interventions.")

Phase 1: Problem Presentation

This step is called *problem presentation,* a term used by physicians before a firm diagnosis is established. For example, a physician's note might read, "The patient presented with recurring headaches." Physicians are taught to treat a patient's initial description of their concern cautiously. A presenting problem of headaches could ultimately be determined to be caused by dehydration or a brain tumor or something else entirely. Each of these would require a very different treatment. Trying to determine the correct solution based only on presented symptoms could lead to making big mistakes—jumping to a conclusion can mean jumping to a confusion! We follow the physician's caution at this early stage and, as always, base our work on evidence and the data that will be collected later in the process.

Objectives for Phase 1   There are three objectives for this initial phase of the problem-solving process. The first objective is to obtain a general understanding of the concern, and the second objective is to develop a plan for collecting any data or information. This additional data is used to determine the actual target problem and help set appropriate goals and design an effective intervention plan. This data moves us from considering the initial presenting problem to the targeted, defined problem in Phase 2.

The third objective for Phase 1 is to get a better understanding of your collaborative partner's beliefs about education and teaching, background, experience, teaching style, and philosophy. You will collaborate with the teacher in the second phase of the problem-solving process to develop a targeted intervention plan designed to specifically address the concern. If such a plan is going to be effective, regardless of how carefully it has been designed, then it must first be implemented. Developing a plan that does not adequately reflect the teacher's personal philosophy of instruction, cannot be easily implemented because of the way the teacher has organized the classroom, or requires specific knowledge, training, resources, skills, or experience that the teacher does not have will probably result in a plan that never gets off the ground, let alone one that can be used effectively.

This problem presentation phase is a crucial one in the problem-solving process and frequently requires more skill than you might initially think. There are differences between how veteran and novice problem solvers approach a presented problem. Experienced and skillful problem solvers know that a key to their success is to be certain that all subsequent efforts are directed to the actual problem, not a supposed problem or a proxy problem. Novice problem solvers can find themselves intimidated very early in this phase, in part because within moments of hearing the problem being described, they often begin a frantic mental search for the solution to the problem. Sometimes they may even begin to carry on an anxious internal dialogue: "Oh, yikes! I've never had to deal with a problem like this one before. I have no idea what should be done about this! What am I going to say to this teacher? Why did I ever think I could be a coach anyway? I'm a complete fraud and the teacher is soon going to figure this out." Anyone who is busy thinking these thoughts and feeling this apprehensive about what solution to suggest cannot be listening intently to the actual information being presented or attending to the more subtle contextual information.

Veteran problem solvers approach this initial phase differently. To begin with, experienced problem solvers know that there is never the perfect solution to any problem, so they waste little mental energy trying to come up with one. These problem-solving pros also know that it is not their responsibility to come up with a solution. Expert problem solvers bring their knowledge about skillfully directing and managing the process, thoroughly engaging in the process at each step, and finding the balance between efficiency and effectiveness. Although one goal of coaching is always to attempt to solve the referred problem, achieving this goal is not the coach's responsibility alone; it must be a shared responsibility. More important, veteran problem solvers also know that the problem being initially described may not even end up being the targeted concern. Why worry about a possible solution at this early initial stage? These experienced problem solvers stay cool, calm, and collected throughout this process.

The Process of Phase 1   The problem presentation meeting between the teacher and SFC coach usually takes the form of an informal interview. (*Note:* Chapter 8 provides detailed information about the process of conducting problem-solving interviews with colleagues.) The teacher completely describes the current status of the problem, shares information about the student or students who are the focus of the concern, presents a bit of history about when the problem started, and describes what has been tried so far to address the problem. The teacher may also provide other details that can help you get a more complete picture of the concern, such as whether the student is receiving any special services or significant details the teacher may have about the student's background or family situation. Although there is important work to be done in Phase 1, we recommend only devoting 15–20 minutes for this meeting because you are only discussing the teacher's opinion of the problem. You will need to spend more time later accurately defining the problem (and ultimately developing a targeted action plan) once you have collected the appropriate information.

Obtain a Description of the Problem   You want to be efficient during Phase 1 so you can obtain as much relevant information as possible from the teacher about their perception of the problem. Be prepared to ask specific questions such as the following:

- Is the problem/concern currently getting worse? Better? Is it fairly stable?

- What interventions have you tried?

- Has the student's family been involved?

- Have other teachers been involved?

It can be helpful to have the teacher bring some data to an initial discussion with a coach, and some schools even require this. This can include information such as the following:

- The student's attendance history

- How often does the student complete assigned work? Always? Usually? Sometimes? Rarely? Never?

- Is the quality of the work satisfactory?

- Does the student do well in one subject but not in another?

If the problem is an academic concern, then it can also be helpful to analyze some of the student's work samples or even review the results from an informal assessment. Chapter 8 provides a guide for collecting information for collaborative problem solving.

Obtain Relevant Contextual Information   Along with the specific, concrete details of the concern, a coach must be fully attentive to other information, and sometimes this happens between the lines. Although some of the critical contextual details may be obtained by skillfully asking questions, some of the more sensitive information may have to be gleaned through careful observation of a teacher's body language, their choice of words, where the pauses or hesitations are made when presenting the information to you, and their sense of ownership or blame regarding the problem. A coach must pay special attention during the Phase 1 interview to gather critical contextual information about the teacher's tolerances, philosophy, background, skills, teaching style, and so forth. We describe this as having your coaching antenna turned on while working through problems with your colleagues. Again, all of this is important in your first collaboration with a teacher. Once you have established a professional relationship, you will already have a sense of this kind of background information when you collaborate in the future, which will allow you to move more quickly through this phase of the process.

Thinking and Responding Strategically: The Coach With Two Brains   One way beginning coaches can emulate veteran problem solvers is to approach the problem presentation phase of the SFC Collaborative Problem-Solving Process using two different (imaginary) brains—the one in the front (that has access to your mouth) and the second one in back. The task of the "front brain" is to listen intently to all the information being presented. This brain reminds us to use our best communication skills from Chapter 4:

- Use the SOLER position

- Fully engage in active listening

- Reflect feelings/affect: nonjudgmental, concise, acknowledging

- Paraphrase

- Ask questions

- Summarize

- Avoid jargon and slang

- Interrupt only if necessary

- Use nonverbal minimal encouragers

The coach carefully and fully attends to the content being shared. The coach accepts, without judgement, the information being presented as the speaker's vision of the problem and understands that they must have a clear picture of the presenter's interpretation or perception of the concern, regardless of its accuracy, to ultimately address this issue effectively. This front brain is also the one using a special, sensitive coaching antenna, which should be actively noting any subtle clues to things such as the teacher's belief systems, tolerances, and philosophy.

In contrast, the job of the coach's second "back brain" is almost the exact opposite. This brain is maintaining the stance of the skeptic and remains thoroughly unconvinced of the presented information: "Maybe this student's reading is really as low as the teacher is saying; maybe the problem is just inadequate curriculum materials; maybe this teacher has tried 'everything in the book' before calling me in to help." Staying at least somewhat dubious at this stage of the process can help guide a coach to fully explore the true nature of the problem, understanding that teachers who have lived with a challenging problem for a period of time may have lost their objective perspective about the facts and may be so emotionally involved that they have difficulty presenting relevant details in an unbiased manner. But this second brain is in the back—without access to the mouth—for a reason. None of these skeptical thoughts are shared with your colleague. They simply help guide the process of determining the data that should be obtained to move from the presenting problem in Phase 1 to a clearly articulated and defined problem.

Hidden Agendas   You could find yourself working with a teacher who you feel is editing the information being shared with you. Perhaps your colleague is trying to paint a picture of the situation that is somewhat different than objective reality. At times, a teacher may want you to help with a hidden agenda and, for a variety of reasons, may not want to discuss this openly. For example, a teacher may be having an issue with a student and intensely wants them to be moved out of the classroom but feels uncomfortable stating this aloud. Instead, the teacher may give you a mixed message by saying aloud, "I'm hoping that by working with you I can find some way to help Gerald improve his performance in my classroom," while thinking, "If this goes the way I hope it will, Gerald will be out of my classroom soon."

Teachers may not believe that some of their problems can or should be addressed by a classroom intervention. They may believe that some problems are due to external conditions, such as a student's home situation, their racial or cultural background, or another consideration that may not be socially acceptable to discuss openly. A teacher might be reluctant to say, "Well, you and I both know that Maria's reading skills are not going to get any better no matter what we try. Her family members don't even speak English, and Maria told me neither of them even knows how to read. Anyway, none of the kids who live in that apartment complex ever do well in school, ever. I've worked with enough of them to know." It is certainly challenging and discouraging to work with teachers who have a hidden agenda or strongly held negative beliefs about students and/or their families. But just like teachers cannot pick which students they work with, we as coaches must work to the best of our abilities with every teacher.

We have found that engaging in a skillfully managed SFC Collaborative Problem-Solving Process can sometimes bring a new awareness and an attitude shift for some teachers. It also may be necessary, however, to confront a teacher and challenge that teacher's ideas about what some students can or cannot do. Such a challenge is not about picking a fight, but it is an invitation for a colleague to reexamine some internal thinking or external behavior that seems to be self-defeating, harmful to others, or both and ultimately to change those patterns. Keeping that skeptical back brain and your coaching antennae actively engaged will help you cope with these challenging, but hopefully rare, situations.

Developing Questions or Hypotheses   One important objective of Phase 1 is to determine how you will collect data or information to define the actual problem more fully so that appropriate goals can be set and an effective intervention developed. During the initial activity in Phase 1 of listening—with your two brains and activated coaching antennae in play—to the presented problem and learning more about your colleague, the coach needs to have been mentally formulating a list of questions or hypotheses about the presented information that should be addressed. You will be developing this mental list at the same time you are listening to the teacher's version of the concern. While your front brain is listening attentively and empathetically to the factual information being presented, and the antennae are busy picking up any subtle background issues, your back brain is reacting with suspicion to each piece of information presented.

These questions or hypotheses are important because they will help guide you and the teacher to collect additional, important information to either help confirm the problem as presented or provide an alternative vision of the concern. Either way, additional data will help toward an overall successful outcome in almost every case. Table 6.1 provides some examples of questions or hypotheses that you may come up with while listening to a teacher present a problem.

Table 6.1.   Forming questions and hypotheses

Teacher comments	Questions (Q) or hypotheses (H)
"Joshua cannot read any of the materials I'm using in my classroom."	Q: What is Joshua's current reading level? Q: Is the problem primarily a decoding problem, a comprehension problem, or a combination of both? H: This is the first year this teacher has been teaching fourth grade. Perhaps this teacher has little experience with students whose reading skills are below grade level.
"I've tried everything I know to help Abigail, and I don't know what else to do!"	Q: What specific interventions have been tried? For how long? With what kind of results? H: Perhaps the teacher's knowledge of effective interventions is limited. H: Perhaps the teacher did not adequately implement a potentially effective intervention (too short of a duration, an instructional program not accurately conducted, or another reason).
"I know Teisha can do the work. She's just not trying hard enough."	Q: Is this a "can't do" problem, a "won't do" problem, or a combination? H: Perhaps this teacher does not know how to modify or adapt curriculum materials for students who are struggling academically.

Certainly, some of the questions that form in your mind during the problem presentation should be asked directly during this initial meeting, or you can at least use questions to probe and see whether a hypothesis seems to be confirmed or should be rejected. For example, if a teacher says, "Joshua cannot read any of the materials I'm using in my classroom," and you hypothesize that this teacher may have little experience teaching students at this grade level, then you can simply ask a few direct questions about this: "Am I correct that this is your first time teaching this grade level? Have you had any previous experience teaching at this level?" Yet, some of the questions or hypotheses will be best addressed by data collected outside of this meeting. For instance, if the teacher says, "I know Teisha can do the work. She's just not trying hard enough," then perhaps you might formulate this question in your back brain in response: "Is this a 'can't-do' problem or a 'won't-do' problem?" or "I wonder if this teacher is using this as an excuse because she's not sure how to help Teisha?" Completing a classroom observation and conducting a one-to-one interview and/or assessment with Teisha herself might be the best way to answer this question.

Developing a Plan for Data Collection   At this point, you should move toward bringing closure to this phase. Part of your responsibility as a coach is to manage the entire problem-solving process skillfully. Information obtained at this stage can only reflect the teacher's perceptions about the problem until more objective data can be collected. Spend just enough time to provide a general sense of the teacher's view of the problem and a focus for the next step—planning for data collection.

Move to developing the plan for data collection by 1) briefly summarizing your understanding of the presented concern, 2) asking the teacher whether your summary is correct, and 3) asking whether the teacher wants to add any additional information. Then collaboratively develop a plan to collect any additional information you both agree will help facilitate the development of the final, accurate problem definition in the next phase of the process. You might say, "As I shared with you during my overview of the Collaborative Problem-Solving Process with you, the next step is for us to decide how we will collect any additional data we might need to come up with the best plan possible."

In most cases, especially if you are working with a teacher for the first time, this will often involve conducting a classroom observation, which is always a rich source of the critical contextual information necessary for problem solving. (Chapter 8 provides detailed information on how to conduct and debrief classroom observations and collect other key data for problem solving.) We also suggest that you find ways to develop a collaborative approach to this problem by involving the teacher in the data collection process, as appropriate. Following is an example of how a coach might close this Phase 1 meeting:

> Thank you for sharing all this helpful information. I think I have a pretty good understanding of your concerns about James's reading problems. I don't want to take up more of your valuable time than is necessary. As I explained earlier, our next step will be to schedule another meeting where we can start discussing what we can do to help James. Before we have that meeting, I usually find it very helpful to schedule an observation of James's reading lesson. This gives me some important firsthand information we can use to make decisions about how to help improve things for James. Always good to get a second set of eyes on the situation! I'd also like to have a chance to visit with James and perhaps conduct some informal assessments to nail down what may be going on. You mentioned that you haven't talked to his teacher from last year. How would you feel about contacting the teacher to see whether you can find out whether James was

also having problems last year and whether she tried anything that was particularly helpful? Do you think it would be beneficial for you to take some notes during the time you are working with James on his reading, noting errors he's making or other things you are noticing about his reading? When we get back together, we can discuss what we've both learned and then set some goals and develop a plan of action. How does that sound? Great. What time looks good for you to have me come into your class to watch James's reading group?

If the teacher pushes you for a solution or advice, then try to fend off the request with the reminder that you should not offer a suggestion without fully understanding the specifics of the problem. Point out that classroom challenges are often complex. Jumping to a conclusion can result in jumping into confusion. But also promise to get to a possible solution as quickly as possible. Collect the data and information identified in the data collection plan before proceeding to Phase 2.

REFLECTION

We suggest that you use Figure 6.1 and Figure 6.2 to record your thoughts and write down any questions that you might need to clarify before implementing this problem-solving process. You might also decide that you want to try out this much of the problem-solving process. If this is the case, then select a colleague who is willing to practice Phase 1 with you.

Phase 2: Define the Problem, Set Goals, Develop the Targeted Action Plan

The second phase of the SFC Collaborative Problem-Solving Process also involves the coach meeting with the teacher. This is perhaps the most involved face-to-face step of the process.

Objectives for Phase 2   There are four important objectives to achieve during this phase: 1) accurately defining the problem based on an analysis of comprehensive and concrete data; 2) helping the teacher set some appropriate, realistic, and achievable goals; 3) developing a plan to evaluate the achievement of those goals; and 4) developing a targeted intervention plan to address the concern and reach the identified goals included in the TAP (i.e., who, what, when, where). This fourth objective also includes mapping out how you can support the teacher to successfully implement the TAP in their classroom.

The Process of Phase 2   The role of the coach in collaborative problem solving includes skillfully managing the process. There are a lot of important tasks involved in Phase 2. Try to find a way to complete all of them carefully and completely, being mindful of the time constraints of the teacher. Because so much needs to be accomplished in Phase 2, it may need to be conducted over a series of meetings that may take an hour or more in total.

Define the Problem   The first step in Phase 2 is to collaboratively define the actual problem that will serve as the focus for the TAP. The process of defining the problem has three steps: 1) sharing the data that has been collected,

2) collaboratively analyzing that data, and 3) coming up with a shared definition of the problem to be addressed.

Sharing Collected Data   The coach begins this next part of the process by determining whether the plan to collect additional data was carried out. If not, the meeting should perhaps be rescheduled. If sufficient information has been collected, then it should then be shared and analyzed collaboratively by the teacher and the coach. It is helpful to model effective problem solving to the teacher and continue to build the important collaborative relationship by thinking aloud as you examine any newly collected information, asking the teacher to voice opinions: "Hmmm, this is interesting. What do you think about this? This is what this says to me . . ."

If the collected data included a classroom observation, then begin the presentation of that information by asking an important question: "Was that day I was in your classroom to observe James's reading group fairly typical?" If the teacher does not consider that the observation was conducted on a typical day, then that teacher will not believe the collected data, so you should not waste too much time presenting it. In such a case, have a conversation about why the day was not a typical day and schedule another observation. If the teacher does consider the day of the observation to be reasonably like a typical day, then you can present the information. Always try to start with some positive comment about what you saw, if possible. As you present the information, you may find that the teacher begins to have an "ah-ha" moment about what is happening. Classroom observation data can be so powerful and informative that sharing this information alone can give the teacher some ideas for the next steps to take with their student.

Present and reflect on any other collected information. Try to keep the focus on the key elements—those points that will lead to an accurate problem definition—rather than presenting and reviewing every piece of data in detail. All the findings you share must be easily understood and interpreted by the teacher. You may find it helpful to translate data into a more easily interpretable format. Transforming data (e.g., the number of errors made while reading, results from a behavioral observation) into charts or graphs can make data more easily understandable.

As you listen to the teacher present any information they collected, be sure to clarify or modify inaccurate or incomplete statements to ensure an adequate understanding of the information. Direct the focus to the conditions most relevant to the problem. The teacher may need help in understanding or interpreting the data so that the next part of the process goes smoothly. For example, if you collected some on-task/off-task data that shows the student was off task during 23% of the observed lesson, or that the student is performing at the 45th percentile on a comprehensive academic measure, then it may be helpful to provide some information about what these figures mean and how to determine their significance to the problem you are working with the teacher to resolve.

Collaboratively Analyze Collected Data   All this information was collected to help more clearly define the actual problem. Interpreting the data involves a careful look at the information broadly to see if there are patterns or clues to why a problem developed in the first place and why it may be continuing. As the coach, you need to help the teacher notice and understand the significance of any such patterns or clues so that you can formulate an accurate problem definition. We are using this process to provide effective PDL, not to just address or solve a problem.

You must be sensitive to the teacher's self-respect during this analysis. Conduct your analysis in a manner that would not be perceived as accusing or blaming teachers for their actions or lack of action or implying fault or blame. That is not the way to begin an important collaboration. The focus of the discussion and data analysis must be on the influence and impact of the teacher's actions on the student. For example, instead of implying that a teacher is not skillful because a student was given reading materials that were too easy, you might say, "Based on the assessment I conducted of James's current reading level, it appears that he may well be able to read material that is more challenging than you had initially suspected. We can take a look at the difficulty level of the material he is trying to read. Making some adjustments there may be part of the plan we develop together." We discuss tips for holding these data-sharing conversations in Chapter 8: "Gathering Information for Problem Solving."

Problem Definition   After you and the teacher have reviewed and analyzed all the information you have collected, you take the lead to summarize what you have both observed and state a concise, accurate, and complete definition of the problem. This problem definition may or may not match the original problem description from Phase 1. It must reflect a synthesis of the review of the collected data that you and the teacher have just completed. You may need to narrow the scope of the problem or focus on one part of a complex cluster of problems to develop an effective intervention plan. Some problems have obvious priorities. If a student is a danger to themselves or others, then this has to be the immediate focus of your efforts. If one of the concerns is a serious problem with attendance, then this becomes the primary focus. The student needs to be attending school regularly before academic, behavioral, or social-emotional concerns can be addressed.

You should present the problem definition as a proposal that is open to amendment, revision, and input from the teacher:

> After looking over all this information, I would say that it appears that James is having problems with his reading because of some underlying skill deficits. He is reading almost 2 years below grade level, and we identified some problems with both decoding and fluency, both of which are affecting his comprehension and his motivation. Is this your sense of the situation? Is there anything you want to add? Do you think we might want to target one of these skill areas to address first?

Set Goals   Now that the actual problem has been carefully defined and targeted, many teachers will naturally want to start talking about the solution. A lot of time and energy has been invested already, so it is completely understandable that the teacher is ready to hear the solution. Coaches, however, need to help their colleagues understand that there is an important intermediary step that must take place first—setting goals. Moving the conversation to setting goals can be a nice change of pace because up until this point the entire conversation has been focused on the teacher's worries and concerns about the problem, what is going wrong, or what is it that the student cannot or will not do or always does inappropriately. We start thinking about potential positive outcomes when we set goals. We get to dream about how much better things will be in the future. That can be a relief, and it starts the process of coming up with a plan from a more encouraging and constructive place.

Goals involve determining what this student will do differently if the plan being developed works. Most teachers have had little experience with goal setting, so this is another PDL opportunity. Coaches should work with a teacher to set a reasonable number of goals, typically one to three, that are sufficiently concrete and measurable. There must be at least one goal to focus the work, but identifying too many goals can also undermine the process.

Goal setting leads directly to the development of a plan to evaluate the effectiveness of the TAP in Phase 4. The success of an intervention should be determined by the degree to which each goal was reached. Evaluations can be formative, providing information during the implementation of the plan, and summative, providing information at the conclusion of the intervention. The coach can use formative data to help support the effective implementation of the TAP, whereas summative data is probably most helpful in deterring the degree to which the goals have been met after a period of implementation. Chapter 9 discusses the specifics of setting goals and creating an evaluation plan.

Develop the Targeted Action Plan   We have reached the point in the process in which a coach works with a teacher to help develop an intervention to address the identified concern and achieve the goals. It should be clear how the process helps you, as the coach, approach problems or concerns like a veteran problem solver. You have completed a thorough analysis of a problem and verified issues by collecting objective data. A specific problem has been identified and clearly defined, and some reasonable and achievable goals for the student have been developed. Along the way you have provided your colleague with a model of how to thoughtfully and systematically address a problem that arises in their classroom. Now you are in a good place to begin developing the TAP with your collaborative partner, the teacher.

While developing the TAP, it is also important to discuss the processes that the coach will use to provide support and assurance while the teacher attempts to make changes in the current patterns of interaction with the target student. If the teacher knew how to implement these great new ideas already or could do them easily and consistently, then they might not have needed any help from a coach in the first place. The details of this work are described in Chapter 9.

Final Steps in Phase 2   As in Phase 1, the coach should wrap up this part of the process by 1) briefly summarizing the problem definition, goals, and TAP, including the plan for collecting evaluation data; 2) asking the teacher whether your summary is correct; and 3) asking whether the teacher wants to add or change any information. The final details also include a review of all the steps that need to be taken to get ready to implement the TAP. What needs to be done? Who will do it and by when? An agreement on when and how to begin to implement that plan will be the final step of this phase.

REFLECTION

At this time, we suggest that you continue to use Figure 6.1 and Figure 6.2 to record your thoughts and write down any questions that you might need to clarify before implementing this phase. In addition, if you selected a colleague with whom to practice implementing Phase 1 of the problem-solving process, then contact them about practicing Phase 2.

Phase 3: Implement the Targeted Action Plan

This is the phase in the SFC Collaborative Problem-Solving Process for deep and permanent learning. When teachers try new procedures in their own classrooms it is far more likely that these procedures will continue to be used successfully in the future if teachers receive sustained support from a coach.

Objectives for Phase 3   The teacher now takes the lead in Phase 3. Phase 3 has two objectives, and both are for the teacher: 1) to successfully implement the TAP and, we hope, in the process, 2) practice the new instructional methods, strategies, and skills that are part of the TAP.

The Process of Phase 3   For the length of time specified in the TAP, the teacher implements the new teaching strategy, uses additional instructional materials, sees that the student receives tutoring, or whatever help was specified in the plan. Along the way, any formative evaluation data that was specified in the evaluation part of the plan should be collected.

It is important to fully support the teacher in actually getting the TAP started. This seemingly simple step is a common stumbling block in the real world. Despite the best intentions and commitment to "start the new TAP for James next Monday," when Monday rolls around, it turns out James is absent or the teacher forgot that this was a field trip day, or many other unexpected circumstances. Check in with the teacher the night before or on the first day of the plan, if possible, to help ensure and support a successful start. If things did not go as originally planned, then help the teacher do a reset.

The coach takes a background role during the implementation of Phase 3, but it is a role of vital importance to the success of these efforts. Coaches provide support to the teacher so that the TAP gets implemented accurately and completely and to ensure evaluation data is collected as planned. Even though a plan may initially specify what to do, for a specified period the coach and teacher should be making collaborative decisions along the way. The teacher should certainly be taking note of what is happening daily in the classroom. If possible, the coach should also visit the classroom to see how things are proceeding or at least have a system for regularly checking in via a phone call, video chat, e-mail, or text. The teacher and coach together can determine whether the interventions should be continued, modified, or ended based on ongoing informal observations and check ins, along with analysis of any other formative data that is being collected.

In most cases, it will be appropriate to let the TAP run for the predetermined length of time and then complete the final phase of the process. The plan can be modified or adapted at any point, however. Rather than completely restarting with Phase 1, you and the teacher can revisit the data collected in Phase 2 and determine if more information needs to be collected, the problem definition needs to be revised, the goals need to be modified, or some components of the TAP itself should be changed. The SFC Collaborative Problem-Solving Process has given you a lot to work with to be successful if you need to troubleshoot.

> REFLECTION
>
> *Stop and record your thoughts on Phase 3 using Figure 6.1 and Figure 6.2. What steps will you take to hold yourself accountable for providing support during this phase? How will you know if your support makes a difference? What will you do if the teacher gets frustrated and wants to stop working the TAP? If you worked with a colleague to practice the problem-solving process, then you might respond to these questions based on that experience.*

Phase 4: Evaluate Goals and Next Steps

At the end of the implementation of the TAP, the teacher and coach sit down with all the information that was collected as part of the evaluation plan developed in Phase 2, which may include both formative and summative data.

Objectives for Phase 4   The final phase of the SFC Collaborative Problem-Solving Process has two objectives: 1) to evaluate the success of the TAP implementation by determining which if any of the goals have been met and 2) decide on next steps for your work with the teacher.

The Process of Phase 4   The SFC coach and teacher will analyze available data and use the results to decide about the next steps. Should the TAP be ended, continued as is, or modified? You collaboratively make this decision by examining each goal separately.

If a goal was achieved, do we want to

- End the TAP immediately or phase it out over time?

- Go back to the problem definition, look at other concerns, and begin the process of developing a new goal or two and then a new TAP to address the new goals?

If a goal was not achieved, do we want to

- Adjust the goal?

- Eliminate the goal?

- Adjust or modify in the TAP?

- Simply let the TAP run a bit longer? (The student might not yet have fully achieved the goal but has made progress.)

Even if you and the teacher find that all the goals were achieved, a couple of decisions still must be made. If the teacher believes that the original concern has been sufficiently addressed and feels no need for continued coaching at this time, then you can shake hands, give each other a hug or high five, or praise each other's good work and move on, hopefully leaving with a positive professional relationship in place and some new learning or understanding for both participants. Even though the concern that caused the teacher to seek out your assistance in the first place has been completely resolved, they may now have other reasons to continue working with you. The teacher might want to address some different issues, perhaps involving the original target student, or there may be other problems or other students for which the teacher might need your help. In this case, you simply restart the process, returning to Phase 1 and continuing through the next three phases. The SFC Collaborative Problem-Solving Process often goes much faster the second time through because a trusting collegial relationship has been established, and you both have a much better sense of each other's communication style, philosophies, knowledge base, and so forth.

REFLECTION

Stop and record your thoughts about Phase 4 on Figure 6.1 and Figure 6.2. What are your overall thoughts of this problem-solving process? What do you see as strengths or challenges? If you practiced with a colleague, what did you learn?

MANAGING THE SFC COLLABORATIVE PROBLEM-SOLVING PROCESS

The SFC Collaborative Problem-Solving Process is successful when the coach and the teacher fully commit to working together to help address a student's concern. The roles of the two participants in this process differ, however. The teacher is the person primarily responsible for helping to describe the concern and presenting the critical contextual information. The teacher is usually the person who carries out the TAP developed to address the problem. The coach helps to decide what additional information is needed to fully define the problem; guides the development of the goals, TAP, and evaluation plan; and supports the teacher to successfully implement and ultimately evaluate the effectiveness of the TAP. The coach also has an additional solo responsibility—to manage the process effectively. Managing the SFC Collaborative Problem-Solving Process involves using time management strategies and skillful communication, along with attentiveness to larger goals, which include helping a teacher learn how to engage independently in an effective and systematic problem-solving process when future problems with students arise.

Streamlined Problem Solving

This chapter described a multistep process for SFC coaches to use to address the sometimes quite complex problems that can arise in school settings. Completing this process can involve a significant investment of time. Those of us who work in schools know all too well that time is often in short supply and, of course, needs to be used wisely. It is also true that not every concern that comes your way as a coach will need to be addressed through such a systematic and detailed process as we have described.

In 1995, Karen Carey wrote a wonderful article about the realities of providing coaching in school settings. She said that coaches in schools should be taught a problem-solving method that is feasible to use in the real-world of schools. Carey mentioned the need for coaches to understand the limited time available to teachers who have "too many students with too many problems" (p. 399). She talked about learning to coach "on the fly," "on the way in from the parking lot in the morning, while walking to mailboxes, down hallways, and during playground duties" (p. 399). These are still wise and important suggestions for coaching today.

Carey (1995) was still talking about using some kind of problem-solving method or process on the fly, not just whipping out your magic wand and solving teachers' problems on the spot. It means adhering to the phases of problem solving but moving through them quickly and much less formally. We suggest using these criteria to guide your decision about the speed and formality of the process:

- *Have you worked with the teacher before?* Consider engaging in a streamlined version of the process if you already have a trusting, mutually respectful professional relationship and the problem presented by the teacher appears to be rather straightforward and narrowly focused.

- *What is the complexity of the problem to be addressed?* You will probably want to follow the steps of the four phases more formally if you have not previously engaged in the SFC Collaborative Problem-Solving Process with the teacher and/or the problem presented seems to be complex and multifaceted.

Jan recalls an incident from her days working as an instructional coach that serves as a good example of successfully using a more informal, streamlined process. She had worked in an elementary school for a number of years, originally as a reading specialist and then as the literacy coach. She knew most of the teachers well, had been in their classrooms often, and had a good understanding of their personal styles, philosophies, and depth of skill, knowledge, and experience. Many of these teachers also clearly respected Jan as a colleague and came to her often for guidance or support.

One day Katy, a second-grade teacher, walked up to Jan in the corridor and said, "What should I do about Ashley? She takes forever to finish her work and even then, she's not doing the quality of work that I know she can do." Katy had some of her students' papers with her and showed Jan a copy of Ashley's work (see Figure 6.4) with a note at the top, clearly written in frustration: "2 hrs. 5 min. total time on this sheet!" with only two of the seven questions answered and with poor handwriting. Jan asked Katy what she had already tried, and, on the spot, gave her a suggestion to try. Jan again saw Katy in the faculty room a week or so later. Katy came up to her and said, "Hey, thanks for your help. It really worked!" and showed Jan two of Ashley's recent worksheets, with all items successfully completed (see Figures 6.5 and 6.6). On one sheet Katy had written "The best ever!" with a giant, smiling star added for good measure.

Katy and Jan had worked together before. They had formed a mutually respectful professional relationship. The problem presented by Katy came with concrete evidence (see Figures 6.4–6.6)—it was more than just a presented problem and Katy's concern was well described and narrowly focused. Her goals for Ashley—to get her work done in a reasonable amount of time with good quality—were appropriate and achievable. All this made this informal encounter in the hallway completely appropriate for a fast-track to a suggested solution such as Carey's (1995) "coaching on the fly."

We believe it is important to reiterate that Katy requested Jan's support in this scenario, and they had already established a relationship. In addition, Katy was very specific when making her request and had evidence to share with Jan. Because of this, it made sense for Jan to offer a recommendation on the spot. This also would have been an instance in which Jan might have agreed to observe in Katy's classroom and provide feedback (Hasbrouck & Christen, 1997).

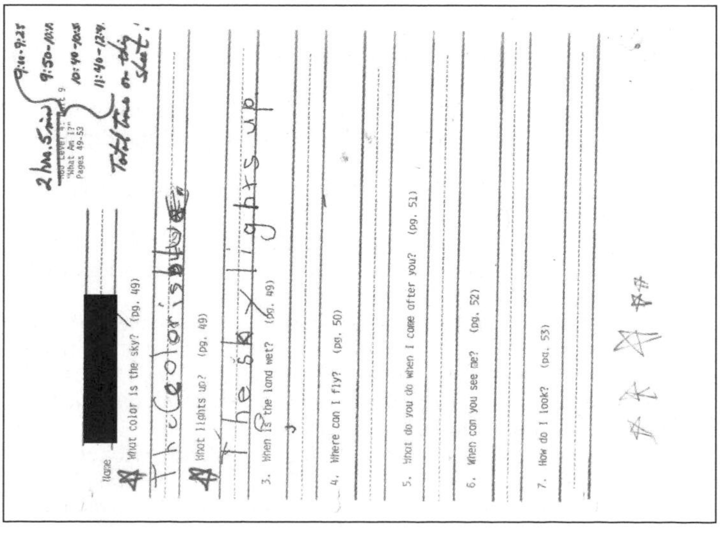

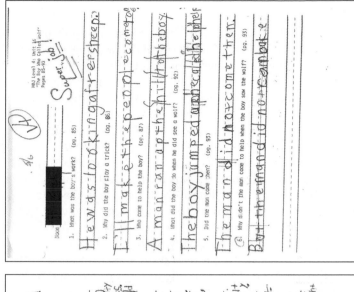

Figure 6.6. Student sample 3.

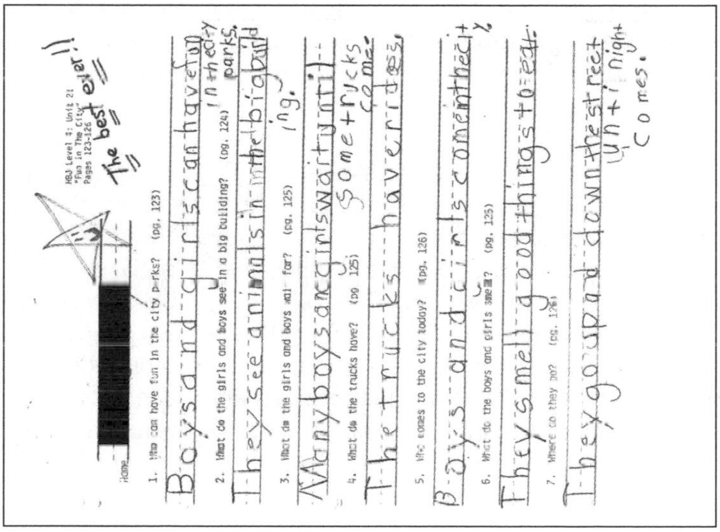

Figure 6.5. Student sample 2

Figure 6.4. Student sample 1.

CONCLUSION

This chapter outlined a highly systematic process so you will have a technique you can use to approach any kind of problem that comes your way as a Student-Focused coach. At the same time, we want you to function as a coach in a way that addresses the needs of the people with whom you are working. You may want to consider moving more quickly through a problem-solving process when time is short and a problem is straightforward. Yet, you may want to follow the Collaborative Problem-Solving Process to the letter when a problem is long standing and complex or you are providing coaching support to a teacher you have never worked with before. There is no single, lockstep approach. Load up your professional toolbox with several effective options for the Collaborative Problem-Solver role of coaching. The next chapter describes the efficient Team Problem-Solving Process as an additional method you can use when working with a group of multiple stakeholders, which is discussed in the next chapter. We hope this chapter has helped you add to your problem-solving toolkit.

Before proceeding to the next chapter, revisit your responses to the questions at the start of this chapter and make any adjustments based on new knowledge or insights gleaned. Also, take time to make any changes or updates to the application exercise.

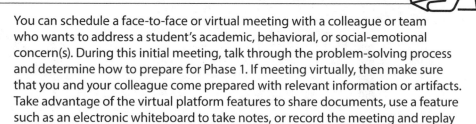

VIRTUAL COACHING TIP

You can schedule a face-to-face or virtual meeting with a colleague or team who wants to address a student's academic, behavioral, or social-emotional concern(s). During this initial meeting, talk through the problem-solving process and determine how to prepare for Phase 1. If meeting virtually, then make sure that you and your colleague come prepared with relevant information or artifacts. Take advantage of the virtual platform features to share documents, use a feature such as an electronic whiteboard to take notes, or record the meeting and replay it before moving into other phases.

REFERENCES

Carey, K. T. (1995). Consultation in the real world. *Journal of Educational and Psychological Consultation, 6*(4), 397–400.

Denton, C. A., Hasbrouck, J. E., & Sekaquaptewa, S. (2003). The consulting teacher: A case study in responsive systems consultation. *Journal of Educational and Psychological Consultation, 14*(1), 41–73.

D'Zurilla, T. J., & Goldfried, M. R. (1971). Problem-solving and behavior modification. *Journal of Abnormal Psychology, 78*(1), 107–126.

Fuchs, L. S., Fuchs, D., Hosp, M. K., & Jenkins, J. R. (2001). Oral reading fluency as an indicator of reading competence: A theoretical, empirical, and historical analysis. *Scientific Studies of Reading, 5,* 239–256.

Gick, M. L. (1986). Problem-solving strategies. *Educational Psychologist, 21*(1 & 2), 99–120.

Hasbrouck, J. E., & Christen, M. (1997). Providing peer coaching in inclusive settings: A tool for consulting teachers. *Intervention in School and Clinic, 32*(3), 172–177.

Hasbrouck, J., & Denton, C. (2010). *The reading coach 2: More tools and strategies for student-focused coaches.* Sopris West Educational Services.

Hayes, J. R. (1989). *The complete problem solver* (2nd ed.). Lawrence Erlbaum Associates.

Hughes, J. N., & Hasbrouck, J. E. (1997). *The Consultant Evaluation Rating Form (CERF) training manual.* Department of Educational Psychology, Texas A&M University.

Hughes, J. N., Hasbrouck, J. E., Serdahl, E., Heidgerken, A., & McHaney, L. (2001). Responsive systems consultation: A preliminary evaluation of implementation and outcomes. *Educational and Psychological Consultation, 12*(3), 179–202.

Knight, J. (2011a). *Unmistakable impact: A partnership approach for dramatically improving instruction.* Corwin.

Knight, J. (2011b, October). What good coaches do. *Educational Leadership, 69*(2), 18–22.

Krulik, S., & Rudnik, J. A. (1984). *Sourcebook for teaching problem-solving.* Allyn & Bacon.

Sprick, R., Coughlin, C., Garrison, M., & Sprick, J. (2019). *Interventions: Support for individual students with behavior challenges, Third edition.* Ancora Publishing.

VanGundy, A. B. (1987). *Creative problem-solving: A guide for trainers and management.* Quorum Books.

Voss, J. F., Tyler, S. W., & Yengo, L. A. (1983). Individual differences in the solving of social science problems. In R. F. Dillon & R. R. Schmeck (Eds.), *Individual differences in cognition* (Vol. 1, pp. 205–232). Academic Press.

7

Team Problem-Solving Process

Before reading this chapter, consider the following questions. Jot down some notes on your current understanding, and then at the end of the chapter, we will revisit these questions to assess the knowledge and insight you gained during your reading.

- What problem-solving process do you use, if any, when meeting with teachers?

- What training, if any, do you have in leading meetings? If you have received little or no formal training, then who would you contact and what support would you need?

- Who is in charge when meeting with a team of teachers (i.e., leads the meeting, determines the topics, sets the agenda)? In what way(s) might you improve or strengthen your approach?

- How would you describe meetings with teachers? For example, ongoing learning that is focused on one topic; differentiated, sustained learning based on individual teacher need; informational or compliance focused.

APPLICATION EXERCISE

In your role as an SFC coach, it is highly likely that you will be asked to assist with behavioral and academic concerns. This chapter builds on the content you learned in Chapter 6, except the focus is on using a structured problem-solving process in a group setting. We suggest that you take time to practice after you learn about the two processes designed to strategically address either academic or behavioral concerns. Contact colleagues, inform them that you are seeking volunteers to take part in a Team Problem-Solving Process, and stress that this will give you an opportunity to practice. After securing a few volunteers, prepare for and implement the behavior or academic Team Problem-Solving Process. We encourage you to write down what you are doing and noticing about yourself as you prepare and implement. Stop after each step as you practice and debrief. Did you do the step correctly? Did the suggested process work well for you, or are there modifications you would make? These reflections might come in handy when you start actually implementing one of the processes with a teacher.

INTRODUCTION

Sometimes it can be more efficient for a group of people to tackle problems, rather than having a coach work one-to-one with an individual teacher. Some schools have implemented a process in which a team of teachers and often other school-based professionals such as special educators, school psychologists, reading specialists, and counselors collaborate to address students' behavioral and/or academic concerns. Such teams have been given different names, including (but not limited to) intervention teams, PLCs, networks, and learning partnerships (City et al., 2009; Fullan, Quinn, & McEachen, 2018; Hall & Hord, 2015). Teams have been used to address students' problems because 1) the more people at the table working on a problem, the wider the diversity of possible solutions; 2) research on school restructuring has identified the benefits of collaboration and teamwork; and 3) ideas generated by a team can sometimes spread and have a broader impact than a single teacher and student (Kampwirth & Powers, 2015).

Yet, as anyone who has tried solving a problem in a group well knows, the potential benefits of any kind of team problem-solving approach can be easily outweighed by some serious difficulties, including the challenge of simply finding time on the calendars of a group of busy professionals for scheduling regular meetings. Other difficulties can include the tendency of some individuals to dominate a situation, the length of time it can take to allow everyone to fully participate in a group process, the greater potential for the discussion to drift off topic, and the different individual working styles of each participant that may create frustrations within the group.

One way to capture the benefits of using a systematic, collaborative problem-solving process with a group of professionals and simultaneously addressing potential pitfalls is to use a structure that controls the time and roles of each participant. Sprick, Booher, and Garrison (2009) outlined a process they called *Team Problem-Solving: An Efficient 25-Minute Process*. We have shared this method with SFC coaches across the country for many years and have received positive feedback about how their team meetings were finally running efficiently, with useful and functional plans being developed. The coaches using this method found it to be an efficient way to have a group of school-based professionals available to address students' problems in a strategic and effective manner. The 25-Minute Team Problem-Solving Process walks participants through a procedure that mirrors Collaborative Problem Solving, starting with an overview of the problem and any related background information, defining the problem to be targeted and setting a goal, brainstorming proactive strategies to address the problem, and finally creating a TAP with specified evaluation strategies. (We provide more information about planning and managing effective meetings in Chapter 10.)

THE 25-MINUTE TEAM PROBLEM-SOLVING PROCESS

There are two separate processes that both use the 25-minute format—one for behavioral concerns and another to address academic issues. Of course, many students will have concerns in both areas; to keep the process efficient, it is important for a teacher to separate the concerns and address individual concerns in separate meetings, if necessary. Each process is specifically tailored to address either behavioral or academic issues, but both have identical tasks that must be completed before holding a team problem-solving meeting, which includes forming the team and assigning roles to three individuals within the team. In addition, both the academic and behavioral processes mirror the more detailed problem-solving processes described in Chapter 6.

Forming the Team

The actual makeup of the team is flexible; every school will have different key people who should serve on a problem-solving team. Some schools have found it helpful to have the student's family attend these meetings, whereas others do not include family members on a regular basis. (If family members are invited to attend these meetings, it is important for a team member to carefully explain the process to them before the meeting. Otherwise, family members may feel as if they are being rushed or that their child is being shortchanged.)

Some schools find that rotating team members is a good idea, perhaps making participation in the problem-solving team a shared duty along with supervising hallways or working on the school social committee. Along with rotating members, there may be some individuals who attend every meeting. Depending on your staff, these regular members might include the school counselor, social worker, school psychologist, nurse, content specialists, or the instructional coach.

As valuable as it might be to have many of these specialists at the table for each meeting, another consideration is the size of the team. Teams with four or fewer members seem a bit small, and teams with 10 or more individuals often feel too big. We typically suggest that a team be comprised of between five and eight members.

Assigning Roles: Manager, Timekeeper, Recorder Both processes for addressing behavior and academic problems begin with assigning specific roles to three participants—Manager, Timekeeper, and Recorder. Each person who takes on one of these roles also participates in the process. Sprick et al. (2009) suggested that the teacher presenting their concern about a student not serve in any of these roles so they can fully concentrate on accurately sharing the information about their concern and listening to the comments, questions, and suggestions of their colleagues. These roles can be assigned to different people from meeting to meeting. For example, the coach, department heads, or building administrators should not always be the meeting Manager because that might imply that they have some additional power or authority that does not come with that role.

The Manager Role The Manager's responsibility is to oversee the group process and make sure that each person on the team has an equal opportunity to participate (no one individual dominates the conversation); the team stays focused on each step of the process, following the specified order of topics; and the amount of time allocated for each step is followed. The team problem-solving strategy will break down if the Manager does not stick to recommended time guidelines for each step in the process. Of course, there will be occasions when the team is making great strides on a step, but time simply runs out. In that case, the Manager may make a recommendation to the group to consider extending the time a bit (e.g., "We aren't quite done with our work on this step. Would everyone agree to extend this step by 2 minutes?"). Also, the opposite sometimes happens when the group wraps up all the work they need to accomplish on a step before the time runs out. In that case, the Manager would check with the group to determine if there is agreement on moving on to the next step. There is no provision for saving unused minutes (or seconds) from one step to another; that would ultimately become too confusing.

Although the basic structure of this process is designed for a 25-minute meeting, there are alternative time lines for a 35- or 50-minute meeting (see Tables 7.1 and 7.2). Some teams find it helpful to use the 35-minute structure for their first few meetings. Once team members are comfortable with the process, they may want to continue to allocate 35 minutes for future meetings, spending the first 10 minutes reviewing evaluation data from previous problem-solving meetings and then subsequently using the 25-minute time line for the meeting itself. The 50-minute option was created to be sure more complex problems could be thoughtfully and thoroughly discussed. It is essential to discuss and agree on which time option should be used before the meeting is scheduled.

Table 7.1. Recommended time lines for the Team Problem-Solving Process (behavioral concerns)

Structured intervention planning for behavioral concerns	25-minute meeting	35-minute meeting	50-minute meeting
Step 1 Present Background Information	6 minutes	7 minutes	10 minutes
Step 2 Identify the Problem and Set Goals	2 minutes	3 minutes	4 minutes
Step 3 Specify Responsible and Irresponsible Behaviors	4 minutes	6 minutes	8 minutes
Step 4 Determine Corrective Consequences	2 minutes	3 minutes	4 minutes
Step 5 Brainstorm Proactive Strategies	4 minutes	6 minutes	8 minutes
Step 6 Create the Targeted Action Plan (TAP)	3 minutes	4 minutes	8 minutes
Step 7 Final Details: Evaluation and Support	4 minutes	6 minutes	8 minutes

Source: Sprick, Brooher, and Garrison (2009).

Table 7.2. Recommended time lines for the Team Problem-Solving Process (academic concerns)

Structured intervention planning for academic concerns	25-minute meeting	35-minute meeting	50-minute meeting
Step 1 Present Background Information	6 minutes	8 minutes	10 minutes
Step 2 Identify the Problem and Set Goals	3 minutes	5 minutes	9 minutes
Step 3 Brainstorm Proactive Strategies	8 minutes	10 minutes	12 minutes
Step 4 Create the Targeted Action Plan (TAP)	5 minutes	7 minutes	10 minutes
Step 5 Final Details: Evaluation and Support	3 minutes	5 minutes	9 minutes

Source: Sprick, Brooher, and Garrison (2009).

The Timekeeper   The Timekeeper's role is to follow the guidelines for the number of minutes assigned to each step in the process and inform the Manager when the time for each step is about to expire, typically when about 30 seconds are left.

The Recorder   The Recorder has the primary responsibility of logging the key agreements at each step of the process and distributing copies of the final plan to all relevant parties. The Recorder should not feel as if they need to become an official courtroom stenographer, writing down everything that is said. At the conclusion of the meeting, the notes are typically handed to the teacher(s) who sought assistance from the team. Teachers are best served with short and succinct notes—the key ideas and a copy of the TAP developed by the team.

Getting Started

Little formal training is needed to make this problem-solving process successful, and everyone who is going to participate should know ahead of time about a few basic compliance rules:

- Participants should have learned about the steps of the process before the first meeting. We have provided a one-page form for both the behavioral problem-solving process (see Appendix 7.1) and the academic problem-solving process (see Appendix 7.2). It is helpful for every team member to have a copy of the appropriate form during a meeting.

- Team members must agree to adhere to the topic and purpose of each step.

- Everyone needs to follow the time guidelines, with only minor adjustments to extend a step or move on if the work on the current step is complete.

- Team members should fully participate in the problem-solving process so that all the possible good ideas are shared.

We highly recommend that SFC coaches give serious consideration to helping establish a problem-solving team in their building as one tool for developing a schoolwide approach for helping every student succeed.

Introduce the Team Problem-Solving Process to your colleagues by recording a mock run-through so everyone can get a better understanding of how the process works (and why it has so many advantages). Discuss the two versions, behavior and academic, and why it is important to address concerns separately. Walk everyone through the steps of the process and explain the options for meeting lengths (25, 35, or 50 minutes). A team problem-solving meeting generally involves one teacher bringing evidence on one student for the group to discuss. At upper grades when students may have multiple teachers in a building, a group of teachers may request a meeting to discuss a shared concern about a student. Develop a system for teachers to request a meeting to help them develop a plan for one or more of their students and how four to seven additional teachers or administrators will attend the meeting as members of the problem-solving team.

REFLECTION

What connections, if any, can you make between the individual problem-solving process covered in Chapter 6 and the Team Problem-Solving Process covered thus far in this chapter? If you are currently implementing or participating in team problem solving, how is it similar or different from the SFC Team Problem-Solving Process (e.g., focus on behavioral or academic concerns, roles, time frame)?

TEAM PROBLEM-SOLVING: STUDENT BEHAVIORAL CONCERNS

Prior to meeting, collect any relevant data related to the student's behavioral concerns (e.g., observations, office records). Contact family members as school policy or the situation requires. Assign the roles of Manager, Timekeeper, and Recorder.

Step 1: Present Background Information

This step begins with the teacher(s)

- Describing the concern about the student (problem presentation)

- Providing as much detail as possible about the problem behavior (e.g., when, where, how often, for how long has the problem been occurring)

- Describing the student's strengths

- Identifying the strategies that the teacher(s) has already tried

Team members may ask questions to get a better sense of the situation; however, no solutions may be offered at this early step. Also, leading questions or comments that imply what a teacher(s) should have done must be avoided (e.g., "Didn't you use positive reinforcement with this kid right off the bat?" "It sounds like you didn't establish a very positive relationship with this student"). The team's function is to help and support, not critique or embarrass, a colleague. The presenting teacher(s) should also share previously attempted interventions or strategies.

Step 2: Identify the Problem and Set Goals (Problem Definition and Goal Setting)

The team works with the teacher(s) to narrow the scope of the problem as necessary and identify one to three goals. See Chapter 6 for more criteria on achievable, realistic goals.

Step 3: Specify Responsible and Irresponsible Behaviors

The team specifies concrete examples of responsible behaviors and/or student strengths to encourage as well as examples of irresponsible behaviors to discourage. This step is essential because the teacher(s) who work with the student will need to be clear and precise about what they want the student to do and not to do. The teacher(s) must be consistent in the administration of any consequences or reinforcement. To be consistent, the desirable and undesirable behaviors must be carefully defined to the teacher(s) and ultimately to the student.

Step 4: Determine Corrective Consequences

The team determines whether irresponsible or inappropriate behavior will be corrected, ignored, or whether a consequence will be implemented by the teacher(s).

Step 5: Brainstorm Proactive Strategies

The team brainstorms ideas for how to encourage the student to increase responsible personal behaviors. The Manager should elicit as many ideas as possible from all attendees. Avoid discussing, criticizing, or dismissing ideas as they come up or promoting your own ideas as being the best. The teacher(s) presenting the problem behaviors can ask clarifying questions about the suggestions.

Step 6: Create the Targeted Action Plan (TAP)

At this step, we encourage all team members to simply listen as the presenting teacher(s) takes the lead in reviewing all the ideas suggested in Step 5 and selecting one or more to implement. Team members can, of course, answer any direct question from the teacher, but they should not play an active role in creating the TAP unless requested to do so by the presenting teacher. The plan has to be created by the teacher(s) who will actually be implementing it in their own classrooms. They create this plan by reviewing all the suggestions provided by the team and selecting the ones they believe will be useful in their classroom settings with their students.

Step 7: Final Details—Evaluation and Support

After developing the TAP, the team

- Helps develop at least two ways to determine the plan's effectiveness in achieving the goals identified in Step 2

- Identifies what other adults can do to assist the student and the teacher(s) to be successful (i.e., be as specific as possible: who will do what, where, by when)

- Identifies who will discuss the plan with the student and/or family and when this discussion will take place

Before the meeting ends, schedule a follow-up meeting to track the effectiveness of the plan. At that meeting, the same questions raised in Phase 4 of the Collaborative Problem-Solving Process (see Chapter 6) should be addressed: Should the TAP end, continue as is, or be modified? Address each goal separately. If the goal was achieved, then do we

- End the TAP immediately or phase it out over time?

- Want to go back to the problem definition, look at other concerns, and begin the process of developing a new goal or two and then a new TAP to address the new goals?

If the goal was not achieved, then do we

- Want to adjust the goal?

- Want to eliminate the goal?

- Want to make changes in the plan?

- Want to let the plan run a bit longer? (The student might not yet have fully achieved the goal but has made progress.)

The Manager ends the meeting (on time) with a summary of the plan and the ideas for support offered by the team members. The Recorder shares copies of the notes with the presenting teacher(s) (and others as relevant).

REFLECTION

Which step(s) do you believe will be easiest? Which do you think will be most challenging? What support will you need and from whom for a step(s) that you believe will be challenging? How do you think your colleagues will respond to following this process?

TEAM PROBLEM-SOLVING: STUDENT ACADEMIC CONCERNS

Chapters 9 and 11 provide more information about developing and implementing effective interventions for academic concerns. It could be beneficial for the coach to review those chapters—or even conduct some PDL based on those chapters—before participating in a team problem-solving meeting.

You will notice that the Team Problem-Solving Process for academic concerns has fewer steps than the process for behavioral concerns. This is due in part to the fact that teachers who bring academic concerns to the team need to collect relevant data before the meeting to share with team members.

Prior to the meeting, the presenting teacher(s) should

- Conduct appropriate assessments, including informal reading inventories, running records, oral reading fluency checks, or other relevant assessments in the academic area of concern (e.g., math, spelling). The teacher(s) should bring copies of results to share with team members.

- Collect and analyze student work samples and bring copies to the meeting.

- Conduct one-to-one diagnostic teaching sessions with the student to assess the student's skills and school success strategies such as notetaking, study skills, and organizational strategies. The teacher(s) observes the student while the student completes an academic task (e.g., reading a passage and answering questions, calculating answers for a series of math problems, writing a paragraph, describing how they would study for a test). The teacher(s) brings observation notes to the meeting.

- Contact family members as school policies or the situation requires.

Step 1: Present Background Information (Problem Presentation)

The presenting teacher(s) begins by describing the student's academic problem and presents and discusses information collected prior to the meeting. The teacher(s) also describes the student's academic strengths. If the team believes more information is needed, then the Manager should stop the meeting and reschedule so that meetings remain data driven.

As in the behavior team meeting process, team members may ask questions to get a better sense of the situation; however, no solutions may be offered at this early step. Also, leading questions or comments that imply what teacher(s) should have done must be avoided (e.g., "Why haven't you been doing fluency drills?" "This kid obviously needs to be in special education").

Step 2: Identify the Problem and Set Goals

As in the behavioral process, the team works with the teacher(s) to narrow the scope of the problem if necessary and identify one to three goals.

Step 3: Brainstorm Proactive Strategies

The team brainstorms ideas for how to help the student meet the identified goals. Ideas may include

- Changes in the classroom structure and organization, including how material is presented and assessed

- Targeted instruction or intervention to specifically address the student's academic or learning challenges

- Accommodations for adjusting the amount or difficulty of the student's workload or other appropriate modifications

The team brainstorms ideas for how to encourage the student to increase responsible academic behaviors. The Manager should elicit as many ideas as possible from all attendees. Avoid discussing, criticizing, or dismissing ideas as they come up—or promoting your own suggestions as being the best.

Step 4: Create the Targeted Action Plan (TAP)

At this step, we encourage all team members to simply listen as the presenting teacher(s) takes the lead in reviewing all the ideas suggested in Step 3 and selecting one or more to implement. Team members can, of course, answer any direct question from the teacher, but they should not play an active role in creating the TAP unless requested to do so by the presenting teacher. The plan has to be created by the teacher(s) who will actually be implementing it in their own classrooms.

Step 5: Final Details: Evaluation and Support

Finally, the team

- Helps develop at least two ways to determine the plan's effectiveness in achieving the goal(s) identified in Step 2

- Identifies what other adults can do to assist the student and the teacher(s) to be successful (i.e., be as specific as possible: who will do what, where, by when)

- Identifies who will discuss the plan with the student and when this discussion will take place

Before the meeting ends, schedule a follow-up meeting to track the effectiveness of the plan. At that meeting, the same questions raised in Phase 4 of the Collaborative Problem-Solving Process should be addressed. Consider if the TAP should end, continue as is, or be modified. Address each goal separately. If the goal was achieved, then do we

- End the TAP immediately or phase it out over time?

- Go back to the problem definition, look at other concerns, and begin the process of developing a new goal or two and then a new TAP to address the new goals?

If the goal was not achieved, then do we

- Adjust the goal?

- Eliminate the goal?

- Make changes in the plan?

- Let the plan run a bit longer? (The student might not yet have fully achieved the goal but has made progress.)

The Manager ends the meeting (on time) with a summary of the plan and the ideas for support offered by the team members. The Recorder shares copies of the notes with the presenting teacher(s) (and others as relevant).

REFLECTION

How, if at all, is this process similar to existing processes at your school? How would you help a teacher select valid, reliable data to bring to this meeting? As a coach, what would your role be in helping the teacher prepare the problem presentation?

CONCLUSION

The 25-Minute Team Problem-Solving Process can be a wonderful tool for SFC coaches to use with their colleagues. It is an efficient way to harness the power of a team of teachers to address a student's academic or behavioral challenges while keeping the process focused on the outcome. Having a team engage in systematic problem solving using this structured process is a great way to participate in PDL beyond having a coach doing that work alone. It is empowering to a broader group of colleagues to collaborate and address each other's classroom challenges. Using the 25-Minute Team Problem-Solving Process can help create a positive, effective, collaborative community of educators who are focused on helping teachers support student success.

Before proceeding to the next chapter, revisit your responses to the questions at the start of this chapter and make any adjustments based on new knowledge or insights gleaned. Also, take time to make any changes or updates to the application exercise.

VIRTUAL COACHING TIP

Whether discussing academic or behavioral concerns with colleagues, take advantage of the many virtual tools available for team problem solving. It could be helpful for the Recorder to start a Google Doc for tracking the information to be shared (goals, brainstormed strategies, the TAP). During Step 1, have the teacher share their screen to present valid, reliable data or create a slide(s) to highlight background information. During the collaboration steps (2–5 for behavior and 2 and 3 for academic plans), allow the allotted time for colleagues to help the teacher identify one to three goals and brainstorm strategies for the intervention. When the presenting teacher creates their TAP, that can be recorded on the Google Doc, along with plans for evaluating the success of the intervention.

REFERENCES

City, E., Elmore, R., Fiarman, S., & Teitel, L. (2009). *Instructional rounds in education: A network approach to improving teaching and learning.* Harvard Education Press.

Fullan, M., Quinn, J., & McEachen, J. (2018). *Deep learning: Engage the world change the world.* Corwin.

Hall, G., & Hord, S. (2015). *Implementing change: Patterns, principles, and potholes.* Pearson Education.

Kampwirth, T. J., & Powers, K. M. (2015). *Collaborative consultation in the schools: Effective practices for students with learning and behavior problems.* Prentice Hall.

Sprick, R., Booher, M., & Garrison, M. (2009). *B-RTI: Behavioral response to intervention: Creating a continuum of problem-solving and support.* Pacific NW Publishing.

Sprick, R., Coughlin, C., Garrison, M., & Sprick, E. (2019). *Interventions: Support for individual students with behavior challenges, third edition.* Ancora Publishing.

The Team Problem-Solving Process for Behavioral Concerns

Prior to meeting: Collect relevant data from observations, office records, and so forth, if possible. Contact parent(s) or guardian(s) as school policy or situation requires.

STEP 1: PRESENT BACKGROUND INFORMATION (6, 7, OR 10 MINUTES)

- Describe/present the behavioral concerns. Identify when, where, how often, and how long the problems occur.
- Describe the student's strengths and needs based on gathered information. Share previous interventions.

STEP 2: IDENTIFY THE PROBLEM AND SET GOALS (2, 3, OR 4 MINUTES)

- Narrow the scope of the concerns, if necessary.
- Identify one to three goals for improvement.

STEP 3: SPECIFY RESPONSIBLE AND IRRESPONSIBLE BEHAVIORS (4, 6, OR 8 MINUTES)

- Provide clear examples of responsible behavior and/or student strengths to encourage and irresponsible/inappropriate behaviors to discourage.

STEP 4: DETERMINE CORRECTIVE CONSEQUENCES (2, 3, OR 4 MINUTES)

- Determine if irresponsible or inappropriate behaviors will be corrected, ignored, or whether a consequence will be implemented.

STEP 5: BRAINSTORM PROACTIVE STRATEGIES (4, 6, OR 8 MINUTES)

- Brainstorm strategies to encourage responsible behaviors.

STEP 6: CREATE THE TARGETED ACTION PLAN (TAP) (3, 4, OR 8 MINUTES)

- Teacher(s) select a manageable set of strategies to implement. Team members answer questions only from the teacher(s).

STEP 7: FINAL DETAILS: EVALUATION AND SUPPORT (4, 6, OR 8 MINUTES)

- Evaluation: Identify ways to determine if the targeted action plan (TAP) is working.
- Support: Identify things other adults can do to assist the student and the teacher(s). Be specific: who does what, where, by when.
- Summarize plan and support plan.

Source: Sprick, Coughlin, Garrison, & Sprick (2019).

The Team Problem-Solving Process for Academic Concerns

PRIOR TO MEETING

- Administer appropriate assessments.

- Collect work samples.

- Conduct one-to-one diagnostic teaching sessions.

- Contact parent(s) or guardian(s) as school policy or situation requires.

- Be prepared to share assessment results with team members. Consider creating summaries of key findings.

STEP 1: PRESENT BACKGROUND INFORMATION (6, 8, OR 10 MINUTES)

- Describe/present the academic concerns using the collected information. (*Note:* If more information is needed, then stop here and reschedule.)

- Describe the student's academic strengths and needs based on gathered information.

- Share strategies or interventions already tried.

STEP 2: IDENTIFY THE PROBLEM AND SET GOALS (3, 5, OR 9 MINUTES)

- Target specific areas to provide assistance to the student (interventions and accommodations as appropriate).

- Identify one to three goals for improvement.

STEP 3: BRAINSTORM PROACTIVE STRATEGIES (8, 10, OR 12 MINUTES)

Brainstorm ideas for

- Changes in the classroom structure and organization.

- Targeted instruction or interventions.

- Accommodations for adjusting the amount or difficulty of the student's workload or other appropriate modifications.

STEP 4: CREATE THE TARGETED ACTION PLAN (TAP) (5, 7, OR 10 MINUTES)

- Teacher(s) select a manageable set of strategies to implement. Team members answer questions only from the teacher(s) at this step.

APPENDIX 7.2

STEP 5: FINAL DETAILS: EVALUATION AND SUPPORT (3, 5, OR 9 MINUTES)

- Evaluation: Identify ways to determine if the targeted action plan (TAP) is working.

- Support: Identify things other adults can do to assist the student and the teacher(s). Be specific: who does what, where, by when.

- Summarize TAP and plan for support.

Source: Sprick, Coughlin, Garrison, and Sprick (2019).

8

Gathering Information
for Problem Solving

Before reading this chapter, consider the following questions. Jot down some notes on your current understanding, and then at the end of the chapter, we will revisit these questions to assess the knowledge and insight you gained during your reading.

- Think about current problem-solving processes that you use to determine and prioritize student academic, behavioral, or social-emotional concerns.

    - What qualitative or quantitative data do you use?

    - How do you decide what data you need?

    - How do you analyze this data and with whom?

- What approach do you follow to set goals, decide on an action plan, and evaluate your plan?

- Are the problem-solving processes you are using being adequately supported by the data you are currently collecting and analyzing? Are there changes you need to consider making?

APPLICATION EXERCISE

Talk to several teachers to learn about their problem-solving processes when dealing with an academic, behavioral, or social-emotional concern. Record your findings and then analyze to determine how teachers approach problem solving.

- Is there a common process? If so, what is it for each type of concern?

- If it is not the same, what is different? How might you use this data when meeting with teachers to come up with a common approach?

INTRODUCTION

The road to learning and academic success is relatively smooth for some students. Others stumble over obstacles along the way that keep them from reaching their potential. Some obstacles are related to the students themselves; some are associated with the kind of instruction the students are receiving. The obstacles frequently spring from a combination of the teacher, the instruction and materials, and the student. Being an effective coach means working to help identify and analyze those often-complex relationships so when you put on your Collaborative Problem-Solver hat you can successfully apply the SFC Collaborative and Team Problem-Solving Processes that were presented in Chapters 6 and 7 to achieve the following outcomes: 1) provide targeted and sustained PDL to your teacher colleague, 2) solve the identified problem to improve outcomes for students, and 3) build critical professional collaborative relationships.

COLLECTING DATA

This chapter describes how to gather the information needed to clarify problems and help overcome the barriers that cause students to struggle with their learning. This data typically falls into four general categories, including data obtained from conducting interviews, observations, academic assessments of the target student, and a review of the student's records. A combination of these is often used. Much of the information gathering you will be completing as a coach occurs between Phase 1 (problem presentation) and Phase 2 (define the problem, set goals, develop the TAP) of the problem-solving process. Coaches also collect data during Phase 3 (implementing the TAP) to inform the decisions involved in Phase 4 (evaluation of goals and next steps). This chapter also provides guidance on how to give useful feedback to the teachers you work with, which occurs in Phases 2 and 3.

Identify Questions That Need to Be Answered

Identifying the questions you want to answer is the first step when considering how to collect any kind of data. Clearly identifying these questions helps determine if you should be thinking about conducting interviews or observations, reviewing academic assessments of the target student, reviewing the students' records, or some combination of these. As part of the SFC Collaborative Problem-Solving Process, these questions arise during Phase 1 as you and the teacher discuss the presenting problems. You might want to know things such as

- When does Eric seem to have the most trouble with his reading?

- What aspects of writing are hard for Santiago?

- Is Kiara actively engaged during class activities?

- Why does Tyrell seem bored when asked to do his assignments?

- Does Rosa struggle to understand the directions when she is doing her homework?

- Does Mrs. Aguirre have routines in place so students know what to do when their work is done or when it is time to change to a different activity?

The techniques we describe in this chapter will help you answer questions like the ones we have listed so you can get an idea of the obstacles that struggling students in your school are facing and then use that data to accurately identify the target problem and develop the best intervention possible (i.e., TAP).

GATHERING INFORMATION USING INTERVIEWS

Much of the information you need in the SFC Collaborative Problem-Solving Process comes from interviewing teachers, family members, and students. Your initial teacher interview, the first step in the structured process outlined in Chapter 6, helps you clarify the initial presenting problem. But interviewing one teacher is sometimes not enough. Different people will usually have different views of the same situation. Conducting interviews with a range of people involved directly, or even indirectly, with the presented concern can help the coach include multiple perspectives, which can lead to a more accurately defined target problem.

Interviewing the student's classroom teacher can help the coach answer two types of questions. First, it can reveal details about the nature of the difficulties the student seems to be having and the times and situations in which problems occur. Second, it can open a window into the classroom teacher's perception of the student and the student's difficulties.

You might want to review the sections of this book on getting started (see Chapter 2) and communication for collaboration (see Chapter 4) as you prepare for an interview. You will want the person being interviewed to feel comfortable by establishing a relationship of trust based on your sincere respect for their ideas and feelings. To a large degree, your nonverbal communication expresses so much information. Using the SOLER strategy we presented in Chapter 4 can help you remember to assume a posture that conveys concern and keeps you focused and attentive. Both your verbal and nonverbal responses to any comments and questions will help determine the success of an interview and possibly the future of the collaboration.

Interviewing Teachers

The initial interview with your teacher colleague is an opportunity to review the SFC Collaborative Problem-Solving Process with them. Teachers who bring their concerns to a coach are seeking assistance and solutions. They may believe that the process begins and ends with this initial meeting—they tell you about their problem, you listen carefully, and then you present them with a fully formed solution on the spot. It is important to clarify how the problem-solving process will proceed so the teacher will not have incorrect expectations.

Although you want to establish a warm and congenial tone at this first meeting, do not allow the interview to drift off course and become a friendly chat or the kind of informal conversation about students that sometimes occurs in the teachers' lounge or workroom. Remember, your goal is to establish and maintain a professional problem-solving relationship that results in improved outcomes for students, as well as to obtain key facts and context information. Sometimes this means you must skillfully redirect the teacher's responses to refocus on the student's specific challenges.

To keep an interview on track, it can be helpful to start with some agreements about the length of time to spend on this step in the process. As the person in charge of managing the problem-solving process—including the amount of time spent—the coach needs to be aware of the time constraints of all participants and spend only as much time as necessary gathering the information and establishing a collaborative relationship. Teachers often work in situations that keep them somewhat isolated from other adults, and when they have a chance to share their problems and concerns with someone, especially a skillful listener such as an SFC coach, they may want to extend the session longer than may be productive. Consider beginning the interview with a statement such as, "I'm glad we found this time to talk about your concerns about James. I have about 20 minutes now. Does that work for you?" Then you should try to keep the interview to that amount of time or less. If you are approaching the end of your agreed-on time limit and you are still engaged in productive work, then take note of the time and specifically ask your colleague if working for another 5 or 10 minutes is acceptable. Being aware of the time and respectful of agreements is part of skillfully managing the process.

The most productive interviews are usually somewhat structured. Taking time to write down the questions you want to address ahead of time can help you keep an interview on track. At the same time, the questions you ask should be open ended and not easily answered with a simple "yes" or "no." This will give the teacher the freedom to express both observations and opinions concerning the student and the feelings accompanying the relationship between student and teacher.

The questions in an initial Phase 1 interview may relate to experiences the teacher has had with the struggling student. Here are some examples:

- When does James seem to have problems? How would you describe these problems? How long has this been going on?

- At what time(s) of day or situations does James seem to do better or worse? How does James respond to large-group, small-group, or individual instruction? What have you noticed when James completes work independently?

- What contributions or feedback, if any, have you received from James's family members or other teachers?

- What interventions, if any, have you tried thus far? What was the result?

- What assessments have you administered recently? In what way(s) did the results help you identify some specific skills strengths or weaknesses?

As you interpret the teacher's responses, keep in mind that they reflect the teacher's beliefs about the student's problems. These beliefs may or may not be supported by other information you will be gathering. The teacher provides the presenting problem, which is an important piece of the puzzle but may or may not fully explain the student's difficulty completely or accurately.

Once you believe the teacher has presented sufficient information about their concern, provide a brief summary of your understanding of the concerns presented, ask whether your summary is correct, and see if the teacher wants to add any information. For example, you might say, "It sounds like you are concerned because James doesn't finish his independent work in reading class and doesn't pay attention during reading instruction. You also seem to be concerned about the quality of his work. His grades in reading are low, especially on assignments to read a passage and answer questions about it. Did I get this right? Is there anything you need to add?"

Finally, you and the teacher should agree on whether more information is needed before moving ahead to develop goals and a TAP, which will almost always be the case. You will likely want to conduct an observation of James during his reading class, so you will need to determine a good time to do this. You may ask the teacher to make notes about specific things they observe related to James's performance and collect relevant work samples. You or the teacher (or both) may plan to administer some assessments to determine the knowledge and skills James needs to learn. Perhaps additional interviews should be considered such as the student's family members, other teachers who currently or previously worked with the student, or even the student themselves. It can also be helpful to review a student's cumulative school records. If this interview is part of a Phase 1 meeting, then set another time to meet—after the pinpointed information has been collected—for the Phase 2 meeting to define the problem, set goals, and develop the TAP.

Interviewing Family Members

Many of our comments about Phase 1 teacher interviews also apply to interviews with students' families. Family members know their children well and can provide an important perspective that can be essential to address some of our students' more complex problems. If you do interview family members, then showing your respect for them and openness to their input will go a long way to establish a productive and cooperative relationship. Careful attention to communication skills is especially important when you interact with families. People who work in schools have their own ways of doing things, and even their own language (with words such as *on task*, *high-stakes tests*, or *objectives*), that may be unfamiliar or even a little overwhelming to some people. Some families may have had unpleasant experiences when they were in school and may have cautious or negative reactions to some aspects of schooling.

All families, including those whose cultures or languages are different from yours, should be encouraged to communicate in ways that make them feel comfortable. It is beyond the scope of this book to provide strategies for working with diverse families, but this is an important consideration for everyone working with students, their families, and their communities. Remember to clearly explain your role in the school and your relationship to their child's teachers.

It is just as important to prepare for the family interview as for a teacher interview. Questions you ask might ask family members include the following:

- What have you noticed when listening to or watching James read?

- Have you noticed James having trouble when he is doing homework?

- Does James have any vision or hearing problems that might affect his reading? If you are aware of problems, then how might this affect his reading? Are there any physical difficulties or medical conditions? If so, how might this condition affect his reading or ability to complete his homework?

- What kinds of things does James say about reading or about school?

- Is there anything else that you think it would be helpful for me to know?

Interviewing Students

Sometimes the best way to find out what is not going well for students is simply to ask them. When you visit the doctor, you are normally asked to talk about how you have been feeling. Doctors use this information along with information gathered from tests and their own observations. In much the same way, conducting structured interviews with students may provide you with insight into their attitudes and feelings and their sense about the times and situations when they have the most trouble. Once again, use communication strategies that allow the student to feel comfortable talking with you.

REFLECTION

How, if at all, do you conduct interviews with different stakeholder groups? If you have a process, then review your questions and make sure that most are open ended. In addition, make sure that you have an agreed-on time limit for this step in the process. If you do not have interview protocols established, then what additional learning or support will you need?

GATHERING INFORMATION USING OBSERVATIONS

Academic and behavior difficulties are rarely, if ever, caused only by conditions in the student. For example, if students are easily confused, then the kind of instruction and feedback they receive can have a big effect on their ability to understand concepts and apply the skills they are learning. It is important to observe instruction in the classroom to fully understand students' challenges, how to improve the instruction they receive, and the interactions among conditions in the classroom, the instruction, and the student.

We know that classroom observations can raise many challenging issues. From our experience, most educators are somewhat to very uncomfortable about being observed by other adults, especially when the observer is assumed to be an expert with a deep knowledge and high expectations about what they are observing. In addition, many coaches themselves have anxieties about conducting observations. You may not have experience doing this and may find the process overwhelming and intimidating. No one expects perfection. We hope you will invest the necessary time to learn how to skillfully conduct observations and improve your skills through a lot of practice. The large amount of tremendously valuable information obtained by observations are most definitely worth the effort. Remember the role-playing activities we suggested in Chapter 4 for practicing your collaborative communication skills? To obtain the practice you need to strengthen your observation skills and build your confidence in conducting classroom observations, seek out a willing colleague and conduct some observations in which the data being collected is not for any high-stakes or emotionally charged purpose.

Making the process as transparent as possible is one way to help your teacher colleagues feel more comfortable having you conduct observations. Be sure to let the teacher know what observation process or protocol you will be using and the purpose for the observation. Always give them a chance to look over any recording sheets or protocols and ask questions ahead of time. Although you certainly will be observing the teacher's actions, the focus of the observation is the student the teacher has concerns about. You might share a personal story about a time when you were observed and received helpful feedback. Having a second set of eyes revealed aspects of your teaching you never realized were there.

We find it helpful to leave some kind of note for the teacher immediately after completing a classroom visit, perhaps a written note left on their desk or a quick text or e-mail. This note is not a summary of your findings or conclusions. It is a way to reassure the teacher about your impressions. Always try to say something positive and encouraging, but honest. If you did observe a chaotic classroom situation, then you might say something such as, "Thanks for letting me visit today. Wow! Your classroom is a high-energy place! I was able to see some things that Ronda was doing that I think will be helpful to us in coming up with a plan to help her. I'm glad we are working together! See you soon."

Observing the Student in the Classroom

The kind of observation you conduct depends on the questions you want to answer. If you want to try to identify specific situations in which the student seems especially frustrated by academic tasks, then you may want to conduct a functional observation that tracks what happens before (antecedent) a behavior occurs and after (consequence) the behavior (ABC; Epstein et al., 2008). We discuss ABC observations a bit later in this chapter. If you want insight into a student's off-task behavior during instruction, then you may record the amount of time the student is on task, off task, or disruptive during different instructional formats (e.g., whole class, small group, collaborative partners, independent work). In our experience, tracking both the student behavior simultaneously with the activity structure is most likely to provide you with useful information about the student's interactions with the teacher and the classroom environment during academic activities.

We suggest you follow a basic plan to prepare for a classroom observation. The seven steps in the process are as follows:

1. *Select an observation format or protocol to match the kind of information you need.* For example, if you need to get a general sense about how the target student is behaving in the classroom, then a functional ABC observation may be conducted. If more detailed information is needed about the relationship between the instruction and the behavioral outcomes, then you may want to use a more formal process. On your first visit to the classroom, you may want to jot down some anecdotal notes about how the classroom is set up, how instruction is scheduled, what other students do while the teacher is teaching small groups, and so forth.

2. *Review the directions for conducting the observation you select.* Be sure you feel comfortable with collecting information using this format. (You may need to do some practice observations first, perhaps in the classrooms of teachers you have worked with in the past.)

3. *Decide how many times, and for how long, you will observe.* It is normally better to observe in a classroom more than once. If you observe only one time, then you might choose a day on which the teacher or student is not feeling up to par or when the class activities are atypical. Normally, you will get a more accurate picture of a classroom and a student's behavior if you conduct two or three 20-minute observations rather than one 50-minute observation.

4. *Schedule a time for the observation with the teacher.* Be sure to observe at the time of day and during the class when the teacher has indicated that the student has the most difficulty. Before you conduct a more formal observation, it can be helpful to go into the classroom for a brief (5- to 10-minute) informal observation with two goals: Getting a general sense of how the classroom works and letting the students and teacher become used to having you in the room so that they will behave naturally when you conduct the actual observation. If your target student is easily distracted, then it may be necessary to conduct more than one of these brief classroom observations to get them used to your being there. Be sure that the teacher knows that they have the option to ask you to reschedule an observation if, for example, the student is having a bad day or the teacher does not feel well.

5. *Prepare the teacher for what you will be doing.* As discussed, many teachers are uncomfortable being observed by an adult, especially when that person takes notes throughout the observation. Be sure that the teacher understands the purpose of your observation. Stress that you will be observing the student and will share your observations with the teacher. Also, assure the teacher that you will not discuss what you observe with anyone else, including the administrator or the student's family members. Those initial, short, informal visits to the classroom before the formal observation may go a long way to help the teacher, as well as the students, feel more comfortable with your presence in the room.

6. *Assemble your materials.* Take your computer/tablet or a clipboard to hold any paper observation form because it is unlikely that a desk or table will be available. Some types of observations also require a timer. If doing a paper-based observation, then take along two pens or pencils. (It is always a good idea to have a backup.)

7. *When you enter the classroom for the observation, find a place where you are as unobtrusive as possible.* Make sure you have a clear view of the teacher and the student you will be observing. In some classrooms, students move from one area of the room to another during a lesson. Be prepared to change your position, if necessary, so you can see the teacher and the student. Knowing where to position yourself is another good reason to do at least one early visit to the classroom before conducting your formal observation.

Observing Student–Teacher Interactions in the Classroom

Conduct a functional ABC observation if you want to collect information about how a student responds to situations in the classroom. As we noted earlier in this chapter, the ABC stands for *antecedent, behavior,* and *consequence.* We are going to explain what each of these words mean. Before we continue, you may be wondering why, in a book written for instructional coaches, are we now talking about observing students' behaviors? Your focus as an SFC coach is to help maximize every teacher's knowledge and skills to enhance student learning. We know that many students who have academic difficulties often demonstrate challenging behaviors in the classroom. We are suggesting that it may be helpful to observe students' behavior to help you understand the possible obstacles to academic progress that students face in their classrooms and to help teachers develop and successfully implement interventions that may help make instruction more successful.

Let's start with the behavior component of the ABC observation. Let's suppose that you are working with Jessie, a fifth-grade boy who told you during your interview that he feels embarrassed when he is asked to read aloud in class. When you assessed his oral reading fluency, you found that his reading was slow and labored for a student his age. Jessie's teacher reports that he is often highly disruptive during social studies, science, or reading class when students are taking turns reading the text out loud. This behavior may be linked to Jessie's difficulties with fluent oral reading. Another student, Samantha, is in second grade. Her teacher is concerned that Samantha does not pay attention to instruction and rarely finishes assigned independent math work. From your informal assessment of Samantha, you know that her math skills are weak and there are gaps in her skills. You suspect that her behavior during class may be linked to her academic challenges.

Now let's talk about the word *antecedent*. An antecedent is something that happens just before a behavior and appears to be linked to the behavior in some way. The antecedent may or may not cause the behavior, but it may trigger it. Here is a simple example: When the doorbell rings (antecedent), my dog barks (behavior). Pushing the button on the doorbell does not somehow flip a switch in my dog's throat causing her to bark, but she has learned that part of her job is to let me know when someone is at the door. In our previous story about Jessie, a situation in which students in the class are asked to read out loud seems to be an antecedent to Jessie's disruptive behavior. In other words, there seems to be a connection between the two.

Consequence is the third component of the ABC functional observation. A consequence is something that happens after a behavior and is somehow linked to the behavior. This is the same as talking about the consequences of your own actions. Consequences can be positive, negative, or both. Positive consequences can also be called *rewards* or *reinforcements*. For example, if I decide to have dessert when I go out to eat, then I am rewarded by the enjoyment of the treat. Another consequence might not be so rewarding, however—I could gain a little weight. In our story about Jessie, we find during an ABC observation that his teacher usually sends him to a time-out room when he disrupts the class. Going to time-out keeps Jessie from having to read orally in front of his classmates. Because this strategy works for Jessie—meaning it gets him out of doing the task of oral reading in front of his classmates—he keeps using it day after day. It is a consequence that rewards or reinforces his behavior and makes it more likely that he will behave this way again in the future. It also does nothing to address the likely underlying academic cause of his disruptive behavior—poor reading skills.

Observing Classroom Instruction

Chapter 9 describes research findings on effective classroom instruction. The overall quality of the instruction being provided in the classroom is definitely worth your attention as an SFC coach.

Observing Classroom Ecology and Routine

Rating scales and checklists can be constructed to describe the physical, instructional, and social environment in the classroom. Observations of the physical environment would include things such as lighting, noise, distractions, temperature, comfort of the students, arrangement of the seating, and general layout. The instructional environment includes elements such as access to and adequacy of materials, instructional methods (especially active versus passive student engagement), expectations and demands, modifications, grouping, and scheduling. The social environment is perhaps the most complex aspect of the classroom environment. This includes the nature of interaction between teacher and student, the way the teacher handles behavior management, peer interactions, and the general atmosphere and classroom climate.

Framing these elements of the classroom environment as questions can help guide your observations. Some questions about key aspects of the physical, instructional, and social environments that may affect a student's academic outcomes are as follows:

- Is the noise, temperature, or lighting making it hard for the student to concentrate and learn?

- Is the student's seating placement in the classroom conducive to learning?

- Does the teacher use high-quality materials as part of effective instruction?

- Does the student have access to the materials?

- Are the materials appropriate for this student?

- Does the instruction appear to be purposeful and based on objectives?

- Is the instruction directed at teaching key skills and achieving targeted standards?

- Do the instructional strategies implemented in the classroom promote mainly active or passive student engagement?

- Do the teacher's expectations and demands appear realistic and conducive to learning?

- Does the teacher provide modifications, supports, or scaffolding to ensure a high rate of success for every student?

- Are the grouping formats appropriate for the instructional objectives?

- Does the teacher communicate warmth and enthusiasm toward the students and the subject matter?

- Do the students appear to be aware of classroom routines, rules, and consequences?

- Are most of the students in the class on task and attentive?

- What is the teacher's reaction to behavioral issues?

- Are the rules clear and consequences applied consistently?

- Do teacher–student interactions generally appear positive?

- What is the ratio of teacher comments that are positive, neutral, and negative?

> ### REFLECTION
>
> *How do you currently collaborate with a teacher and plan for a scheduled observation? What tools do you use when conducting observations? Compare your approach to planning for and conducting observations with recommendations and examples we provide. What do you notice? In what way(s), if any, might you alter your existing practices to improve or strengthen how you plan for or conduct observations?*

Providing Feedback After Observations

After collecting all the data from planned interviews, assessments, observations, and records review, you are ready for Phase 2 of the SFC Collaborative Problem-Solving Process—define the problem, set goals, develop a TAP. Take some time to organize all the information in a way that will make the collaborative analysis of the data as easy as possible. You do not want to simply share many pages of observation or interview notes or the scoring sheets from an assessment. Displaying the data as a summary, with key points emphasized, can go a long way to making the data useful in the problem-solving process. Graphs, charts, or short bulleted lists are suggested.

Keep your role as coach in mind as you prepare to share the results of any kind of classroom observation. Remember that SFC coaches help maximize each teacher's knowledge and skills to enhance student learning. Your role is to be a supportive and encouraging colleague; you are not an administrator or evaluator.

At the beginning of the postobservation conference, remind the teacher that your purpose in conducting the observation was to observe the target student within the classroom and collect information that might support you and the teacher as you work together to help the student succeed. Once you have established a focus on the student as the purpose of the observation, it is important to ask the teacher if the observation was conducted on a typical day. It is crucial to get this information ahead of time so the teacher cannot later explain away what you observed with the statement, "But that never happens!" If the observation was conducted on an atypical day, then you need to know so you can schedule another observation and not waste time analyzing possibly misleading information.

At this point, you can begin to describe the student's behaviors you observed in the class. As you talk about things you noticed the student doing or saying, link these observations to the strategies the teacher was using at the time. For example, you can talk about antecedents to a student's behaviors that you recorded during an ABC observation or the percentage of time the student was on task during different types of activity formats.

Try to restrict this description to student behaviors that are directly relevant to academic success. If factors related to the physical or social environment in the classroom appear to be strongly related to the student's academic outcomes, then you will need to discuss some of these factors. We suggest, however, that your main emphasis be on the learning environment, such as access to appropriate and high-quality materials, including age- and achievement-level appropriate texts, instructional methods, especially active student involvement and the elements of explicit instruction, ambitious but realistic expectations and demands, and the effective use of grouping and scheduling.

Giving teachers too much feedback at one time is one mistake made by many beginning coaches (and one we made ourselves at first). We suggest you provide at least three points of positive feedback to the teacher, reinforcing the effective aspects of the lesson. Then choose only one or two important areas in which the teacher might want to focus.

Remember, you cannot fix everything at once by providing a long list of all imperfections. Frame your feedback as merely reporting the facts of what you observed. Describe the data, and let it make the points. Avoid judgmental statements. Always convey an attitude of respect for your colleague as a peer professional. Ask for their opinions. Ask why they make certain instructional decisions during the lesson with sincere curiosity. Teachers often have good reasons for choices they make while teaching, even though they may not be readily apparent to the observer. Continue to convey to your colleague that you are partners in helping the student grow and improve. Remember that the primary goal of all coaches is to support student success.

REFLECTION

Reflect on a time when you provided feedback to a teacher or when you received feedback. What was the plan for the feedback session? What did you notice about yourself when delivering or receiving the feedback? What questions did you ask, or what questions were you asked? Based on your experience(s), what would you do different when planning for or delivering feedback after an observation?

GATHERING INFORMATION USING ASSESSMENTS

Obtaining information from teachers, families, and students using only interviews or observations is typically not sufficient to fully define a student's challenges. You will almost always need more information. If the concern involves a student's academic performance, then conducting some kind of informal or perhaps even more formal assessments might be in order. If the teacher is concerned about a specific academic area such as reading, writing, spelling, handwriting, or math, then there are numerous options available that can relatively quickly and efficiently provide data that can greatly inform the development of a targeted intervention. Concerns such as low levels of spoken language proficiency would also lend itself to considering some informal assessments. It is more likely that a combination of rating scales and observations might be used for behavioral concerns. If there is evidence of a more serious concern, such as one that might ultimately involve an evaluation for a possible disability and special education services, then the referral processes used in your educational setting should be considered. Your role as coach could be to help the teacher initiate that process.

GATHERING INFORMATION USING RECORDS REVIEWS

It is often helpful to get a historical sense of a student's progress and challenges. The easiest way to do this is to look over their school records, which can provide a sense of a student's academic profile over time and can help determine if the current concern is new or has been a chronic problem that has existed for years. Has the student been referred for or served by special education or other special services? If the problem is new, is there something different in the student's life? Does this signal some issues around a student's social or emotional well-being? Has the student moved frequently? Are there health issues that have been previously noted? All this background information can definitely help you and the teacher create a more accurate problem definition, which directly leads to a more reasonable goal and a more effective intervention.

The SFC Collaborative Problem-Solving Process works best when each step is conducted in a way that is as collaborative as possible. The job of collecting the data needed for Phase 2 usually falls primarily to the coach because teachers are busy in their classrooms. It is often a good idea to suggest that the teacher take responsibility for reviewing the student's records to make the task of data collection a bit more equitable. The teacher may have access to information that could be off limits to a coach, so you will want to review school and/or district policies. Reviewing a student's information can also be eye opening for a teacher to learn a bit (or a lot) more about the student that needs support.

CONCLUSION

Our focus on helping students succeed academically must be supported by useful, reliable information about student strengths and needs, the nature of the instruction they receive, and the complex interactions and conditions that exist in their classrooms. Providing effective coaching depends on your ability to identify and understand these conditions in order to help students and teachers overcome obstacles and perhaps learn new skills and strategies. Interviews, observations, assessments, and records reviews are the SFC coach's tools for gathering this important information.

Before proceeding to the next chapter, revisit your responses to the questions at the start of this chapter and make any adjustments based on new knowledge or insights gleaned. Also, take time to make any changes or updates to the application exercise.

VIRTUAL COACHING TIP

Scheduling time to meet with a teacher to discuss a student's academic, behavioral, or social-emotional concerns can occur in a face-to-face or virtual platform. If meeting virtually, then plan ahead so that you and your colleague know the student's specific area of concern. By being prepared, you can engage in deeper conversation and make decisions for who, when, where, and how the data will be collected (e.g., interviews, observations, academic assessments of the target student, review of the student's records). You will also need to determine how you will share your evidence during your next virtual meeting. Take advantage of tools such as a colleague recording themself teaching a portion of a lesson and uploading this recording for you to view. Uploading a file will allow opportunities to review, take notes, identify time stamps in a video, and so forth. Use a share screen feature during the next scheduled virtual meeting to replay portions of videos or use chat or a breakout room to determine next steps.

REFERENCE

Epstein, M., Atkins, M., Cullinan, D., Kutash, K., & Weaver, R. (2008). *Reducing behavior problems in the elementary school classroom: A practice guide* (NCEE #2008-012). National Center for Education Evaluation and Regional Assistance, Institute of Education Sciences, U.S. Department of Education. Retrieved from https://files.eric.ed.gov/fulltext/ED502720.pdf

9

Developing, Supporting, and Evaluating Effective Interventions

Before reading this chapter, consider the following questions. Jot down some notes on your current understanding, and then at the end of the chapter, we will revisit these questions to assess the knowledge and insight you gained during your reading.

- What has been your experience with helping someone set a goal?

- What experience(s) have you had with designing an evaluation plan and monitoring progress toward achieving a goal?

- How, if at all, have you supported others with identifying, selecting, and or implementing evidence-based interventions?

APPLICATION EXERCISE

Identify one teacher (or more) who has sought out your support to work through the SFC Collaborative Problem-Solving Process. Write down what you notice about yourself and the teacher as you work through each phase (listed below). What questions do you pose? What verbal processes are used? What nonverbal cues do you see and when? What might this tell you?

- Problem presentation
- Define the problem, set goals, develop TAP
- Implement the TAP
- Evaluate goals and next steps

INTRODUCTION

Engaging in the Collaborative Problem-Solver role as an SFC coach usually involves using some version of the SFC Collaborative Problem-Solving Process that you learned about in Chapter 6. In Chapter 7, you read about some procedures, tools, and strategies you can use to gather the information needed to identify and define a problem, which occurs in Phase 1 and early Phase 2 of the process, and lays the foundation for developing an effective intervention.

This chapter discusses some procedures that an SFC coach—working collaboratively with colleagues—can use in Phases 2, 3, and 4 of the Problem-Solving Process to set goals, develop a plan, support the teacher, and eventually evaluate the effectiveness of an intervention to help improve a student's academic success. We will start with the goal-setting step in Phase 2.

SETTING GOALS

Once a presented problem or concern has been identified and defined based on the collaboratively collected and analyzed data (starting in Phase 1 and finalized in the early stages of Phase 2), there is more to do in Phase 2. You now move to the process of setting goals. As we mentioned in Chapter 6, identifying the goals before working to develop a TAP refocuses all participants on where they are going rather than where they have been. This step can bring a wave of positive feeling and optimism to the process and provide a clear path to follow in the development of an intervention(s). The goals set at this point can also serve the evaluation process during Phase 4 of the SFC Collaborative Problem-Solving Process in which the success of the intervention is determined and decisions are made about next steps.

If the teacher with whom you are working has little previous experience developing goals for students, then this step in the process may require some direction and leadership from you—an opportunity for PDL around goal setting. It can help explain the rationale for setting goals at this point in the process. Clear, well-defined goals help guide the development of more effective intervention plans, motivate the teacher and student by providing a fixed target for their work, and play a role in the eventual evaluation of your efforts.

Teachers often begin a discussion of goals by talking broadly about their hopes for their student. They may say that the student should "develop a better attitude toward school," "feel more confident about himself," or "start acting like an eighth grader." It will be important to reconfigure these general goals as more measurable ones, focusing on the observable behavior changes that would show evidence of "a better attitude" or "more confidence" or "acting like an eighth grader." You might provide guidance by saying, "That would be a wonderful outcome for Loren indeed! How would we know if Loren develops a 'better attitude'? What would he be doing differently?" Perhaps suggest reframing the goal to say something such as, "A student reads more books or increases participation in class discussions."

The coach should also be ready to help direct the teacher to develop goals that reflect what research has indicated are worthwhile, will be valuable to the student's academic success, and are reasonably achievable. A goal of having a disruptive student "be quiet 100% of the time" would not be appropriate nor achievable. Setting goals may generate a lot of useful discussion about what is worthwhile, valuable, and achievable.

Well-defined goals that can be objectively measured will be needed to eventually evaluate whether the plan has been effective. Consider using Doran's (1981) SMART criteria when writing your goal(s) (see Figure 9.1). Consider also adding an *I* to SMART to highlight how important it is to set a goal that will inspire you (Campbell & van Nieuwerburgh, 2018).

Goal(s)					
Directions: Based on the analysis of data you collected, write the goal(s) in the following table. When you finish writing the goal(s), place an X under each SMART goal element. You want to make sure that each goal meets the criteria.					
Objective(s)	Specific	Measurable	Assignable	Realistic	Time related

Figure 9.1. SMART goals. (*Source:* Doran, 1981.)

- **S**pecific: What is the goal or area of focus?

- **M**easurable: How will you know if you are making progress toward meeting the goal?

- **A**ssignable: Who is responsible for implementing or achieving the goal?

- **R**ealistic: Can the goal be achieved?

- **T**ime related: When should the goal be achieved?

Goals should be directly linked to the problem definition that targeted the area of primary concern. Setting two to four goals is usually preferable, but there needs to be at least one. The goals should be attainable given the resources available, which include time, money, and people who can help as well as the planned length of the intervention. For example, it would be unreasonable to set a goal that a fourth-grade student currently reading at the 1.5 grade level will be reading at the third-grade level in 5 weeks. It is also unreasonable to make perfect scores a goal (100% correct on all written work; zero errors in oral reading). Most human beings cannot consistently achieve at a perfect level. As you can see, there is much opportunity for PDL through goal setting.

Some goals may involve a clearly described baseline, which is the level at which the student is currently performing. The goal must then specify a reasonable performance level for the end of the intervention period. You can determine baseline levels by reexamining some of the observation or assessment data that was collected after Phase 1. Goals that are developed from baseline data can be stated using clear, concrete descriptions of where the student is currently performing and where you can expect them to be performing within a set period of time. For example, if James's teacher begins by stating that she would like to see James become a better, more confident reader, then you might work with her to develop some goals that look like these:

Goal 1: James is currently reading at about the second-grade level based on results of an informal reading inventory (baseline). Our goal is for him to be reading at a third-grade level in 6 months.

Goal 2: James correctly identifies 14/30 (47%) vowel combinations on an informal phonics assessment (baseline). Our goal for him is to correctly identify at least 27/30 (90%) vowel combinations in 6 weeks.

Goal 3: James's oral reading fluency score on unpracticed second-grade materials is currently 68 words correct per minute (baseline). Our goal for James is to have a score of 80 words correct per minute in 6 weeks in second-grade materials.

REFLECTION

Reflect on a goal that you have set for yourself or review a goal that a colleague set. As you review this goal, refer to the SMART criteria and guiding questions. If your goal does not address each criterion, then what would you change? If you were meeting with a teacher who had a goal that did not meet the SMART criteria, then how would you guide the conversation to help them make an adjustment?

Covert Goals

In addition to the goals developed for the student by you and the teacher, there may be times that the coach wants to set goals that are left unstated. Such goals often include desirable changes in a teachers' attitudes or behaviors, such as having a teacher become more positive or patient with students or increasing a teacher's skill level in using assessment data to make instructional decisions. Although such covert goals can be an important part of the SFC Collaborative Problem-Solving Process, they are not goals you discuss openly with a teacher unless they have expressed an interest in considering setting some goals for themselves.

If you sense an openness on the part of your teacher colleague to the idea of setting goals for their own growth, then you may want to propose the possibility: "While we were analyzing the data I collected during the classroom observations, you expressed some concern about the low ratio of positive to negative statements that I recorded during the times I visited your room. I wonder if you might be interested in working toward increasing your positive statements and interactions? Might that be something you'd like to consider setting as a goal for yourself to work toward?"

DEVELOPING AN EVALUATION PLAN

The success of an intervention should be determined by evaluating the degree to which each goal was achieved. If the goals have been well defined, then developing an evaluation plan goes quite smoothly. As we mentioned in Chapter 6, evaluations can be formative, conducted as the intervention is being implemented, or summative, completed at the end of an intervention period. Many evaluations collect both types of information. Formative data can be used to help support the intervention, and summative data is important for the final decisions about the overall success of the intervention plan.

SFC coaches take the lead in developing the evaluation plan by suggesting one or two possible evaluation strategies to consider. Determining whether the student's goals have been achieved might involve using some of the measures described in Chapter 8 that can be used to collect data for defining and analyzing the initial presenting problem, including results from assessments or observations. Although standardized measures are best used for assessing academic growth over a longer period of time, generally a year or more, there are informal assessments that can measure improvement over shorter periods of time. For more information on the use of informal measures for assessing academic skill growth and goal attainment, you can look for books or workshops about curriculum-based assessment or curriculum-based measurement.

DEVELOPING AN INTERVENTION PLAN

Novice coaches sometimes believe that problems are solved by identifying the key (magical) intervention strategy. More expert problem solvers understand that a consistent and skillful implementation of one or more strategies may possibly lead to improvement as long as the strategy is supported by evidence of effectiveness, is linked logically to the targeted problem and goals, and is implemented effectively.

It is vital that you work with the teacher to develop an intervention plan that can, and probably will, actually be implemented in the classroom. Carefully designing a great intervention plan that never gets implemented will not help the student. Researchers have identified some circumstances that contribute to the successful implementation of intervention plans:

- The teacher believes that the intervention will be effective.

- The intervention does not require a lot of time or material resources.

- There is a match between the theoretical underpinnings of an intervention plan and the teacher's philosophies and beliefs.

- The intrusiveness of the intervention on the typical classroom routines and schedules is minimal.

- The teacher has a sense of control of the situation (Burns et al., 2017; Ellis & Bond, 2016).

Maintaining these conditions for successful implementation when developing a plan will go a long way toward ensuring that the teacher will successfully carry out the plan.

Develop a List of Intervention Strategies

Begin collaborating on an intervention plan with a thoughtful and deliberate exploration of possible strategies to use to reach the goals you have identified rather than with a frantic search for the right answer or that elusive magic solution. Brainstorming can be a great way to generate a list of possible strategies. For example, it can be nice for a teacher to have a menu of ideas from which to choose, but realistically there are times when there is only one feasible or acceptable strategy to consider. You can kick off the brainstorming session by saying something such as, "Now that we have decided what goals we'd like to see James achieve, let's think of some ways we can help him meet them. What ideas do you have that you might like to try?"

Once again, if the teacher has had little experience in developing or using effective interventions, then the coach may need to take the lead in this process, perhaps by suggesting one or two possible strategies: "Thinking about the fluency goal we set for James, have you ever used a repeated-reading strategy in your classroom? There are some really good ways that this can be used to make a big difference in a student's accuracy and rate. Would you like some more information about what this could look like as part of a plan for James?"

Sources of Strategies   The wealth of resources and experiences that you undoubtedly have brought to the position of SFC coach will likely be a primary source of strategies you can suggest to a teacher. It is common for coaches, especially novice ones, to worry that they might not have a good idea about what to suggest. We say, "Keep calm." Remember that you serve as a resource for effective ideas and strategies, not the provider of the perfect solution. No single person can possibly know everything about how to help every student. Many students who have academic problems also have significant behavioral and emotional needs. Quite a few come from families that face substantial chronic stress. No coach can be expected to have a bag of tricks or a handy magic wand to tackle every situation. Skillful, confident, professional coaches acknowledge their own level of training and expertise, as well as the limits of their knowledge and skills. Ethical standards in every profession require that a practitioner provide only advice and engage in activities that are within their skill sets and levels of expertise.

You should always be open to turning to other experts who may have specialized knowledge and skills that are different or more extensive than yours. You should be prepared to call on the expertise of others when a situation warrants it. Modeling this openness to your colleague can go a long way to stop the incorrect notion that a coach brings a magic wand to the problem-solving process. It can also help keep your relationship with your colleague on an equal footing, with neither party bringing any perceived superior value to the process.

Bookmark helpful web sites on your computer so you and the teacher can explore them together. There are many evidence-based resources available online, such as Intervention Central (https://www.interventioncentral.org), and numerous research reports are available from the Institute for Education Sciences (https://ies.ed.gov). Be wary, however, of web sites such as Teachers Pay Teachers or the various teacher-focused boards on Pinterest. These and others frequently provide free or low-cost attractive and fun activities for teachers to use, but they rarely have a solid basis of evidence to suggest they might be effective in actually providing successful intervention. SFC coaches should always suggest, recommend, and support evidence-based resources.

It is likely that one or more of your colleagues will believe that any resource they find must be effective. "These resources were uploaded by teachers, right?" "The authors have Ph.D.s, so this must be based on good evidence." You will want to be prepared for these conversations and be able to articulate which resources are based on evidence and which are just attractive and fun. How will you handle this conversation? What will you say, and how will you say it so that the teacher understands that there is a difference?

Evaluating Suggested Strategies   Each intervention strategy you generate with the teacher must be evaluated. Strategies under consideration should be judged on several dimensions to determine the general likelihood of their effectiveness. Again, it is quite possible that the teacher has little or no experience in evaluating intervention strategies, so be prepared to guide this process. Each strategy should

- Have evidence of effectiveness
- Match the problem definition and specific goals

- Be appropriate for the situation (match the age, skill level, and needs of the student)

- Be feasible (match the demands of the context and the available resources)

- Be aligned with the philosophies and beliefs of the teacher

- Be minimally disruptive to the normal routines of the classroom

"I tried that, but it didn't work," is something that you might hear from a teacher colleague on occasion. The teacher may have already tried to implement a version of some of the very intervention strategies that you think should be considered a part of a new, collaboratively designed plan of action. The teacher may be reluctant to try again, believing that they have already attempted that particular solution and determined for themselves that it was not effective. It is possible, however, that the techniques or strategies the teacher tried may not have been used consistently or accurately or were used for an insufficient period of time. If your colleague had been trying to use a strategy for the first time, then it is possible that more training, guidance, or support was needed to implement the strategy effectively. The coach may need to discuss why those "already tried but failed" strategies should perhaps be reconsidered and how those strategies can be adjusted to be more successful.

Selecting Strategies to Implement   Once some possible strategies have been identified and evaluated, the teacher can select some to try. Although the coach can have an input, it is important for the teacher to feel empowered to make the final selection of strategies. After all, the teacher is the one who has to implement the plan in the classroom. The teacher has to believe the plan can work and that they can use the strategies effectively. If you try to sell one or more of the strategies too hard, then your colleague may feel coerced or pressured. You may also need to help the teacher select a reasonable number of strategies to implement at any given time. You can point out that the list can be revisited at any point in the future if any of the strategies selected are not as effective as was hoped or if they prove to be too challenging to implement in the classroom.

REFLECTION

How do you go about reviewing and selecting evidence-based strategies? Select a few strategies that you have used or shared with others and review the evidence base.

THE TARGETED ACTION PLAN

Now—finally—it is time to develop a plan for implementing the strategies. The TAP must be quite specific about how the intervention will be carried out: Who will do what to implement each strategy; how these actions will be taken; and when, how often, or for how long. Remember to include steps for notifying the student and the student's family about the plan.

In some cases, the teacher may need some training to be able to successfully implement one or more of the selected intervention strategies, which may involve observing a demonstration by the coach or another teacher or attending a workshop or in-service training. If training, guidance, or preparation is needed, then it must be specified as part of the overall plan. There may also be data collection forms, charts, or self-monitoring forms that must be created and copied in order to implement the plan. Your plan should list the person(s) who will be responsible for locating or preparing these materials and the date they will be needed. This level of specificity will help ensure a consistent and accurate implementation of the plan. It is usually helpful for the coach to take detailed notes about the TAP and offer to write up the TAP details and distribute copies to everyone who may be involved.

Wrapping Up Targeted Action Plan Development

Once the goals have been set, the evaluation plan is in place, and a detailed intervention plan has been developed and recorded, the coach should finalize this phase of the Collaborative Problem-Solving Process by briefly summarizing the definition of the target problem, the identified goals, the plan for collecting the evaluation data, and then reviewing the TAP. Following your summary, invite the teacher to add any information or make corrections as needed.

It is always a good idea to present the finalized plan with a balance of optimism tempered with realism. We hope the teacher feels empowered by the process in which the two of you have engaged and likely invested a significant amount of time. We also hope your colleague has confidence that the collaboratively developed plan has a good chance of helping the student achieve the specified goals. It is important for the teacher to have realistic expectations, however. A significant period of time and sustained effort will probably be required before you can see improvement in a student's academic or behavior skills. Every plan is, at best, a good-faith effort to help students make some gains and improvements. A good plan that is developed with care and evaluated following the guidelines you have outlined is an important step in the right direction. It is never an ironclad guarantee of success.

PROVIDING SUPPORT TO THE TEACHER

Many interventions require at least some change in the teacher's behaviors or routines and may involve the teacher engaging in new and untried procedures. During the discussion of the intervention, the teacher will probably get excited about the new ideas being discussed and the awareness that help for the student is on the way. In all of this enthusiasm, the teacher may honestly feel confident about successfully completing each of the tasks identified in the TAP. But, when returning to the demanding routines of the classroom, the teacher may be, in fact, a bit unclear about procedures or unable to complete some steps of the plan. This happens more often than not.

Even the most carefully developed and well-designed intervention plans—those viewed enthusiastically by teachers during the planning process—may not be implemented successfully. This happens for a variety of reasons. Maybe the teacher did not sufficiently understand how to do part of the intervention or did not have the skills or resources (e.g., time, money, materials, assistance) to carry it out. Another possible reason for an unsuccessful implementation is that there are rarely instant and positive changes for students when an intervention is first implemented. Teachers may become discouraged and stop prematurely or modify the intervention plan in a manner that lessens its chances for success.

As the coach, you can avoid these pitfalls if you understand the need to provide ongoing support for the teacher. This often involves checking in periodically with the teacher—either in person or by phone, e-mail, or text—to see how things are going and providing help, advice, guidance, and encouragement. It is wise to begin this support just before the initial implementation of the plan. If the teacher has decided to be ready to begin the plan on Monday, then make a note to check in on the preceding Thursday or Friday, or even over the weekend, to see whether they have everything in place to begin implementing the TAP successfully. Be sure to check in again Monday afternoon or Tuesday morning to see how things went on the first day.

The frequency and intensity of the support should match the complexity of the interventions and the expertise and experience of the teacher in implementing interventions. In most cases, the greatest amount of support is needed in the early stages, and support can taper off after things are successfully rolling along. Obviously, inexperienced teachers attempting to implement complex interventions will require more frequent and intensive monitoring than experienced teachers implementing less-complex interventions.

EVALUATING OUTCOMES

If the evaluation component of the intervention contained plans for conducting formative assessments, then the coach should be checking to see if this data is being collected. The information collected formatively—which includes such things as the student's self-monitoring forms, curriculum-based measurement graphs, and scores from weekly progress checks—can be reviewed periodically by the coach and teacher together to allow both parties to make decisions along the way about whether a component of the intervention should be continued as is (adequate progress is being made toward the achievement of the specified goal), modified (progress toward the goal is slow or nonexistent), or phased out (the goal has been achieved). Any summative evaluation procedures specified in the intervention plan should be completed at the end of the specified intervention period, and that information should be analyzed collaboratively by the coach and teacher. Again, this data can be used to guide collaboration on decisions about whether to terminate, continue, or restructure the intervention plan.

If it appears that changes in the intervention plan are needed anywhere along the way, then you can work with the teacher to determine the following:

- Should those changes involve doing essentially the same procedures as outlined in the TAP but perhaps a bit more intensively? Or perhaps more frequently?

- Does the procedure need to be used more systematically?

- Does the teacher need a bit more training or support?

Suppose the TAP you developed involves having the target student work for 15 minutes, three times a week, with a peer tutor to practice oral reading. If the formative evaluation data seems to indicate that progress is insufficient, then it does not necessarily mean that the idea of tutoring should be abandoned. Perhaps you and the teacher should consider having the tutor work with the student for 20 minutes each session rather than 15. Or maybe the tutor can come an extra day or two each week. It could be that the materials used in the tutoring sessions need to be examined—they may be a bit too easy or too difficult to help the student. It is also important to observe the interaction between the tutor and the student. Have the sessions become a time for friendly visits rather than focused, intensive practice? Is most of the tutoring time being spent getting ready, finding materials, or in some other activity besides oral reading? Consider such factors before scrapping the whole idea of tutoring.

If it appears that some new ideas or approaches should be considered, then you do not have to restart the entire Collaborative Problem-Solving Process again. Simply go back to the notes you took during Phase 2 and look at the original list of possible strategies that was developed. It may be time to consider including one of those ideas in the TAP. Be sure to provide the teacher with any training or support necessary when modifications or additions are made to the intervention.

Considering whether the goals were realistic is another aspect of the evaluation process. There are times when a coach and teacher may have been overly optimistic about how much growth or skill improvement would be realistic to expect from a student. It may be that the goal itself should be modified rather than the intervention plan. Lowering a goal or extending the time period for goal attainment can feel discouraging to all participants, but sometimes it is the most logical step to take. If a goal must be changed, then it is important to present that to the student in a way that is as encouraging as possible: "James, you have been working very hard on your reading. I'm so impressed with your efforts, and I hope you are, too! You know that we had hoped to be moving you up to the next level of materials by now, but I think it will be best to stay at this level for a little bit longer. I know what a hard worker you are, and I just guessed that you'd get up to that next level a bit faster. You will get there if you keep working this hard. It will just take a bit longer than we originally thought, and that's perfectly normal!"

Examining the evaluation data may also indicate that one or more of the original goals have been achieved. Congratulations to everyone! This is an exciting moment for sure. This rarely means that the larger goal of helping the student has been achieved, however. If the general goal of a teacher was to help a student "become a more competent and confident reader," then making gains in reading level, reading accuracy, and reading fluency can justifiably be seen as important steps in that direction. Once one or more of the initial goals have been achieved, however, it may simply be time to develop some new goals, revise the TAP, and begin on the next step of this important journey to help the student achieve all reasonable academic and behavioral goals.

REFLECTION

Now that you know more about the SFC Problem-Solving Process, what questions do you have? Which phase(s) do you feel most confident to implement? Which phase(s) do you feel that you will need to seek out additional information or practice?

CONCLUSION

Your job as an SFC coach is to do your very best work as a competent and caring professional to help teachers help their students. You cannot hold yourself—or allow others to hold you—to any higher standard than that. You are not a miracle worker or a magician. Some of the challenges that teachers face are not easily addressed. Problems that reflect issues and concerns that are beyond your expertise will be brought to you as a coach. As an SFC Collaborative Problem-Solver, your professional obligation is to help the teacher develop and successfully implement an intervention that has a good chance for success, not one that is guaranteed to solve the targeted problem. Following the process as outlined in Chapters 6–8 should help you accomplish this and help many teachers and students.

Before proceeding to the next chapter, revisit your responses to the questions at the start of this chapter and make any adjustments based on new knowledge or insights gleaned. Also, take time to make any changes or updates to the application exercise.

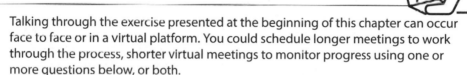

VIRTUAL COACHING TIP

Talking through the exercise presented at the beginning of this chapter can occur face to face or in a virtual platform. You could schedule longer meetings to work through the process, shorter virtual meetings to monitor progress using one or more questions below, or both.

- What progress is being made to achieve the goal?
- What evidence exists to show this?
- Do changes need to be made? If so, what are the reasons for needing a change, and what are the change recommendations?
- If so, what are the reasons for needing a change, and what are the change recommendations?

REFERENCES

Burns, M. K., Riley-Tilman, T. C., & Rathvon, N. (2017). *Effective school interventions* (3rd ed.). Guilford Press.

Campbell, J., & van Nieuwerburgh, C. (2018). *The leader's guide to coaching in schools: Creating conditions for effective learning.* Corwin.

Doran, G. (1981). There's a S.M.A.R.T. way to write management's goals and objectives. *Management Review, 70,* 35–36.

Ellis, A. K., & Bond, J. B. (2016). *Research on educational innovations* (5th ed.). Routledge.

10

The Teacher/Learner Role

Designing and Providing Effective Professional Learning

Before reading this chapter, consider the following questions. Jot down some notes on your current understanding, and then at the end of the chapter, we will revisit these questions to assess the knowledge and insight you gained during your reading.

- What does effective PDL mean for an SFC coach?

- How do you plan for continuous learning about a new skill or strategy rather than a 1-day PD?

- How do you provide differentiated, sustained PL opportunities to meet individual teacher needs?

- What evidence exists to show that PDL at your school maximizes every teacher's knowledge and skills to enhance student learning?

- What do you think about when reading this quote, attributed to Confucius: "I hear and I forget, I see and I remember, I do and I understand"?

APPLICATION EXERCISE

Create a survey and disseminate to all teachers to collect their perceptions about PDL being delivered at your school. Your survey can be organized to collect qualitative and/or quantitative data. Teachers need to clearly understand that the data is being collected and analyzed anonymously; do not ask for any identifiable details. We recommend that you include questions or statements such as the following:

- PDL at my school has a focus, and this focus spirals from one session to the next.
- PDL at my school is always about maximizing every teacher's knowledge and skills to enhance student learning.
- PDL emphasizes evidence- or researched-based ideas.
- My input and voice are evident in my school's PDL opportunities.

Add statements or open-ended questions as you see necessary and capture data in a format that works best for everyone to analyze and understand (e.g., a Likert Scale with the categories strongly agree, agree, neither agree or disagree, disagree, and strongly disagree).

Collect the data and analyze the results. What became clearer to you as you analyzed the survey responses? What would you like to do differently? What is one small step you can take to improve PDL at your school?

INTRODUCTION

One of the primary reasons coaching works is that it provides opportunities to share knowledge and expertise about real-world situations and learn from each other. The best coaches do not see coaching as simply an opportunity to spread their wisdom and experience to other teachers who are less informed or less skilled. Instead, successful coaches are sincerely interested in helping every student become successful and confident, and, in the process of working with peer colleagues to achieve this, they add to their own personal bag of tricks or repertoire of professional tools and strategies. The best coaches see a personal learning opportunity in every coaching encounter. The work that SFC coaches do to provide as well as obtain their own continued PDL happens within the Teacher/Learner role.

This chapter presents specific ways that an SFC coach can support teachers through PDL. When SFC coaches share effective, proven instructional strategies, methods, and techniques with an individual colleague or with small or large groups of educators or even parents, we label those tasks as falling under the Teacher/Learner role. We use the label of Teacher/Learner to underscore that every SFC coach must understand and embrace the importance of viewing themselves—and interacting with their colleagues—as professional equals. SFC coaches certainly have a responsibility at times to teach something to their colleagues, such as providing effective, well-designed, and appropriate PDL to support an individual colleague, or to small or large groups of educators or possibly parents. But, at the same time, SFC coaches must constantly view themselves as learners who are eager and open to gaining new knowledge about effective teaching and coaching.

Coaches have the opportunity to learn from every teacher with whom they interact. The lessons coaches learn are sometimes about providing good instruction, sometimes they are about interacting with different kinds of people, and sometimes they are lessons in patience. Beyond learning from the teachers, an SFC coach has a responsibility to keep learning about instructional practices supported by the best possible research. The coach should continue to read and study, seek out their own PDL opportunities, and gain access to the support of colleagues and outside resources. Coaches should look for ways to continue learning alongside their colleagues, such as attending conferences with others from your school, district, or agency; participating in trainings or webinars together; or collaborating on an article or book study. These shared learning events can establish and/or strengthen the all-important collaborative partnership between coaches and colleagues.

PROFESSIONAL DEVELOPMENT

We introduced PD in Chapter 1 and want to reiterate that the goal of effective PD is not that teachers learn how to go through the motions of implementing an effective instructional strategy. They must understand the strategy enough to be able to know when and how to use it to support student learning and practice it enough to be able to apply it flexibly. This kind of understanding takes time. Joyce and Calhoun (2010) described PD as "coming into being through deliberate actions by the organization . . . to generate learning by educators and to make the school a learning laboratory for teachers and administrators" (p. 9). Fullan (2007) defined *PD* as "workshops, courses, programs, and related activities that are designed presumably to provide teachers with new ideas, skills, and competencies necessary for improvements in the classroom" (p. 35). Cole (2004) referred to PD alone as a way to avoid change. This last statement by Cole might make you pause and ponder what he means, but we think you will understand Cole's position as you continue reading.

Most people know that changing any organization is hard, taking a minimum of 3–5 years (Hall & Hord, 2015), and requires each individual within the organization to make changes. The change needed in a school might be school culture, team collaboration, family and community relationships, teacher retention, or instructional design or delivery. You will not change any of these quickly nor in one PD session. Changing any of these things would take time and focus, and only offering a few PD sessions alone will likely divert attention from the real issue. Keep this question in mind when you are scheduling, planning, or preparing a PD session. Does your PD directly address or simply skirt around the real issue or concern?

Let's explore a few examples of PD that skirt around real change. Elementary reading teachers inform their administrator/supervisor that they are struggling to implement all components of their core reading program, so the administrator/supervisor contacts an outside consultant and schedules a 1-day refresher during an upcoming campus PD day to help teachers with implementation. That is it. Now you have the additional PD needed to effectively implement your core reading program, right? Likely not. Although teachers informed their administrator/supervisor that they were struggling with implementation, they did not specify what components were causing them to struggle. A 1-day workshop, or even a few workshops, will likely not lead to change without additional input or a deep understanding of the problem.

Here is another scenario that avoids change. A district curriculum and instruction specialist noticed a high percentage of students not mastering grade-level standards. This specialist contacts a publisher's sales representative to inquire about intervention instructional materials without receiving input from teachers or an administrator/supervisor. The sales representative shares a few options during their initial call and then schedules a meeting to show the materials. The meeting with the sales representative and the district specialist does not include teachers who will implement these materials nor an administrator/supervisor; however, the specialist believes she has enough information to make a decision. Besides, teachers will not have to attend a meeting, and they will likely appreciate the additional intervention materials for their classrooms. Impressed by the sales pitch, the specialist decides to place an order. As soon as other administrators/supervisors sign off, she will send the teachers a calendar invitation to attend an after-school PD session to learn about the new intervention materials. The publisher's training team will demonstrate the materials during this PD session and share how the program has been successful in other districts.

It is unlikely that either scenario will lead to any kind of meaningful change, and it is quite possible that teachers will not use the materials with fidelity or at all because they had no input during the decision-making process. Always remember how important it is to get input from all stakeholder groups who will be affected by a change.

PROFESSIONAL LEARNING

We also introduced PL in Chapter 1. Fullan and Hargreaves (2016) defined *PL* as "focusing on learning something new that is potentially of value" (p. 3). In this sense, there is a type of structure for learning with a measurable outcome. With PL, there are ongoing opportunities to collaborate with others to build on initial PD.

> The essence of system success is a culture of daily interaction, engaging pedagogy, mutual trust and development, and regular, quality feedback related to improvement. Learning to be better is a function of purposeful collaboration endemic to an organic culture geared for continuous improvement and innovation. (Fullan & Hargreaves, 2016, p. 8)

This quote nicely describes the purpose of a true PLC (i.e., an effective PLC is the ongoing, continuous work with colleagues engaged in authentic discourse in an organic manner). It is not a time or an event like we often see or hear. For example, "our PLC meets on Wednesday from 2:00 p.m. to 3:00 p.m." is a nonexample of a PLC. Because you have a dedicated day and time to meet does not mean that professionals are meeting to learn from each other. In fact, there are times that we have taken part in meetings labeled a PLC in which teachers hardly speak to each other.

You might be thinking PD and PL are one in the same, and to an extent they are. There can be formal learning from a PD session, as well as developmental growth through ongoing PL opportunities. Your challenge as an SFC coach is to ground change initiatives in sustained PL and not only a one-time PD session.

EFFECTIVE LEARNING OPPORTUNITIES

With the knowledge you have gained thus far in this chapter, we hope you understand that PD is not synonymous with an external expert coming to your school for a day, assuming they know what you need, teaching a new strategy, and leaving. What happens after the expert leaves? This way of providing PD does not work well. Teachers may get an overview of a particular teaching approach, pick up some useful ideas, or even "make and take" some things to use in their classrooms, but they rarely learn enough in these 1-day events to make a real difference in their instruction that positively affects student outcomes. These 1-day workshops can easily be "sit and get" sessions or a stand-and-deliver type presentation because the expert has so much to tell you in a short time. There is considerable evidence that this traditional, short-term workshop approach does not typically result in improved instruction or student outcomes (Joyce & Calhoun, 2010).

PD is also not synonymous with randomly selecting a workshop to attend off campus with the assumption that the presenter knows your specific need. Unfortunately, too often, we see administrators/supervisors or teachers attend a conference, learn about the latest trend from an expert, and then schedule that expert to come to their campus to present this latest trend to the staff. Without thinking deeply about your campus needs and including others in the decision making, you could be selecting a solution to a problem that does not exist. It just looks and sounds good in the moment.

Realizing that PDL is a form of teaching is the key to developing and delivering effective PDL. We humans often learn new skills and absorb new concepts best when we can see demonstrations and models, actively participate and practice what we are trying to learn, and have ample opportunities for practice over time with feedback and guidance as we apply the new learning. Teaching is teaching; learning is learning.

We believe it is important for an SFC coach to consider the commonalities between PD and PL throughout all aspects of their work. PD or PL can occur in formal and informal settings and for individuals, small groups, or large groups. They can occur in the form of meeting with small groups of teachers or study groups or observing and coaching individual teachers as they learn to integrate effective instruction into their everyday teaching routines. PDL is necessary if you want teachers to learn a new skill or strategy well enough to know when and how to use it effectively to support student learning. It is important to provide teachers with many opportunities to practice a newly learned skill or strategy so that they will be able to apply it flexibly in their own settings, with their own students. It is also important that teachers engage and collaborate with each other as they continue to learn, improve, and innovate. Teachers must also have opportunities to learn, critically think, and communicate with others beyond a 1-day PD workshop to further develop and grow.

REFLECTION

If talking to someone who was unfamiliar with PD and PL, how would you describe each, including their similarities and differences?

Coach as Continuous Learner

As a coach, you know the importance of keeping others' needs in mind and realize that individuals learn differently and at different paces. Hattie (2012) said,

> Talking is one thing; action is the other . . . to put ideas into action requires having an intention to change, having knowledge of what successful change would look like, and having a safe opportunity to trial new teaching methods. (p. 71)

When taking on the Teacher/Learner role, we believe that an SFC coach has an obligation to continue their own learning in a way that enhances their knowledge or that of others, develops PDL opportunities to communicate this new learning, and delivers content in engaging, meaningful ways.

With this in mind, imagine yourself as a Teacher/Learner who is leading colleagues in implementing a schoolwide intervention model. As the SFC coach, you read more about response to intervention (RTI) and multi-tiered systems of support (MTSS) and ask yourself

- How do campus administrators/supervisors communicate and support the effective implementation of RTI or MTSS?

- What information about RTI or MTSS will colleagues need to understand to implement a schoolwide intervention model?

- How might new learning about RTI or MTSS build on existing processes or systems?

- How could I explain or demonstrate the differences between RTI and MTSS?

As you learn more about RTI or MTSS, you think about what colleagues may or may not know and areas they have expressed wanting to learn more about. You consider how you might present new learning in small chunks over time or in differentiated settings to meet individuals' needs. You know that RTI and MTSS processes rely on student assessment data to guide decision making, so a focus on assessments might be a place to start, including building on existing assessment practices, allowing multiple opportunities for colleagues to practice administering or analyzing assessment data, or providing support for colleagues as they begin to implement any new learning. More specifically, topics might include

- Teaching colleagues about different types of assessments

- Demonstrating how to administer an assessment with fidelity

- Modeling ways to analyze assessment data to differentiate instruction based on students' needs

- Coplanning a lesson using data

- Determining necessary scaffolds to support student learning based on the assessment results

If colleagues already know a great deal about assessment or data analysis, then maybe the focus should be on instruction and intervention strategies. This might include

- Showing a teacher how to teach a newly learned intervention strategy

- Modeling how to differentiate classroom instruction to meet the needs of students with learning disabilities or how to develop classroom management routines

- Arranging for a teacher to observe a colleague teaching a skill or concept

- Coplanning an intervention lesson that supports Tier 1 instruction

- Modeling self-reflection about instruction

As the SFC coach, you have a responsibility to continue to learn about effective, proven instructional strategies, methods, and techniques and teach your learning to others through effective, well-designed, and appropriate PDL. The primary purpose of the Teacher/Learner role is to provide valuable and effective PDL to your colleagues. A second important purpose is committing to your own continued PDL.

Similarities Between Teaching Teachers and Teaching Students

Your role as a Teacher/Learner is to learn the needs of your teachers and scaffold support accordingly. Consider Hasbrouck and Denton's (2005) comparison of how teaching teachers is like teaching students. The characteristics in the bulleted list might help you as you prepare for ongoing PDL opportunities with your colleagues.

- Effective instruction responds to the needs of the learner.

- Effective instruction may take place in different grouping formats.

- Effective instruction in new skills or strategies includes modeling or demonstrations.

- When people learn new skills, they need opportunities to practice with feedback and support.

Just like assessing the strengths and needs of students in a classroom, it is important to assess the strengths and needs of each teacher in a school. This can take many forms, including a survey or questionnaire, classroom observations, individual meetings, or reviewing student achievement data. It is important that you get to know each teacher so that you can appropriately respond to their individual needs. Similar to differentiating instruction for students, differentiate for your teacher colleagues.

PDL can be large- or small-group formats, or it can be provided to an individual. When differentiating, you might conduct a workshop for teachers with similar needs or interests across grade levels, or sometimes for teachers with similar needs in a single grade level. Regardless of the approach or content, remember that people are usually motivated to learn new concepts and skills that are practical and relevant to their personal situation. Reading or hearing about a new instructional strategy is not as powerful as seeing a demonstration. As the coach, you can help build capacity in others by modeling an instructional strategy in a classroom with a teachers' students. You can also schedule time for a teacher or small team of teachers to observe a colleague. These observations are not to critique. Rather, an observation can provide direction for another teacher or offer another approach to deliver a strategy in their classroom. Practice is needed. Humans are creatures of habit in many ways. It can be hard to make changes when we are used to doing something in a particular way. There is nothing wrong with having routines because they can provide a framework for which we can make important choices. Habits can be difficult to break, however. It is important that coaches understand that even if a teacher embraces a new instructional strategy, it will still likely require a lot of practice to integrate into their regular teaching routines. Remember the importance of providing feedback and supporting teachers as they apply new learning.

Differentiate and Sustain Learning Opportunities

Pioneering researchers of coaching (Joyce & Showers, 1980) identified five components of training if the goal is to transfer newly learned skills or strategies to the complex environment of a classroom. These same components remained in their 2002 research findings and include 1) presentation of theory or description of skill or strategy, 2) modeling or demonstration of skills or models of teaching, 3) practice in simulated and classroom settings, 4) structured and open-ended feedback, and 5) coaching for application. Four components are included in Table 10.1, with structured and open-ended feedback implicitly included throughout the other components.

Table 10.1.   Training components and attainment of outcomes in terms of percentage of participants

Training element	Effects on knowledge	Effects on short-term use percentage of participants)	Effects on long-term use percentage of participants)
Study of rationale (readings, discussions, lectures)	Very positive	5%–10%	5%–10%
Rationale plus demonstrations (10 or more)	Very positive	5%–20%	5%–10%
Rationale plus demonstrations plus planning of units and lessons	Very positive	80%–90%	5%–10%
All the above, plus peer coaching	Very positive	90%+	90%+

Source: Joyce and Showers (2010).

Table 10.1 identifies the percentage of participant knowledge and skill gained when learning a new skill or strategy, as well as the percentage of participants who effectively transferred their learning to the complex environment of a classroom. Notice the very low percentage of participants transferring newly learned skills to classroom practice without ongoing coaching support. To think that Joyce and Showers identified these components nearly four decades ago is unbelievable. We have known that coaching works for a long time, but many schools are just getting around to implementing it.

The SFC Coach Professional Development Learning Plan   It seems clear to us that coaches need differentiated and sustained plans to support teachers—a plan that includes teacher input, along with what is known about student assessment data or student perceptions. You can devise your own plan that works for you; however, we wanted to provide an example that we call the *SFC Coach PDL Plan*. This plan includes a few steps; however, we believe it is essential that you gain a clear understanding of the current level of implementation and devise a support plan accordingly. The SFC Coach PDL Plan consists of the following steps:

1.   Assess the need(s) for PDL in the school.

2.   Prioritize the needs(s).

3.   Write an objective(s) to address the need(s).

4.   Plan activities to target the objectives.

5.   Evaluate the effectiveness of the plan.

These five steps should seem familiar as they closely align to the steps involved in our SFC Collaborative Problem-Solving Process (see Chapter 6), as well as what we would expect a teacher to do when planning instruction for students. For example, a teacher may preassess students so they can adequately differentiate instruction throughout a unit. The results from this preassessment provide guidance for a teacher on how they will need to differentiate instruction throughout the unit. Based on the differing needs of students, the teacher writes objectives to 1) challenge and extend the learning for students who have mastered the unit skills or concepts, 2) close the learning gap for students who have not mastered any of the skills or concepts, or 3) provide additional guidance for students who mastered only some of the skills or concepts. There is not a one-size-fits-all instructional approach to meet the needs of all students, so the teacher determines varied approaches and activities and closely monitors progress and provides feedback. This is really no different than what an effective SFC coach does. You assess and prioritize teacher needs—you cannot accomplish everything at one time—and then determine your plan to support that need.

We include examples of forms that you can use to develop your SFC Coach PDL Plan. You can use all of the forms we include in our PDL Plan, some forms, or create your own. It is up to you. You will have to ultimately decide on a PDL Plan that works best for you and your colleagues. If using our forms, then we recommend that you start with the explicit instruction elements or literacy sample questionnaire that we covered in Chapter 3. You would then proceed to the Classroom Observation Summary form (see Figure 10.1). The Classroom Observation Summary form allows you to record evidence from your observations using the same explicit instruction elements or areas of literacy included on the Teacher Priority Survey. This data will allow you to compare your observations with teacher perceptions.

Teacher Priority Survey: Explicit Instruction Elements

Classroom Observation Summary	
Directions: When observing a teacher's classroom, record evidence of explicit instruction elements that you see during your visit. Enter your rating using the same scale used on the teacher survey: 3–*High priority*, 2–*Medium priority*, or 1–*Low priority*. For example, you did not observe the teacher "sequencing skills logically," resulting in student confusion when working independently. Write a 3 for that element.	
Explicit instruction element	**Teacher**
Determine critical content.	
Sequence skills logically.	
Review previously learned material and build on prior knowledge.	
State the lesson's goal and make relevant connections	
Present material in small steps.	
Think aloud and provide step-by-step demonstrations.	
Use unambiguous language to explain or model.	
Provide examples and nonexamples.	
Provide guided and supported practice.	
Ask questions and require frequent responses.	
Closely monitor student performance.	
Provide immediate, affirmative, and corrective feedback.	
Prepare students for successful independent practice.	
Provide immediate, distributed, and cumulative practice opportunities.	

Figure 10.1.   Teacher Priority Survey: Explicit Instruction Elements.   (*Continued*)

Figure 10.1. *(Continued)*

Teacher Priority Survey: Areas of Literacy

Classroom Observation Summary	
Directions: When observing in a teacher's classroom, record evidence of the areas of literacy that you see during your visit. Enter your rating using the same scale used on the teacher survey: 3–*High priority*, 2–*Medium priority*, or 1–*Low priority*. For example, you did not observe the teacher teaching in small groups. Write a 3 for that element.	
Areas of literacy	**Teacher**
Teaching phonemic awareness.	
Teaching phonics.	
Teaching fluency.	
Teaching vocabulary.	
Teaching comprehension.	
Teaching writing.	
Using assessment data to guide instruction.	
Organizing and managing small-group instruction.	
Monitoring student progress in reading and writing.	
Implementing research-based reading and writing programs and resources.	

You will likely be able to draw some conclusions with the teacher survey and classroom observation data alone. Additional data may be needed, however. We include student perception data or student assessment data as a third set of data (see Figure 10.2). We recommend collecting student perception data whenever possible to gain student perspectives of classroom teaching practices. This could be done through individual or small-group interviews.

Student Perception Survey				
Directions: The purpose of this survey is to learn how students perceive experiences in the classroom. The survey includes 10 questions and will take about 30 minutes.				
Inform the student: "I will pause after each question and ask you to respond. I will ask you to give me a rating for most questions. There will be a few questions at the end where I will ask you to provide a description or give examples. For the questions asking for a rating, I will read a statement about something happening during a lesson in your classroom, then ask if this occurs all of the time, some of the time, or never. If there is a statement that you have not experienced or do not know about, then you can say, 'I don't know.' I will be taking notes as we talk, but I will not include student names."				
Classroom experiences	**All of the time**	**Some of the time**	**Never**	**I don't know**
When starting each lesson, my teacher reviews what we previously learned to build on what I already know.				
At the beginning of each lesson, my teacher states the lesson's goal and tells me why, when, or where I will use this skill.				

Figure 10.2.   Student perception data.   *(Continued)*

Figure 10.2. *(Continued)*

During each lesson, my teacher talks out loud and provides step-by-step demonstrations.				
During each lesson, my teacher provides time for me to practice and moves around the classroom to make sure my classmates and I understand what to do.				
During each lesson, my teacher asks a lot of questions and requires all students to give frequent responses.				
At the end of each lesson, my teacher assigns homework that I can successfully complete.				
In this class, I am most motivated when . . .				
In this class, I am least motivated when . . .				
In this class, I learn the most when . . .				
In this class, I learn the least when . . .				

Student Assessment Data

Directions: Use results of assessment data in each classroom to rate students' needs. Enter your rating using the following scale:

3: Most students in this class display a need.

2: Some students in this class display a need.

1: Few students in this class display a need.

0: No student in this class displays a need.

For example, assessment data in one kindergarten classroom indicates that 75% of students have not mastered phonemic awareness skills. You would write a 3 under the heading *Most* for this area of literacy. Enter *Not Applicable* (N/A) if there is an area of literacy that is irrelevant in your grade level or with which you are unfamiliar.

Areas of literacy	Most	Some	Few	None	Not applicable
Phonemic awareness					
Phonics					
Fluency					
Vocabulary					
Comprehension					
Writing					
Other					
Teacher name:					
Grade level:					

If you follow our approach at this time, then you may have three or more sets of data to analyze for each classroom. This is important because your SFC coach role is to provide differentiated, sustained PDL and not a one-size-fits-all approach. Look for patterns or trends as you compare the sets of data you collected. How did teachers respond? How did students respond? What did you learn from your classroom observations? Try to identify one element or area to target for each classroom teacher (i.e., identify one focus area that may have a domino effect on other aspects of instruction if implemented well). You may find that an entire grade level or most teachers in your school have similar needs. If this is the case, then your PDL Plan may not reflect individual priorities. Rather, your PDL Plan will focus on a grade-level, department, or school-wide priority.

As you analyze data sets, know that you may find that teacher survey results indicate a low need of support in monitoring student performance closely, yet your observation data suggests otherwise. You may find that teacher survey data indicates that they provide multiple opportunities for students to respond, yet observation and student perception data indicates this is not happening. You may find that teacher survey data indicates that focusing instruction on critical content, the first explicit instruction element, is a low priority, yet student assessment data is low. You may find that student assessment data is high, yet classroom observation data reveal minimal opportunities for students to practice. This is why we believe it is always a good idea to have ample data to draw conclusions prior to developing your PDL Plan. In some instances, you may need even more data before you are ready to write an objective to focus your support. See Chapter 9 on how to write an ISMART goal.

Once you have analyzed various sources of data and identified one or more objectives, you are ready to complete the rest of your SFC Coach PDL Plan. This plan will guide PDL decisions and activities. When your PDL Plan is fully developed, you must stay focused and implement your plan. Similar to classroom teachers setting goals for student learning, you now have your goal(s) to support teacher success.

Figure 10.3 includes additional columns to finalize your SFC Coach PDL Plan. This form includes a space to identify your target audience, which may be an individual teacher, grade level, department, or all teachers. There is space to record how often you will meet with your target audience, the specific activity to be performed, and resources that you will need. For example, you might meet one time per week with all third-grade teachers to plan small-group instruction during their literacy instructional block. Teachers will need to bring their evidence-based literacy instructional materials as well as student assessment data to determine small-group needs. The final column is to record progress. For example, what evidence will you collect each week when meeting with these third-grade teachers to show that you are making progress toward accomplishing the objective you set? This could be student assessment data, classroom observation data, or something else.

The real work begins now that you have spent ample time collecting and analyzing data and developing an SFC Coach PDL Plan. We have observed many obstacles with teachers transferring newly learned skills to classroom practice or with coaches staying true to their PDL Plan. Lack of classroom implementation is often due to little or no ongoing coaching after colleagues learn a new skill or strategy. Not sticking to the PDL Plan is often a result of coaches who do more administrative work than coaching, coaches who lack sufficient training or learning to adequately support colleagues, schools or districts implementing multiple initiatives simultaneously, or how time is spent when meeting with teachers.

Be cognizant of your approach and stick to your PDL Plan. You did not collect and analyze various forms of data to now focus on something else. Challenge

SFC Coach PDL Plan					
Directions: Record your objective(s) to address priorities at your school. For each objective, include					
Audience: Who will participate?					
Frequency: How often will you convene?					
Activity: What will you do?					
Resources: What research-based instructional materials will you need?					
Progress: What evidence will you collect to measure growth?					
Objective(s)	**Audience**	**Frequency**	**Activity**	**Resources**	**Progress**

Figure 10.3.   SFC Coach PDL Plan.

yourself to focus on the real issue that needs to change, and plan your support based on what is known from research and teacher input. If teachers identify the lack of a vertically aligned instructional system as one major issue contributing to low student achievement data, then focus your coaching time and efforts there. This issue would be a significant undertaking and require additional input to prioritize actions; however, it would keep you and teachers focused on a real issue.

For each action leading to the end goal of having a vertically aligned instructional system, you could plan support that includes theory, demonstrations, practice, feedback, coaching, and evaluation. Each component is important, and evaluating the PDL Plan is essential. How will implementation be evaluated to know whether the PDL Plan is effective? How frequent will the PDL Plan be evaluated—three times per year, quarterly, monthly? There should always be a way to decide whether to continue the plan or make modifications, regardless of what is decided.

REFLECTION

How do you see yourself developing, implementing, and evaluating a PDL Plan? What do you see as the benefit(s) for having a PDL Plan?

Transferring New Knowledge to the Classroom

We recommend that you further your learning by reading Joyce and Showers' (1982) research on what it takes to build the highest level of skill in teachers. The following bulleted list highlights some of their findings, including the approximate time it takes to learn about and implement a new skill or strategy in the complex context of a classroom. These authors suggested

- 20–30 hours to study theory about the skill or strategy (e.g., presentations, readings)

- 15–20 demonstrations or more to observe the new skill or strategy being taught with diverse learner populations (e.g., struggling readers, English learners [ELs], gifted and talented)

- 10–15 times to practice the new skill or strategy with colleagues or small groups of students

This research makes it clear that a 1-day PD workshop will not result in a meaningful change in teachers' practice.

We stressed earlier that planning is the key to providing effective PDL. The following framework is one way to organize your time with colleagues; however, adjust according to your context or needs.

1. Establish a purpose for the session and give teachers the big picture.

    - *Talk about the benefits of the approach, process, or strategy.* Let teachers know what they are likely to gain by learning and using the new approach. Just like delivering a lesson in the classroom, provide the why, when, or where it could be used.

    - *Link session information to needs the teachers have identified.* Let the teachers know that you take their needs seriously by focusing on areas that they have identified and link sessions to these needs.

    - *Focus on student outcomes.* Talk about patterns of student strengths and needs that teachers have identified through assessments and about the potential of the new approach or strategy to help support students' growth.

    - *Create links to research.* A discussion of potential benefits of the approach should include a description of the supporting research. It is important to make links to research so that teachers know why they are being asked to implement something different.

    - *Make it practical.* Stress the practical nature of the new approach or instructional strategy. Help teachers understand that learning this new strategy will make their teaching more effective rather than just making more work for them.

2. Provide modeling and demonstration of instructional strategies.

    - *Model any new or unfamiliar procedures.* For example, model and demonstrate how to engage students in a review of the phonological awareness skills during small-group instruction.

    - *Have teachers demonstrate strategies to each other.* After modeling and demonstrating how to engage students in a review of phonological awareness skills during small-group instruction, have teachers demonstrate to each other in pairs.

3. Plan for active engagement.

    - *Include time for discussion with other teachers.* For example, you might ask for a one-sentence reaction to a question or statement printed on chart paper or included in your presentation. Have each teacher write only one sentence. Then provide a set amount of time for teachers to discuss their responses with a partner.

    - *Have teachers role-play to practice new activities and strategies.* Some teachers may not enjoy role playing because it does not seem real to them. If this is the case, then try modeling a feedback strategy that you have used after conducting a classroom observation. Then show a short video clip of a teacher teaching. After watching the video clip, practice the feedback strategy. One teacher role-plays the teacher teaching and the other teacher role-plays the coach.

    - *Ask teachers to put objectives or activities in order by difficulty level or developmental sequence.* For example, model skills found in a vertical alignment (e.g., kindergarten through 12th grade) for one set of standards (e.g., summarization). Then have teachers work together to order the skills from the lowest to highest grade.

    - *Have teachers practice developing strategies for providing their students with opportunities to practice skills.* For example, teachers could work together to determine ways that students can have repeated exposures to making inferences.

    - *Have teachers practice grouping students based on assessment results.* Ask teachers to bring the results of one or two key assessments they have administered to their classes. Discuss the interpretation of the results and assist teachers in using the results to create small groups of students who have similar instructional needs. Encourage teachers to work together to group students.

    - *Request that teachers create sample lessons or lesson plans.* Assist teachers in creating lessons based on the results of assessments of their students or provide a scenario for a fictitious group of students and include assessment data. You can guide teachers in using assessment data and their standards to plan instruction.

4. Encourage self-reflection and help teachers become problem solvers.

    - *Encourage or discuss live or videotaped lessons.* For example, watch a short video and have teachers only focus on questions being posed to students. After the video, have teachers discuss the types of questions they heard.

    - *Ask teachers to share what has worked well in their classrooms or strategies they have used to identify and solve student problems.* Have teachers bring examples of a routine they have used to increase student time on task or completing independent work in a workstation.

    - *Provide a format for self-reflection.* For example, ask each teacher to bring a student work sample to discuss with colleagues. What was the goal of the lesson? What was the expected outcome? What was the standard? How can I increase the level of rigor?

Read the following scenario and then see which elements from our recommended framework are included in the coach's response to the scenario. (*Note:* We include a few of our connections after the scenario. Compare your notes with our examples or add to the list.)

During a recent meeting with your colleagues, you spent time analyzing beginning-of-year student achievement data to determine an area of focus. Although a few areas had lower-than-expected student performance scores, one area specifically stood out to your colleagues. Student performance in vocabulary is abysmal. To see if this has been an ongoing issue, you and your colleagues review historical data and learn that vocabulary has been an area of need for at least 2 years. Collectively, the team decides that vocabulary development is a real need, and they suggest that this should be a schoolwide effort. Teachers note that vocabulary is an important skill that is taught at all grade levels and in all content areas. A schoolwide vocabulary effort could increase communication between or among grade levels, focus collaborative PDL days on one topic, and structure the planning or support provided by the coach.

As the SFC coach, you share Joyce and Showers's (1982) findings (i.e., approximate amount of time it takes to implement a new skill or strategy in the complex context of a classroom) to see if teachers are really determined to make vocabulary a priority. If so, they will need to understand that this will not be a quick fix. Teachers overwhelmingly agree that they need to develop a deeper understanding of how to teach vocabulary and that a systemwide focus is important. With this knowledge and their permission, you set out to organize an SFC Coach PDL Plan that will include theory, demonstrations, practice, feedback, and coaching. Colleagues understand that a one-time workshop will not change current vocabulary practice, and most teachers are willing to put in the extra time to learn more. You know that your PDL Plan needs to be strategic, yet flexible to meet individual teacher needs. You know that you need to be aware of cognitive overload as you introduce and deepen vocabulary knowledge over time. You also know that you need to continuously remind yourself and teachers that changes in practice will not happen overnight.

You use all available data, collegial input, and additional research findings to develop the following PDL Plan to share with your colleagues.

- *Develop an explicit vocabulary instruction presentation.* You select an article to share with teachers as one way for everyone to understand the importance for explicit vocabulary instruction, including the importance of language development and racial equity (e.g., Julie Washington's *Quest to Get Schools to Respect African-American English* or maybe Hart & Risley's *The Early Catastrophe: The 30 Million Word Gap by Age 3*). You engage teachers in critical discourse and encourage reflection. How do you implement student engagement strategies throughout all parts of your vocabulary lesson? In what way(s) do you encourage students to communicate with others? What does a positive learning environment look and sound like for students? How would you describe your implementation of culturally responsive pedagogies? How do you teach family members about the importance of vocabulary and oral language development? In addition to discussing an article during the first step of the PDL Plan, you will describe what explicit vocabulary instruction is, how students' knowledge of vocabulary influences comprehension or fluency, and revisit the explicit instruction research. You will include opportunities for teachers to review and discuss vocabulary standards to ensure everyone understands grade-level vocabulary expectations.

- *Model or demonstrate how to explicitly teach vocabulary.* As teachers learn more about the importance of explicitly teaching vocabulary and knowing the standards to teach at their respective grade levels, you will select a video to demonstrate what explicit vocabulary instruction looks and sounds like. After the video, you will build in time for teachers to share observations, new learnings, or strategies they might try during their vocabulary instruction. For example, what were students doing in the video? What was the teacher doing in the video? What activities did the teacher use? How did the teacher engage the students when introducing vocabulary words or allowing for partner or team practice? You know from research that colleagues need to see several demonstrations for a newly learned skill or strategy, so you select lessons from teachers' core reading program. Selecting lessons will allow you to demonstrate the routine used in the video with their materials. After each demonstration, ask colleagues to debrief and identify vocabulary elements they saw that would influence student learning in their classroom.

- *Practice in simulated and classroom settings.* After discussing the importance of explicit vocabulary instruction and seeing a few demonstrations, you know that teachers will need numerous opportunities to practice. You arrange time for grade-level teachers to practice with each other first, then schedule time to bring in small groups of students. This additional practice time with teachers and students will allow for ample opportunities to practice with each other and with students before implementing in the classroom. Based on research, you know that there is a much higher chance that teachers will transfer their learning to the classroom if they are confident that they have learned the new skill or strategy.

- *Provide structured and open-ended feedback.* The SFC Coach PDL Plan thus far included multiple opportunities to practice explicitly teaching vocabulary, and teachers feel confident about their learning. Before observing in their classrooms, you ask teachers to assist you in developing a checklist that you or another teacher can use when observing vocabulary instruction in their classrooms. You can provide examples of checklists or ask colleagues to work together to create a checklist. You will also want to spend time determining how teachers being observed want to receive feedback. How soon after the observation will the debrief occur? Will the observer pose reflection questions? Will the observer share a strategy to implement in the classroom?

- *Coach for application.* This is ongoing for the SFC coach. You will continue to observe, learn, provide feedback, and engage in conversation to differentiate based on individual needs to support implementation.

Although the same four elements from our suggested framework are not included in this scenario, you likely found evidence of all four. For example, there is a/an 1) link to the needs the teachers have identified; 2) focus on student outcomes; 3) link to research; 4) practical approach to increasing knowledge of vocabulary instruction; 5) opportunity for modeling or demonstrating; 6) time for teachers to discuss, practice, and plan; and 7) video demonstration. There are numerous variations of how you might assist your colleagues based on their needs and context. Keep in mind that you will want to develop an SFC Coach PDL Plan based on input from teachers. Including their voices is critical to changing a practice.

There is a lot to consider when introducing or learning one new strategy or skill that can cause substantial change. Imagine how overwhelmed a teacher may feel when a school or district requires more than one area of change. What will you do to help teachers manage these additional requirements? How will you help manage resistance so that teachers can remain focused on the one skill or strategy that they plan to change? How will you communicate to your administrator your need to support teachers in their identified area of focus and not the other expectations or mandates? These are a few questions that you will need to answer, along with many others.

Remember that change can be challenging, difficult, and take a long time. In our experiences, we have faced situations in which teachers do not want coaching support, and this is sometimes due to them simply not wanting to change. This could be for any number of reasons, such as their deep-seated beliefs or not understanding why the new skill or strategy is needed nor when or where they will be able to teach it. Do not get discouraged. Direct your attention to those who do want to implement the new skill or strategy. We think you will be surprised when reluctant teachers start requesting your support because they notice positive changes occurring for teachers with whom you are working. As we have said more than one time, your SFC coach role does not come with power or authority. You cannot force someone to want your support or advice.

REFLECTION

What approach do you follow when creating a plan to support teacher needs? How is your plan similar or different from the PDL Plan we propose? What changes, if any, would you make to your current approach?

LEADING EFFECTIVE MEETINGS

You might be thinking that there is no possible way that you have the time to present theory, demonstrate, and allow for practice. We have found that it is possible from our experiences. We see many missed opportunities for PDL. This includes time spent (or wasted) in meetings. We shared 25-, 35-, and 50-minute academic or behavior meeting processes in Chapter 8 and now want to provide additional information about leading effective meetings.

> Monday morning begins with a 20-minute information meeting led by the principals. Nearly all teachers attend these meetings. Communication is one way—from the principals to the teachers—with little time for questions. One of the interviewed teachers compared the meeting with a shopping list, "It is just to tick off the items." (Arlestig, 2007, p. 266)

We realize this quote alludes to an administrator/supervisor leading a faculty meeting; however, we also recognize that this type of meeting happens in many situations, including those led by coaches. As you continue reading, we think you will discover that the research we include relates to most, if not all, types of meetings. Think about connections you can make to your SFC Coach PDL Plan, regardless of the type of meeting in which you lead or take part.

Meetings do not have to be a waste of time. Meetings can serve as opportunities to share new ideas, discuss issues that have arisen in practice, collaborate with others, and evaluate student achievement or educational programs (Klein, 2005). They can serve in this manner if there is proper preparation. Garmston and Wellman (1992) stated that, "All presentations are made twice—first in the presenter's mind, during the design stage, and second, during the actual presentation. Eighty-five percent of the quality of the second presentation is a product of the first" (p. 1). Have a purpose for bringing colleagues together and be prepared in order to enhance learning during meetings. Without a clear purpose, adequate preparations, or a clear focus, you might find yourself leading a meeting in the pressure box environment. Michel (2011), coauthor of this book, conceptualized this as "dominated by the hierarchical chain of commands and emphasizes mandates and expectations rather than what participants say matters most: student learning and teacher development" (p. 131). This pressure box environment is not what you want.

Meetings occur for a variety of reasons and are necessary for the success of any organization. Numerous scholars have identified the necessary features of effective meetings (Arlestig, 2007; Brandenburg, 2008; Francis, 2006; Klein, 2005; Leach et al., 2009; Sexton, 1991). Following is a compilation of ideas from these researchers:

- Adequate preplanning

- Effective and proper training of facilitators

- Encouragement of teacher expression

- Communication that encourages different perspectives and interpretations

- Participant engagement

- Shared decision making

- Establishment of safe and nurturing environment

- Collectively designed ground rules

- An agenda with relevant topics for participants

- Effective use of time and punctuality

- Appropriate meeting facilities

We want to stress the importance of effectively using time to focus on student learning during meetings. It is not how much time you have; it is how you use each minute that is important.

Using Meetings for Professional Development and Learning

From our experiences, there is often too long of a lag between meetings to effectively learn, practice, and plan for the delivery of the new skill or strategy. Fortunately, based on what we have presented about meetings, we know meetings can be optimal times for ongoing PL. Should you and your colleagues decide that meetings will be your avenue to learn about a new skill or strategy, then the following example might help you think about breaking down content into manageable sections over time. Although we discuss using several meetings to determine an area of focus with colleagues (e.g., theory, demonstrations, practice), your plan might include more or fewer meetings. You will need to work with colleagues to develop a plan and meeting sequence.

Meetings 1–4: Determining Needs and Theory

During your first meeting, consider spending time communicating your responsibilities as an SFC coach, building relationships, becoming familiar with individual preferences and philosophies, or understanding teachers' needs. Teachers will need to know that you are there to work collaboratively with them in a non-evaluative role. Revisit the SFC coach definition in Chapter 1 or our description of the SFC coach in Chapter 2. The work of an SFC coach remains the same no matter what—to guide and support the planning and implementation of effective, evidence-based instructional practices to support student progress.

During your second meeting, you might spend time analyzing student achievement data with teachers to determine an area of focus. Collectively, you learn that students have low performance in vocabulary, and grade-level teams decide that vocabulary should be a schoolwide effort. You engage colleagues in an activity to determine why students struggle in the area of vocabulary (e.g., EL and language barrier, little emphasis on vocabulary instruction in the core reading program) by writing all of their reasons on a sheet of chart paper or posting on a whiteboard using sticky notes. You can then work together to determine which reasons are within your area of control or influence and which are outside your area of control or influence. This is an important step because it helps to reduce the number of reasons why students struggle with vocabulary and moves the discussion forward in identifying a possible root cause for low performance in vocabulary. If time allows, you can have colleagues read an article such as *Are You Looking Out the Window or in a Mirror?* by Rick DuFour (2004) and discuss. If time runs short, you could have teachers read the article prior to the next meeting. This article can help put into perspective the need to focus on a can-do attitude rather than an if-only attitude and direct the conversation to what you have control or influence over. Prior to teachers leaving this meeting, distribute and ask them to read a research article about oral language and vocabulary development before coming to the next meeting.

During your third meeting, you engage colleagues in conversation about the research article they read about oral language and vocabulary development. You might also quickly discuss the DuFour article if you did not have time during the previous meeting. Reading and discussing research with teachers is an important step so that everyone has a clear understanding of why this focus is so important. For example, the coach and teachers might consider what oral language development has to do with reading instruction. Why is it important to explicitly teach vocabulary? In what way(s) does vocabulary affect comprehension or fluency? The questions are endless, and questions can lead to further questions or research opportunities. Prior to leaving this meeting, ask colleagues to come to the next meeting with their grade-level vocabulary standards, which will allow you and the teachers to review and see how vocabulary skills build over time. It will also be an opportunity to discuss and emphasize grade-level vocabulary standards as well as vocabulary standards above and below their grade level should teachers need to scaffold instruction for students who struggle or need to extend their learning.

During the fourth meeting, the SFC Coach PDL Plan provides time to analyze standards, including grade-level standards and standards taught before and after your grade level. When studying grade-level vocabulary standards, you ensure that colleagues understand what they need to cover. For example, do not assume that each third-grade teacher knows the words *affix, palindrome,* or *root.* You also do not assume that each third-grade teacher knows how to teach the meaning of an affix, palindrome, or root word. As an SFC coach, you might learn during this meeting that one or more colleagues need additional support in learning about grade-level standards, whereas others need to learn more about how to scaffold and use previous skills for struggling readers. Before colleagues leave this meeting, ask them to come to the next meeting prepared to discuss how they currently teach vocabulary or share successful practices they have used in the past when teaching vocabulary.

We hope that you see a pattern in the meeting processes. There is a common focus based on the initial meeting with colleagues. By sticking to this common focus, you validate teachers' input and help them develop their skills to improve in one area. You also do not fall victim to the 1-day PD and avoid change. Keep meetings focused and colleagues actively engaged, regardless of the amount of time you have. You are providing a structure that allows for critical discourse: facilitating, listening, and asking questions. By doing this, you are building capacity in your colleagues and implicitly modeling ways they can build capacity in their students.

Meetings 5–7: Demonstrations

During the first 4 weeks, the SFC Coach PDL Plan allowed teachers to gain a deeper understanding of many aspects surrounding vocabulary. You can shift the focus to demonstrations for subsequent meetings. Recall from Joyce and Showers' (1982) research the need to provide multiple demonstrations in various contexts, which can be in the form of face-to-face demonstrations with colleagues or use of a video. When demonstrating, include examples of diverse learners or learners similar to your school setting. For example, what does it look or sound like when explicitly teaching vocabulary to ELs, students with disabilities, or gifted and talented students? After a few initial demonstrations with teachers, you might demonstrate how to teach vocabulary with ELs. In another meeting, you might demonstrate how to teach vocabulary with gifted and talented students. Know your student population and teacher needs and use this information to help guide your decision making.

Meetings 8–10: Practice

At this point, the SFC Coach PDL Plan might include scaffolds for colleagues to become more proficient in teaching vocabulary. This might mean organizing practice opportunities in which colleagues work in pairs, with other grade-level colleagues, or with small groups of students. You know from the research that colleagues need many opportunities to practice before implementing in the complex environment of a classroom. During one meeting, you might allow time for colleagues to practice the implementation of a new vocabulary routine. During another meeting, you might work with teachers and select academic vocabulary words to teach from their core reading programs. By working alongside teachers, you will have a firsthand look at who may need additional support in the future.

As mentioned earlier and based on our experiences of providing support for coaches nationally, we see many lost opportunities to increase teacher learning. We sometimes observe PD that appears as one-way communication, coach to colleagues; meetings in which colleagues view or analyze more data but do not spend time focusing on how to use the data to guide instructional decision making; or meetings that are all about mandates or expectations. Please know that this does not have to be the norm. Focus your attention on the real issue (and learning) and determine other ways to share mandates or expectations.

This is not to say that we have only seen lost opportunities. In a few instances, we have observed meetings used to deliver a small amount of PD followed by several weeks of intense PL. We delivered a 1-day interactive PD session on peer coaching in one school. Then, during subsequent onsite visits, we engaged teachers in ongoing PL to deepen their understanding of peer coaching through collaboration. These subsequent learning opportunities took place during 40-minute grade-level meetings and included the use of an adapted, structured Tuning Protocol developed by Joseph McDonald (1992) for the School Reform Initiative. The collaborative dialogue included student work samples and teacher lesson plans. Following is how the work evolved into PDL.

- *Post a working agenda to guide the meeting.* For example, post a working agenda with topics to cover prior to colleagues arriving to the meeting. This includes the same information that was e-mailed several days before the meeting so that everyone knew how to prepare or what to bring. The working agenda allows for flexibility and the ability to make adjustments. The working agenda also allows colleagues to understand the flow of the meeting.

- *Post and review working agreements.* Working agreements are similar to group norms; however, they are predetermined and adjusted when needed. For example, you might post working agreements such as

  - Balance listening and speaking

  - Speak with candor

  - Presume good intentions

  - Provide thoughtful feedback; not challenging others' opinions

  - Ask questions

We defined each working agreement and provided examples or nonexamples during a successful first meeting with colleagues. Each individual then selected and wrote down one working agreement to focus on throughout the meeting. For example, a colleague who often talks a lot chose to balance listening and speaking so that others could contribute more. During subsequent meetings, colleagues referred to the posted working agreements and selected their focus. *Note:* If you decide to include working agreements during your meetings, then know that you can always select one agreement on which everyone focuses. You would choose an agreement for everyone if colleagues' behaviors during a prior meeting affected how others participated or contributed. For example, a few colleagues dominated the conversation during the meeting by talking over others and not allowing others to be heard. They interrupted each other or were inattentive when they did not want to hear others' thoughts. You decide that during next week's meeting everyone will focus on "providing thoughtful feedback; not challenging others' opinions." The effective implementation of working agreements, just like rules or routines in a classroom, is a preventative measure so that your time with colleagues remains focused, nonjudgmental, and respectful.

- *Select a Facilitator.* Initially, we modeled this role; however, we released responsibility so that others could facilitate. This was a way to build capacity in others, and the hope was that grade-level teams would continue to use this process. In this example, the designated Facilitator kept the conversation focused on the student work sample or lesson plan, engaged colleagues, listened attentively, and reminded colleagues of the working agreements when needed. *Note:* being the Facilitator does not mean directing or controlling the conversation. It is a role similar to that of the Manager in the 25-Minute Problem-Solving Process presented in Chapter 7.

- *Share artifacts.* Each colleague briefly shared the artifact they brought to the meeting. "I brought a student work sample from yesterday's math lesson on three-digit addition." "I brought my lesson plan for tomorrow's lesson on root words." Colleagues selected one artifact to discuss because of time constraints; however, everyone was responsible for bringing an artifact.

- *Provide additional context.* During the previous step, colleagues selected one student work sample or lesson plan for the whole group to analyze. During this step, the chosen colleague, referred to as a *presenter,* provided additional detail about the student work sample or lesson plan, including the goal of the lesson, expected student outcomes, instructional method(s) used to deliver the content, instructional scaffolds, student diversity, and other important details. After providing the additional context, the presenter posed a guiding question for others to discuss. The guiding question is what they wanted others to talk about to provide feedback or other suggestions, leading to new learning or a way to improve. They posed a question for which they did not have an answer. For example, does the independent activity included at the end of this lesson demonstrate mastery of the lesson goal? Does this lesson plan allow for critical thinking or encourage student collaboration? Does the lesson adequately address the learning goal?

- *Converse and listen.* Before colleagues began talking about the presenter's question, they asked a few clarifying questions based on what was presented. It was important that colleagues had the knowledge needed to engage in a productive conversation that would provide the presenter with additional insight or recommendations. After a few clarifying questions, colleagues discussed the question posed by the presenter. The presenter remained silent and took notes during the discussion time. They did not engage in the conversation or add additional information. This was not their time to defend their decisions; if they posed a meaningful question to which they did not have an answer and provided sufficient context, then they did not need to try to interject.

- *Share your learning.* After a short amount of time, the presenter summarized what they heard from their colleagues' conversation, including new learning, strategies they had not thought about previously, or a realization that their lesson was low-level rigor or activities did not relate to the lesson goal.

Colleagues engaged in critical discourse about the student work sample or lesson plan, asked clarifying or probing questions, and provided feedback to each other in a nonthreatening manner. As the SFC coach, you will need to talk through and model each step if you decide to implement this protocol. We believe that after ample practice you will quickly understand and appreciate this process. From our experiences, colleagues take on more ownership, engage in authentic discourse, and provide each other with recommendations that were previously unknown.

> ## REFLECTION
>
> *How would you describe meetings that you lead or meetings where you are a participant? What do you notice about yourself? What do you notice about others? If you were in charge, what would you do differently?*

CONCLUSION

Improvement "is more a function of learning to do the right things in the setting where you work than it is of what you know when you start to do the work" (Elmore, 2004, p. 73). As an SFC coach, model findings from research through your everyday actions and words as well as in your daily planning. Your deliberate actions can serve as a model of how to work independently and collaboratively. Your deliberate actions can also demonstrate how to maintain a focus on student learning.

Before proceeding to the next chapter, revisit your responses to the questions at the start of this chapter and make any adjustments based on new knowledge or insights gleaned. Also, take time to make any changes or updates to the application exercise.

VIRTUAL COACHING TIP

Creating an SFC Coach PDL Plan can take place face to face or in a virtual platform. Make contact with one or more teachers who have sought out your support, create a plan, and execute the plan. If using a virtual platform, then plan ahead for how you will model strategies, engage participants, or allow time to practice. Colleagues will need to make sure that they have access to all necessary materials ahead of time. Take advantage of the many features included in virtual platforms, such as the breakout room, chat, whiteboard, poll, and hangout.

REFERENCES

Archer, A., & Hughes, C. (2011). *Explicit instruction: Effective and efficient teaching.* Guilford Press.

Arlestig, H. (2007). Principals' communication inside schools: A contribution to school improvement? *The Educational Form, 71,* 262–273.

Brandenburg, S. (2008). *Conducting effective faculty meetings* (Doctoral dissertation). Retrieved from Dissertations & Theses. (Publication No. AAT 3316300)

Brennan, W. (2018). *Quest to get schools to respect African-American English.* Retrieved from https://www.theatlantic.com/magazine/archive/2018/04/the-code-switcher/554099/

Cole, P. (2004, December). *PD: A great way to avoid change.* Centre for Strategic Education.

Doran, G. (1981). There's a SMART way to write management's goals and objectives. *Management Review, 70*(11), 35–36.

DuFour, R. (2004). Are you looking out the window or in a mirror? *Journal of Staff Development, 25*(3), 63–64.

Elmore, R. (2004). *School reform from the inside out.* Harvard University Press.

Francis, A. (2006). *A comprehensive model of meeting dynamics: The influence of purpose, structure, process, and characteristics of individual participants* (Doctoral dissertation). Retrieved from Dissertations & Theses. (Publication No. AAT 3237408)

Fullan, M. (2007). Change the terms for teacher learning. *Journal of Staff Development, 28*(3), 35–36.

Fullan, M., & Hargreaves, A. (2016). *Bringing the profession back in: Call to action.* Learning Forward.

Garmston, R., & Wellman, B. (1992). *How to make presentations that teach and transform.* Association for Supervision and Curriculum Development.

Hall, G., & Hord, S. (2015). *Implementing change: Patterns, principles, and potholes* (4th ed.). Pearson.

Hart, B., & Risley, T. (Spring, 2003). *The early catastrophe: The 30 million word gap by age 3.* Retrieved from https://www.aft.org/sites/default/files/periodicals/TheEarlyCatastrophe.pdf

Hasbrouck, J., & Denton, C. (2005). *The reading coach: A how-to manual for success.* Sopris West Educational Services.

Hattie, J. (2012). *Visible learning for teachers: Maximizing impact on learning.* Routledge.

Joyce, B., & Calhoun, E. (2010). *Models of professional development: A celebration of educators.* Corwin Press.

Joyce, B., & Showers, B. (1980). Improving in-service training: The messages of research. *Educational Leadership, 37,* 379–385.

Joyce, B., & Showers, B. (1982). The coaching of teaching. *Educational Leadership, 40*(1), 4–10.

Joyce, B., & Showers, B. (2002). *Student achievement through staff development* (3rd ed.). Association for Supervision and Curriculum Development.

Klein, J. (2005). Effectiveness of school staff meetings: Implications for teacher-training and conduct of meetings. *International Journal of Research and Method in Education, 28*(1), 67–81.

Leach, D., Rogelberg, S., Warr, P., & Burnfield, J. (2009). Perceived meeting effectiveness: The role of design characteristics. *Journal of Business Psychology, 24*(1), 65–76.

McDonald, J. (1992). Tuning protocol. Retrieved from https://schoolreforminitiative.org/doc/tuning.pdf Michel, D. (2011). *An analysis of faculty meeting content and processes: A multi-case study of three south Texas schools.* (Doctoral dissertation). Retrieved from Dissertations & Theses. (Publication No. AAT 3501081)

Rosenshine, B. (2012). Principles of instruction: Research-based strategies that all teachers should know. *American Educator, 36*(1), 12–19, 39.

Sexton, D. (1991). *Conducting faculty meetings: A new direction for principals* (Unpublished master's thesis). St. Cloud State University.

11

Delivering Effective Instruction and Intervention

Before reading this chapter, consider the following questions. Jot down some notes on your current understanding, and then at the end of the chapter, we will revisit these questions to assess the knowledge and insight you gained during your reading.

- How would you describe what explicit instruction looks and sounds like in a core and intervention classroom? What are the similarities between these two settings? What are the differences?

- As an SFC coach, how would you communicate and support the campus or district MTSS or RTI model?

- If you were in a coaching role, what evidence would you collect to demonstrate that your position affects student learning?

APPLICATION EXERCISE

This chapter introduces the SAILS acronym (Standards, Assessment, Instruction and Intervention, Leadership, and Sustainability). Find an example(s) to demonstrate how you support or plan for each component. For example, throughout this school year, teachers at your school are learning how to identify and teach academic vocabulary words using a peer coaching model. As a coach, you have no idea what the future holds with funding and continuing this intense learning. You also know that teachers get frustrated when each school year starts with something new. They want some consistency and time to better their craft in one area before moving onto something new. With this knowledge, what is the plan to sustain learning in academic vocabulary?

INTRODUCTION

Research supports the need for explicit, targeted, and intensive instruction, especially for struggling students (Archer & Hughes, 2011; Hempenstall, 2016; Rosenshine, 1987, 2012). It is essential for all instructional coaches, including those using the SFC model, to be deeply informed about this research so they can support and guide their teacher colleagues to effectively implement this kind of instruction in their classrooms to maximize student success. Recall that Goal 1 for SFC coaches involves working to help teachers, parents, and everyone in the system to use the best possible strategies and support to help every student successfully achieve their academic, behavioral, and social-emotional potential. Knowing the research about explicit instruction is definitely a big piece of this required knowledge for coaches.

Rosenshine (2012) described explicit instruction as teachers teaching a small amount of material and then guiding or assisting students as they practice. Hasbrouck and Denton (2005) referred to *explicit instruction* as "telling it like it is" (p. 8). Archer and Hughes (2011) defined *explicit instruction* as an "unambiguous and direct approach to teaching that incorporates instruction design and delivery" (p. 1). All essentially reinforce the need to be systematic and direct and include the following elements:

- Determine critical content.

- Sequence skills logically.

- Review previously learned material and build on prior knowledge.

- State the lesson's goal and make relevant connections.

- Present material in small steps.

- Think aloud and provide step-by-step demonstrations.

- Use unambiguous language to explain or model.

- Provide clear examples and nonexamples.

- Provide guided and supported practice.

- Ask questions and require frequent responses to explain learning.

- Monitor student performance closely.

- Provide immediate affirmative and corrective feedback.

- Prepare students for successful independent practice.

- Provide immediate, distributed, and cumulative practice opportunities.

No item in this list can happen by chance. Each item requires the identification or selection of content, appropriate and adequate lesson design and delivery, and sustained, differentiated opportunities for students to practice.

Let's say that your SFC coach role this year requires you to support middle school mathematics teachers in teaching order of operations. Although mathematics may not be your area of expertise, you should be willing to seek out additional resources to guide your own learning and effectively support teachers. You can learn together. You start by studying how to best teach order of operations and learn about key vocabulary, necessary foundational skills, strategies, and resources. You realize from your research that teaching order of operations may take several days when initially introduced to students because of the many prerequisite skills (e.g., solving inside parenthesis, knowing what an exponent means).

As you continue your learning and preparations to support the middle school mathematics teachers, you come across a poster in one of the middle school classrooms with the mnemonic device of PEMDAS. You ask the teacher how she uses this mnemonic device and learn that she teaches students the phrase "Please excuse my dear Aunt Sally" so that they remember the correct sequence of steps. You ask the teacher if you can take a photo of the poster to use during an upcoming meeting with the middle school mathematics teachers. You want to emphasize the importance of students understanding the meaning behind order of operations and not only memorizing a mnemonic device.

You are prepared when it is time to meet with the middle school mathematics teachers. You know the research, student performance data, and want to ensure that teachers have the content and pedagogical knowledge to explicitly teach order of operations. As a collaborative team, you engage in discourse about student expectations, purpose for teaching order of operations, real-world connections, prior challenges when teaching order of operations, and more. As the SFC coach, you stress the importance of students understanding the meaning behind order of operations and not only memorizing a mnemonic device. You proceed and show teachers the expression $4 + 2^4 \div 8 \times 5 + (12 - 3)$. You then discuss misconceptions. For example, would a student correctly solve this expression if following the PEMDAS poster without a clear understanding behind order of operations? The answer is probably not. Imagine a student solving what is inside parenthesis first, then the exponent, and then the next step on the poster—multiply. You already know this is trouble if students do not have the clear understanding that the next step is to multiply or divide, whichever comes first left to right. After this discussion, you model how a teacher might explicitly teach order of operations.

The meeting continues, and the team decides that order of operations is not a skill to rush through. Collectively, teachers decide that the first lesson will include explicitly teaching key vocabulary such as *expression* and *variable*, as well as parenthesis in an expression. The second lesson will build on vocabulary and parenthesis and add exponents. The third and fourth lessons will show how to multiply and divide or add and subtract in an expression ensuring that students have a clear understanding that when they reach the step to multiply and divide or add and subtract that they solve whichever comes first from left to right. You feel good at the end of this meeting. You guided the middle school mathematics teachers in learning more about order of operations, discussed misconceptions, modeled teaching, and determined a lesson sequence to gradually increase complexity. When you meet with these teachers again, you plan to continue to work on order of operations by analyzing student work samples, reviewing teacher lesson plans, sharing resources, and more.

Although the explicit instruction elements outlined earlier may seem like common sense and routinely implemented, our experience unfortunately suggests otherwise. Whether we are observing a novice or an experienced teacher, we see many discrepancies from research-based instructional practices when observing in classrooms as coaches. This sometimes includes what appears to be a lack of clarity on how to determine critical content, differentiate instruction appropriately, or deliver skills or concepts in small, manageable chunks coupled with continuous monitoring and immediate, corrective feedback. Sadly, we too often see teachers dominating the lesson by talking too much, posing and answering their own low-level questions, assigning irrelevant practice opportunities or problems emphasizing test-taking strategies, or providing minimal feedback to curb student misconception or misunderstanding.

Instructional coaches must have a strong knowledge base of what it means to support explicit instruction in the classroom, which includes how the coach implements these same elements when modeling for or meeting with teachers.

REFLECTION

In a coaching role, how would you support colleagues to learn about or implement the explicit instruction elements?

THE SAILS FRAMEWORK FOR EFFECTIVE SCHOOLS

To further elaborate and demonstrate how an SFC coach might support the successful implementation of the most effective, research-based instruction by teachers, we will use the SAILS acronym as a framework for effective schools developed and originally described by Hasbrouck and Denton (2005) in *The Reading Coach*. The five components in the SAILS model are well cited in effective schools' research and all play a critical role in achieving high levels of academic achievement.

Standards

Ornstein and Hunkins (2013) said this about standards:

> Standards, and particularly national standards, assume that all students, all communities, all teachers, and all school districts are alike and that they face the same challenges, possess the same values, and have students of the same intellectual abilities, the same intellectual interests, the same behavioral dispositions, and the same cultural and ethnic backgrounds. Standards imply that all school districts define the worth of a particular objective with the same metric. This is not reality. (p. 193)

Quite the statement, right? Albeit determined by policy, power, or other reasons, standards exist as a road map for what students should master at various grade levels. Standards help teachers and administrators/supervisors develop and maintain instructional vision and direction. When this is understood and implemented effectively, teachers and administrators/supervisors study the standards, discuss the standards at grade level and across grade levels to establish instructional focus, and apply the standards to set high performance goals for all their students, including students in special education.

As an SFC coach, you play a critical role in helping teachers identify and understand essential learning standards for the grade levels they teach. You also have a role in providing guidance to teachers when a student has or has not met grade-essential standards. Take teaching the concept of inference as an example. We make inferences on a regular basis, and we make inferences in all content areas in the school setting. Making inferences is a higher level thinking skill that can be difficult for some students if not explicitly taught. Consider a fourth-grade struggling reader learning about making inferences. A classroom teacher who does not know how to scaffold learning for this student may continue to teach like business as usual; however, this approach will not sufficiently address the gap in the student's learning. Rather, the SFC coach must provide the support needed to help scaffold instruction. This may include modeling strategies that focus on inferencing; however, it may require a more in-depth scaffold such as helping this student make connections to background knowledge or develop vocabulary. Defined by Graves and Braaten (1996) from a compilation of research on scaffolding, "Scaffolding—[or] provid[ing] a support to help learners bridge the gap between what they know and can do and what they need to accomplish in order to succeed in a particular learning task—is often identified as one of the most effective instructional procedures available" (p. 169). Here is a way to help teachers learn about standards:

- Identify an individual teacher, grade level, or department who has sought your support.

- Provide an overview of the explicit instruction research.

- Select one standard. (We recommend choosing a standard that is currently being addressed or one that will be addressed soon.)

- Learn about the standard with the teacher, grade level, or department, and determine how to explicitly teach the standard.

- Determine ways to scaffold instruction for students needing remediation or those needing extension.

- Decide how you will support the teacher, grade level, or department to successfully implement the lesson.

If you think back to our definition of SFC, this exercise demonstrates cooperation, mutual engagement, maximizing a teacher's knowledge and skills, and focuses on enhancing student learning. Remember, you are a Facilitator, Collaborative Problem-Solver, and Teacher/Learner. Empower educators, engage them in authentic conversation, and allow them to take ownership over their learning.

Assessments

The word *assessment* can bring about a great deal of anxiety. Based on conversations with some educators, there does not seem to be a shortage of tests being administered. Rather, it sometimes seems like testing takes precedence over instruction. There is often too much time taken for testing, little time to analyze all of the data, and even less time trying to figure out how to use the data to differentiate instruction. Hargreaves and Fullan (2012) told us in *Professional Capital: Transforming Teaching in Every School* to "be informed by the evidence, not numbed by the numbers" (p. 173) and "decide what data you need and use it judiciously" (p. 172). In other words, find what is necessary and use it.

We administer assessments for a variety of decisions needed to gauge student performance and guide instructional planning. That is, we determine where instruction must begin, for each individual student, in order for each to successfully achieve an end goal as determined by benchmarks or standards. With this in mind, it is important to know whether assessments are reliable and valid. In simple terms, do results remain the same when answering similar questions on the same test or when someone else administers the assessment? That is, is the assessment reliable? Does the assessment align with the content taught and provide instructionally useful information? Is it valid?

Educators in the most effective schools collect and use assessment data to 1) screen students for academic needs, 2) diagnose specific academic concerns, 3) monitor student progress continuously, and 4) evaluate student outcomes toward the achievement of academic standards.

- Screening assessments are designed to help educators answer the following question: Which of our students might possibly need some extra assistance in order to be successful academically?

- Diagnostic assessments are administered individually and are designed to help educators answer the following question: What are this student's academic strengths and instructional needs?

- Progress monitoring assessments help to answer the following questions: Is learning happening? Is my teaching working for this student?

- Outcome assessments are designed to answer the following question: Did our students make progress toward meeting the standards?

Administrators/supervisors at effective schools find ways to provide PL opportunities for their teachers to help them understand why assessments are administered. Only with such foundational knowledge can educators select and use assessments in a manner beneficial to students.

Assessments may be formal or informal, norm- or criterion-referenced, or formative or summative. Educators must understand the type and purpose for each assessment they administer. Several assessment details we believe an SFC coach should know are as follows:

- Formal assessments administered and scored using prescribed methods or procedures. An example would be any of the curriculum-based measures, including the assessment of oral reading fluency (e.g., the Dynamic Indicators of Basic Early Literacy Skills–DIBELS), or tests such as the Comprehensive Test of Phonological Processing.

- Informal assessments administered without standardized methods or procedures. Examples include teacher-made tests or observations.

- Norm-referenced assessments used to compare a student's performance against a norm (i.e., what is expected at a given age or grade level). Examples include the Scholastic Assessment Test or American College Testing.

- Criterion-referenced assessments used to compare a student's performance with a predetermined expectation. An example may be your state assessment, which may also have state-level norms.

- Formative assessments that provide information to monitor and guide student academic progress. Examples include unit tests or district-developed benchmarks.

- Summative assessments often given at specific times to measure student achievement. Examples may include a semester exam to measure student achievement at specific time intervals.

We recommend that you stop and take time to consider the assessments administered by one teacher or one grade level. Ask the teacher(s) to list all of the assessments they administer and then categorize by the type(s) of assessments.

We suggest listing assessments for one content area first. For example, list all literacy assessments administered in first grade, including a weekly spelling test, if a teacher administers a spelling test, and all other literacy assessments. Next, ask the teacher(s) the purpose for each assessment and whether the assessment helps to answer questions such as, Who needs help? What kind of help do they need? Is the student meeting standards? Finally, help the teacher(s) decide which assessment(s) will best inform instructional decisions and maybe do away with those that are not helpful.

With assessments, comes test items. As an SFC coach, you may be asked to help write test items. If this is the case, then take time to conduct research and learn how to write test items before you begin. It is not easy to sit down and construct well-written test items, and you cannot rely on well-written test items or assessments coming from a program or product. You, collaborating with a teacher(s), must have a clear sense of what will be expected of students at the end of a unit and what you will accept as evidence of mastery.

From our experience, teachers often write test items or whole assessments because of a mandate or personal decision whether they know the research. As mentioned in the previous paragraph, you must know or seek out the research. Research informs how to write test items and how to create an assessment blueprint. What is an assessment blueprint? The blueprint includes critical content (i.e., grade-level essential standards or student expectations) you will assess at the end of the unit, the number of questions for each critical content area, and the cognitive-complexity level for each question (e.g., Bloom's Taxonomy, Depth of Knowledge). Figure 11.1 is an adapted example originally developed by Kubiszyn and Borich (2013)

Essential standard	K	C	AP	AN	S	E	Total number of questions

Figure 11.1.   Assessment blueprint sample. (*Key:* K, knowledge; C, comprehension; AP, application; AN, analysis; S, synthesis; E, evaluation)

If a blueprint does not exist prior to teaching a unit, then how will you assess student performance at the end of that unit? In other words, what are the essential standards students must know at the end of this unit, and what evidence will show that students mastered these standards? We all know that there are many standards to teach, so it is important to determine which are critical. For example, one essential standard might be to compose an informational text. Other skills not listed in the blueprint, but could be taught and monitored, include handwriting, spelling, sentence construction, research, and organization.

As an SFC coach, you play a role in helping teachers understand the need for a blueprint, including how to create one. This is an important step prior to teaching a unit, as this guides lesson planning and formative assessments throughout a unit. Kubiszyn and Borich (2013) outlined and described how to write test items such as binary- and multiple-choice items, completion items, and essay items.

Before proceeding to the next component of SAILS, consider how you support teachers with understanding assessments or assessment terminology. What assessment area(s) do you feel confident in teaching? What assessment area(s) do you need to learn more about?

Instruction and Intervention

Instruction and intervention that meets the needs of all students, at all levels of abilities and skills requires that teachers

- *Organize and manage the classroom environment.* This includes establishing rules and routines and organizing space so that students and teachers can interact, materials can be accessed with ease, students can use scaffolds (e.g., a sound wall, anchor chart), and teachers can see what is happening in all parts of the classroom at all times. It also includes organizing space for whole- and small-group instruction. Archer and Hughes (2011) distinguished the difference between a rule and goal saying that a goal reflects values, and a rule is a specific statement of a value. One example of a goal is that drivers should be courteous, whereas a rule is that the speed limit is 65 miles per hour or stop for pedestrians in a crosswalk. Rules "promote safety and create a positive learning environment in which teachers can teach and students can learn" (Archer & Hughes, 2011, p. 117).

  As the SFC coach, you may find the need to support teachers who post goals rather than rules or help teachers learn more about rules. A few things you should keep in mind is that rules should

- Be few in number

- State the desired behavior in a positive manner

- Be unambiguous, short, simple, and begin with a verb

- Define behaviors clearly (Archer & Hughes, 2011)

It is also important for teachers to understand the need to introduce and post rules, develop lessons to teach each rule, and review rules continuously. It must be stated that rules apply to everyone in the classrooms—students and adults.

Classroom efficiency requires routines. Teachers must establish routines to maximize instructional time and help students effectively monitor and manage their own social behaviors. Clear routines promote order as well as safety in early childhood settings through high school. Routines also set the stage for positive learning environments. Similar to rules, you may find that teachers whom you coach need help with developing routines. This means helping a teacher determine routines needed, outlining or defining each routine, and reviewing as needed. Routines require explicit instruction, so you may want to revisit the explicit instruction elements described earlier in this chapter. For example, students do not learn your expectation for walking down the hallway without explicit instruction. This means you must model, practice, provide corrective feedback, and revisit as necessary. You might also stress to teachers that they consider cognitive overload when presenting routines. Introducing too many at one time may cause confusion, resulting in students not learning the routine.

- *Plan core lessons and focused interventions.* This includes understanding results from assessment data and appropriately supporting individual students with learning critical content articulated in standards. Short- and long-term goals can help teachers with planning core and intervention lessons as well as deciding on experiences to address specific needs or acquire new knowledge and skills.

- *Use validated instructional strategies and materials.* Paper does not teach; teachers teach. Select and use materials that have evidence of effectiveness, are appropriate to the students' ages and skill levels, are directly related to the lesson objectives, and are motivating and intriguing to students.

Teachers can provide high-quality instruction and intervention by organizing and managing the classroom environment, carefully planning core lessons and focused interventions, and using validated instructional strategies and materials.

Before proceeding to the next component of SAILS, consider how you can support teachers with planning and delivering effective instruction and intervention that meets all learners' needs. In addition, think about how you would help a teacher establish a safe, orderly classroom environment with rules and routines.

Leadership

In order to understand the idea of leadership within the SAILS framework, coaches must first understand the idea of a system. Langley et al. (2009) defined a *system* as "an interdependent group of items, people, or processes working together towards a common purpose" (p. 37). To know if this exists in your organization, you will need to gain a deep understanding of the current system. For example, what is the vision? Why does your organization exist? What is an area of reform? Once you can respond to who you are or an area of reform, you can move on to reducing variation within the systems' outcomes. You cannot reduce variation if you do not know where you are going. You might consider one or more of the following elements and determine what the current level of systemwide implementation looks like for each (Hiebert & Stigler, 2017).

- Learning goals are written for students at each stage of their school careers and are written as precisely as possible.

- Curriculum is written to support the learning goals and is improved as teachers implement lessons and experiment with alternative techniques.

- Measurement data is collected and analyzed, including qualitative data to examine evidence of implementation, or quantitative data to monitor student achievement.

- Differentiated, sustained PDL is focused on improving the methods of teaching and their outcomes; it is not focused on an individual.

If clarity within your system lacks one or more of the elements, then you might collaborate with others to help clarify, define, or articulate what each should look like.

Peter Northouse (2013) defined *leadership* as "a *process* whereby an individual influences a group of individuals to achieve a common goal" (p. 5). Leadership supports the system, and we stress *process* because any change to the system will take time. Hall and Hord (2015) said change in practice requires 3–5 years. Why?

Because each individual within the organization must change for organizational change to occur. This is no small feat when you may have resistant stakeholders who do not understand the change or reason for a change. As you read in the system and leadership definitions, you must work toward a common purpose or influencing a group of individuals to achieve a common goal. Be cognizant that "effective change processes shape and reshape good ideas as they build capacity and ownership among participants" (Fullan & Quinn, 2016, p. 14). Thus, know your purpose or goal and commit to action.

Systems and leadership have the capacity to affect school change. Research suggests the following levers to affect change.

- Supportive and distributed school leadership with a clear vision

- Supportive teacher community in which there is allocated time to collaborate and have transparent communication

- Organizational redesign in which you reduce the number of reforms, resources, and strategies; reframe goals or practices based on input or implementation; remove duplicate efforts; and provide ongoing, job-embedded PD

- Quality external support that is aligned to your purpose or reform area and not something new

- Interschool networks to share or model practices and cultivate engagement among different stakeholder groups (Fullan & Quinn, 2016; Li, 2017)

We believe that these levers should be part of the SFC coach's responsibilities and aligns with our definition of SFC: A cooperative, ideally collaborative, professional relationship with colleagues mutually engaged in efforts that help maximize every teacher's knowledge and skills to enhance student learning.

Before proceeding to the final component of SAILS, consider how your role affects change or leads to improved or strengthened systems.

Sustainability

Sustainability is the final SAILS component. Hasbrouck and Denton (2005) referred to *sustainability* as a "lasting agreement among all school faculty and administrators to adopt a no-excuses intervention model, making a firm pledge to work together to help every student" (p. 18). They went on to highlight terms such as *relentless, sense of urgency, passionate, realistic, high expectations, collaboration,* and *transparent communication* that can lead to successful reform. These terms align with Li's (2017) findings about successful reform processes:

- *Focus and build:* Set direction and vision as well as identify a pilot group to be involved in an experiment.

- *Manage resistance:* Use various strategies to address resistance against the reform and maintain focus on the direction and vision.

- *Transfer of skills:* Provide external support to guide a pilot group to develop new skills and celebrate successes that strengthen commitment and entice others to join.

- *Scale up:* Engage other teachers in the reform and use pilot teachers as leaders in the reform area.

- *Deepen and broaden reform:* Expand reform to other areas within the organization, deepen knowledge of leaders, enhance collaboration opportunities, and share or model practices internally or externally.

- *Address new challenges:* Deepen and broaden reform through leadership, flexibility, immediate response to concerns, or cohesiveness.

Focus on an area and seek out a few pilot teachers to implement a new practice or initiative before everyone is expected to implement it. What works? What does not work? What challenge(s) occurred when implementing? What additional data might we collect to understand the challenge(s)? What aspect of the reform area could we sustain and how?

Understand that any change to a practice or reform requires time. In the leadership section of SAILS, we highlighted Hall and Hord's (2015) research in which they said that change requires 3–5 years to implement, and it takes longer if trying to transform an organization. A nonexample of successfully implementing change is when administrators/supervisors select teachers to come together for annual curriculum writing. First, this is problematic because curriculum writing requires a great deal of knowledge and expertise in standards, curriculum, test blueprint design, and more. Second, rewriting curriculum annually is problematic because standards or core programs do not usually change that often. Third, with annual changes, the change initiative starts over each year. It is likely that few educators become comfortable with the curriculum in 1 year. Continuous change can lead to a lack of trust, confidence, and perception that people making decisions do not know what they are doing. Do not fall into this trap.

REFLECTION

How would the elements of SAILS play a critical role in achieving high levels of academic achievement in your setting?

APPLICATION TO INSTRUCTIONAL COACHING

You have learned about the types of assessments, how to create blueprints, the need to understand how to write test items, and the elements of effective instruction. Now what? Your role as an SFC coach likely includes assisting teachers in using data to guide instruction, and this may include helping teachers plan for whole-class instruction, small-group instruction, or independent practice. It may also include determining ways to use data to monitor progress for a whole school goal. This does not mean doing all of this on your own; you want to build capacity and engage others.

Effective systems include examining and discussing assessment results and keeping the focus on students' needs (Hargreaves & Fullan, 2012). They understand the importance of meeting (e.g., at least beginning, middle, and end of year), sharing data in a public manner, and being nonjudgmental. Everyone must work together—not in silos—to meet all student needs. Using a protocol is one way to facilitate a data conversation. We present Data Driven Dialogue, a protocol developed by the Teacher Development Group (2017), and describe how an SFC coach might use this protocol.

- *Predictions*: You select a data set and describe it to teachers without showing the results. For example, you select a diagnostic data set from a first-grade beginning-of-year assessment that includes results for phonological awareness and comprehension. You do not share results—simply describe the assessment, when it was administered, the skills it assessed, and the number of students and subpopulations who were assessed. Teachers then think about what was described and make predictions. This may include statements such as, "I assume that the data . . ." or "My predictions are that . . ."

- *Go visual*: You distribute the data set and provide an overview similar to that shared during the predictions phase. You provide teachers with notebook paper, chart paper, markers, or other materials they may want to use to make sense of the data. Their role is to determine how they might recreate this data in a manner that makes the most sense to them, which may be in the form of a line graph, bar graph, or other depiction. In addition, the analysis may be in the form of calculations, trends, or other means. As the coach, you are facilitating a conversation with teachers and allowing them to make sense of the data set. Also, keep in mind that teachers—not you—infer what these results might mean. It is also important to point out that teachers are recreating the data in visual form only. They should only focus on facts; not drawing conclusions, sharing strategies, or trying to defend reasons why the data looks like it does.

- *Observations*: Teachers record factual observations from their visuals—no inferences, justifications, or rationales. For example, teachers review the visual(s) they created and write down facts: "I notice that three students . . . ," "50% of students mastered . . . ," or "When looking at phonological awareness scores, students performed best in . . . ." You might tell teachers to record their observations on sticky notes before sharing with others.

- *Inferences*: It is time to make an inference. What conclusions can you draw from your observations, and what is your evidence? What additional data might you need to determine an area of need? Is there enough evidence to recommend a solution?

The data-driven dialogue protocol requires you to facilitate, pose questions, challenge assumptions, probe, and much more. From our experiences, it is common for some people to look at a data set and immediately start thinking about strategies. It is premature to make decisions immediately without deep analysis. Take the time to identify the right problem so that you determine the right solution.

Teachers who take part in the data-driven dialogue likely have a better picture of their next steps. So, now what? In some instances, maybe you offer PDL, which may include the whole school, grade level(s), department(s), or individual(s) and may be in a formal or informal setting. Consider how to provide differentiated, sustained PDL to meet individual needs, regardless of the setting or participants. Not all teachers will need the same support. We find it disheartening when teachers share frustrations in which they are 1) required to attend PD sessions that are irrelevant or do not meet their needs, 2) overwhelmed by what appears to be competing resources or initiatives, 3) consistently learning or being introduced to new concepts or skills that are not connected to prior learning, or 4) receiving support that is not helpful to improve student learning. This tells us that a coach must focus and plan support to meet individual learner needs.

Schmoker (2011) titled the first chapter "The Importance of Simplicity, Clarity, and Priority" in his book *Focus: Elevating the Essentials to Radically Improve Student Learning*. Consider this for a moment. What comes to mind when you think about each word (i.e., *priority, clarity, simplicity*)? Do you think of definitions, examples, situations, or something else? What comes to mind when thinking about your coaching role? Let's connect these words to an example presented earlier—teaching order of operations. Student data shows that students struggle with order or operations, so this becomes a priority. Using a data-driven dialogue-facilitated protocol, you become more aware of why students struggle with order of operations; you have clarity. Designing an instructional sequence to explicitly teach the order of operations brings simplicity (e.g., Lesson 1: Teaching key vocabulary explicitly, such as *expression* and *variable*, as well as parenthesis in an expression; Lesson 2: Working with exponents; Lessons 3 and 4: How to multiply and divide or add and subtract in an expression). This step-by-step process was designed because of a priority and can now lead to ongoing PL with support from peers.

Starting with Joyce and Showers's work in the 1980s, researchers have long emphasized the need for ongoing peer coaching if teachers are to transfer newly learned skills to the complex environment of a classroom. Study of theory, practice, and demonstration alone lead to minimal change. Unfortunately, from our experiences, these actions alone occur all too often. We often hear stories of teachers attending a PD session—or abbreviated training because of time constraints—and are then expected to implement immediately. This clearly goes against any research on peer coaching or effective PL practices. For example, some teachers might say that they spend the first 5 days of a new school attending trainings that seem to have no purpose or connection to a school focus. This is an ineffective practice, and there is plenty of evidence to articulate why. We are not saying this cannot work, but there needs to be a clear focus and alignment.

Imagine if you could convince administrators/supervisors to minimize the amount of PD being provided at one time using research and data as your justification. What plan would you put forth? For example, you notice that end-of-year kindergarten data indicates low phonological awareness scores. You conduct research and find an article written by Moats (2020) that included the following:

> The recognition of printed words depends first on awareness of the speech sounds (phonemes) that the alphabetic symbols represent and then on the brain's ability to map sounds to letters and letter combinations (graphemes). As reading develops, the mapping of speech to print includes recognition of letter sequences, including syllable patterns and meaningful units (morphemes). The reading brain gradually builds neural networks that facilitate rapid processing of symbol-sound and sound-symbol connections. Once these networks for mapping speech to print are developed, the brain can recognize and store images of new printed words with little conscious effort. (p. 11)

You know the need to have a prevention mindset, and you likely know the importance of building a strong foundation for future reading success. You schedule time to meet with your administrator/supervisor and, rather than the unaligned 5-day back-to-school PD, you propose the following plan for kindergarten teachers.

> Day 1: Use the Data Driven Dialogue protocol outlined and described earlier in this chapter. After completing the protocol's four phases, you engage kindergarten teachers in a conversation to discuss reasons why students struggle at the end of the year in phonological awareness. Teachers come up

with many reasons why students struggle, and you guide the kindergarten teachers in determining actions within their control, including changes to instructional delivery, planning, or student activities.

Day 2: You engage kindergarten teachers in learning more about phonological and phoneme awareness. For example, you print an article about these topics including (but not limited to) why to explicitly teach them. You then work with the teachers to explore and learn more about phonological standards.

Day 3: You deliver a session on the phonological awareness continuum. The presentation includes an overview of each skill in the phonological awareness continuum, demonstration of each skill, and practice opportunities. You spend time reviewing the phonological and phoneme awareness sections in the core reading program to determine if these skills are explicitly taught or need to be enhanced with other evidence-based supplemental resources. You also explore how phonological and phoneme awareness skills spiral throughout the year in the core reading program or how skills affect other parts of a lesson, such as phonics, vocabulary, fluency, or comprehension.

Day 4: You guide teachers in planning phonological and phoneme awareness lessons using standards, core reading program materials, and explicit instructional strategies. You also include time for kindergarten teachers to teach lessons to one or more of their colleagues.

Day 5: You provide additional time for teachers to practice delivering their lessons and provide guidance on ways to teach phonological and phoneme awareness in small groups or practice skills in workstations.

Although you may not have the entire day with kindergarten teachers, your plan provides structure and guidance to strengthen these foundational skills. If your administrator/supervisor agrees with this plan, then you might find yourself creating similar plans for other grade levels.

As a reminder, an SFC coach builds capacity in teachers. Your role is not to print spreadsheets; collect data; or disaggregate, analyze, or summarize data on your own. In addition, your role is not to do the planning or implementation for others. If you spend your time doing the work for teachers, then how are you building capacity? If you spend your time doing for others, when are you coaching? We want to continue to emphasize the need to build capacity in others; not for others to solely rely on you.

REFLECTION

What structure(s) or system(s) have/would you put in place as an instructional coach to build capacity in others?

RESPONSE TO INTERVENTION/MULTI-TIERED SYSTEMS OF SUPPORT

Many states and districts are supporting their instruction and intervention efforts by embracing the frameworks providing RTI or MTSS. Coaches often have a key role in supporting the success of these frameworks. You have likely heard about or have knowledge of these terms; however, we include the following definitions to avoid confusion.

- RTI integrates assessment and intervention within a multilevel prevention system to maximize student achievement and reduce challenging behaviors. Schools identify students at risk for poor learning outcomes, monitor student progress, provide evidence-based interventions and adjust the intensity and nature of those interventions depending on a student's responsiveness, and identify students with learning disabilities or other disabilities (American Institutes for Research, 2017a).

- MTSS is a framework designed to respond to the needs of all students within a system that integrates, but is not limited to, tiered behavior (e.g., positive behavior interventions and supports [PBIS]) alongside academic (e.g., RTI) supports. MTSS is a whole-school, data-driven, prevention-based framework for improving learning outcomes for all students through a layered continuum of evidence-based practices and systems (U.S. Department of Education, 2017).

We realize that districts and states across the nation vary in their definitions and implementations of RTI and MTSS. There may be three or more tiers of services, the framework or model title may include instruction and intervention, or something else. Regardless of the way in which RTI or MTSS is implemented in your school system, the key is to provide high-quality instruction or behavioral support for all students. The American Institutes for Research (2017b) highlighted the following levels of intensity for prevention, and we will use these levels interchangeably with tiered levels often cited in other research.

- Tier 1: High-quality core instruction; school- and classroomwide behavior systems for all students, staff, and settings

- Tier 2: Evidence-based and coordinated intervention to supplement (not supplant) high-quality core instruction; specialized group systems for students with at-risk behaviors

- Tier 3: Individualized, evidence-based intervention in addition to high-quality core instruction for students who show minimal response to the secondary prevention; individualized systems for students with high-risk behaviors

As an instructional coach, you play a key role in supporting teachers to deliver high-quality instruction and intervention. As we have said several times in this book, the best intervention is high-quality instruction or behavioral systems during Tier 1 instruction. Some students, however, may need more intensive support and focus beyond Tier 1 instruction. Students receiving Tier 2 services are provided with additional support to learn grade-level essential academic and/or behavioral standards. Students receiving Tier 3 support are provided with the most intensive instruction to close the achievement gap. Some students receiving Tier 3 services may have IEPs and/or individual behavior plans, and some might have been identified as having a disability. Tier 3 helps provide the requirements of their IEPs. Later in this section, we provide additional details regarding a multitier prevention model for instruction and behavior. We begin with instruction.

Tier 1 should include both whole-class or small-group instruction, independent practice, or independent or collaborative workstation time. Teachers purposefully plan how they will deliver the essential grade-level standards, which includes the explicit instruction elements described earlier in this chapter. Purposeful planning also means considering ways in which you deliver content in a positive, supportive, and nurturing manner. Teachers determine how they will teach lesson content in small chunks and check for understanding. This means teaching a small portion of the lesson, allowing for practice opportunities, checking for understanding, providing feedback, and more. Then, the teacher can increase the complexity of instruction if students demonstrate success. If a teacher reaches the end of the lesson with minimal opportunities for students to practice, then they may find that their instructional delivery lacked explicitness and many students did not understand the lesson's goal. This is a teaching problem. As a coach, you can support planning and delivery of a lesson that keeps students actively engaged throughout.

When planning for Tier 2 intervention, maintain focus on skills or concepts covered in Tier 1. Tier 2 is an opportunity to reinforce skills or concepts delivered during Tier 1 instruction in which some students struggled or needed additional practice opportunities. This means Tier 2 grouping is fluid and remains flexible because different students may struggle or need additional practice with skills or concepts covered during core instruction. Think of this as providing additional time for some students to learn or master the standards. The classroom teacher is best suited to deliver Tier 2 instruction because they taught the skill or concept during Tier 1. If someone besides the classroom teacher provides Tier 2 intervention, then there must be opportunities for collaboration between the classroom teacher and interventionist. Without opportunities to collaborate, students who struggle or need additional practice may be asked to try to learn new skills or concepts or be instructed through teaching strategies they are unfamiliar with, thus creating even more challenges for them. Intervention instruction delivered via a computerized program also requires additional preparation time to ensure the intervention lesson aligns with core instruction. If not, students may learn a new set of skills or concepts that is not helpful if the goal is to learn grade-level essential standards.

Students receiving Tier 3 services are significantly below grade level or are missing essential skills or concepts from prior grade levels and should receive targeted and intensive intervention. Although we often find teaching assistants, paraprofessionals, or others delivering Tier 3 intervention, we argue that the most highly qualified individuals should deliver instruction. Reading or math specialists, dyslexia teachers, special education teachers, speech-language pathologists, and others possess the knowledge and skills to deliver Tier 3 instruction. Take time to collaborate with one or more of these specialists, or with the teacher, to share skills or concepts covered in Tier 1 so that Tier 3 intervention helps to build the foundational knowledge for that skill or concept.

As the coach, you can play a critical role in guiding teachers with planning instruction, instructing teachers about content they may not know, and providing support and feedback. In addition, your role is to assist with analyzing core programs adopted by your school, determining ways to supplement instruction if skills or concepts are not sufficiently covered, and building capacity in teacher knowledge. Always remember that a program or product is not the solution for high-quality instruction. Building capacity in those delivering the instruction is key.

Now, let's consider behavior. The Office of Special Education Programs (OSEP) Technical Assistance Center on Positive Behavioral Interventions and Supports (2017) provided access to a decision-making guide and self-assessment to determine modifications to behavior plans. This brief included questions such as

- *Are the foundations of a PBIS in place?* This question requires teachers to reflect on the physical arrangement of classroom, routines, and expectations. If these foundations are unclear or nonexistent, then take time to make adjustments. If these foundations are in place, then consider the second question.

- *Are proactive and positive PBIS practices implemented consistently?* This question refers to student engagement levels, teacher support and feedback, and affirmation of specific student behaviors. If these are in place, then proceed to the third question. If not, then revisit the first question or strategies used when answering this second question.

- *Does schoolwide data indicate that challenging behaviors still exist?* If so, determine if the behaviors are minor or major. If minor, then redirect with consequence strategies. If major, then how many students were involved in the incident? If many, then request additional support for staff. If few, then request additional support for students.

Tier 1 behavioral prevention includes organizing classroom space, establishing rules, and determining routines. These also go a long way in contributing to the ability of a teacher to provide the most effective academic instruction. Archer and Hughes (2011) included some of the following questions to consider regarding the physical organization of a classroom.

- Are there designated areas for various activities such as whole class, small group, or workstations?

- Are students in close proximity to teachers during instructional time?

- Are students facing teachers during instructional time?

- Do students have access to communicate with a partner or team during instructional time?

- Are instructional materials organized and readily available for instructional activities such as whole class, small group, or workstations?

- Can teachers and students move freely around the classroom without obstacles?

- Is the student work and other instructional resources posted in the classroom relevant and supportive of student learning?

- Can teachers see all parts of the room and all students during any instructional activity?

An SFC coach can review the previous questions with teachers and provide support modifications, if needed, to ensure the physical environment remains orderly, sets the stage for appropriate behavior, and sets a positive tone for students and adults.

Consider secondary interventions for those students who require additional support or guidance or who do not respond to the primary interventions. This may include

- Teaching students how to use more acceptable, positive behaviors to replace challenging behaviors

- Rearranging the classroom or school environment so that problems can be prevented and desirable behaviors can be encouraged

- Monitoring, evaluating, and/or reassessing the plan over time

It is necessary to observe student behavior and redirect as needed. If a student does not respond to these secondary interventions, then consider tertiary interventions.

An individualized plan is necessary in a Tier 3 prevention for behavior. Tier 3 interventions may be necessary for students who exhibit routine patterns of challenging behavior. Involve students requiring an individualized plan in the goal setting. Tailor Tier 3 interventions to the individual, along with any consequences. Tier 2 prevention strategies may work; however, you may need to develop emergency procedures to deescalate severe behaviors that could danger other students or adults.

REFLECTION

What do you know about your school's or district's multilevel prevention model for instruction or behavior? How have/would you support colleagues with implementing a multilevel prevention model for instruction or behavior? (Note: To assist with this last question, you might explore resources developed by Dr. Randy Sprick and colleagues at Safe & Civil Schools at www.safeandcivilschools.com; the OSEP Technical Assistance Center on Positive Behavioral Interventions and Supports at www.pbis.org; or Drs. Anita Archer and Charles Hughes at www. explicitinstruction.org.)

CONCLUSION

An SFC coach must understand pedagogy, know what content is required for students by state standards and district guidelines, and have the ability to support various stakeholder groups. In addition, coaches must understand the importance of systematic practices and how to lead reform efforts. We also know how important a coaching role is and how much knowledge is required.

Revisit Appendix 1.1 before proceeding to the next chapter. How have your responses changed? What questions do you still have about the SFC model? Are there any chapters that you think you should revisit to gain a deeper understanding? Also, revisit your responses to the questions at the start of this chapter and make any adjustments based on new knowledge or insights gleaned. Finally, take time to make any changes or updates to the application exercise.

VIRTUAL COACHING TIP

Having conversations about explicit instruction, RTI, MTSS, and sustainability can occur when colleagues are face to face or when meeting virtually. Either approach requires planning and preparation. If discussing RTI during a virtual meeting, then ensure that all participants have access to and have reviewed the RTI process. If discussing Tier 1 instruction, then make sure everyone has access to standards, data, or other important resources. Sharing slides on your screen may be needed in a virtual platform, and a breakout room can be used to share strategies, come to consensus, or brainstorm solutions. In addition, the chat feature can allow each participant to share something they have learned, heard, shared, or recommended. Another idea is to record presentations (e.g., explicit instruction elements) and build a virtual library for colleagues to access when needed.

REFERENCES

American Institutes for Research. (2017a). *Essential components of RTI: A closer look at Response to Intervention.* Retrieved from https://mtss4success.org/resource/essential-components-rti-closer-look-response-intervention

American Institutes for Research. (2017b). *Multi-level prevention system.* Retrieved from https://mtss4success.org/essential-components/multi-level-prevention-system

Archer, A., & Hughes, C. (2011). *Explicit instruction: Effective and efficient teaching.* The Guilford Press.

Fullan, M., & Quinn, J. (2016). *Coherence: The right drivers in action for schools, districts, and systems.* Corwin.

Graves, M., & Braaten, S. (1996). Scaffolding reading experiences: Bridges to success. *Preventing School Failure, 40*(4), 169–173.

Hall, G., & Hord, S. (2015). *Implementing change: Patterns, principles, and potholes.* Pearson.

Hargreaves, A., & Fullan, A. (2012). *Professional capital: Transforming teaching in every school.* Teachers College Press.

Hasbrouck, J., & Denton, C. (2005). *The reading coach: A how-to manual for success.* Sopris West Educational Services.

Hempenstall, K. (2016). *Read about it: Scientific evidence for effective teaching of reading.* Centre for Independent Studies Research Report No. 11.

Hiebert, J., & Stigler, J. (2017). Teaching versus teachers as a lever for change: Comparing a Japanese and a U.S. perspective on improving instruction. *Educational Researcher, 46*(4), 169–176.

Joyce, B., & Showers, B. (1980). Improving in-service training: The messages of research. *Educational Leadership, 37*(5), 379–385.

Kubiszyn, T., & Borich, G. (2013). *Educational testing and measurement: Classroom application and practice* (10th ed.). Wiley.

Langley, G., Moen, R., Nolan, K., Nolan, T., Norman, T., & Provost, L. (2009). *The improvement guide: A practical approach to enhancing organizational performance* (2nd ed.). Wiley.

Li, Y. (2017). Processes and dynamics behind whole-school reform: Nine-year journeys of four primary schools. *American Educational Research Journal, 54*(2), 279–324.

Moats, L. (2020). *Teaching reading is rocket science: What expert teachers of reading should know and be able to do.* Retrieved from https://www.aft.org/sites/default/files/moats.pdf

Northouse, P. (2013). *Leadership: Theory and practice* (6th ed.). Sage.

Office of Special Education Programs Technical Assistance Center on Positive Behavioral Interventions and Supports. (2017). *Positive behavioral interventions & supports.* Retrieved from www.pbis.org

Ornstein, A., & Hunkins, F. (2013). *Curriculum: Foundations, principles, and issues* (6th ed.). Pearson.

Rosenshine, B. (1987). Explicit teaching and teaching training. *Journal of Teacher Education, 38*(3), 34–36.

Rosenshine, B. (2012). Principles of instruction: Research-based strategies that all teachers should know. *American Educator, 36*(1), 12–39.

Schmoker, M. (2011). *Results now: How we can achieve unprecedented improvements in teaching and learning.* Association for Supervision and Curriculum Development.

Teacher Development Group. (2017). Data driven dialogue. Retrieved from https://www.schoolreforminitiative.org/download/data-driven-dialogue

U.S. Department of Education. (2017). *Multi-tiered systems of behavioral and academic support.* Retrieved from https://www2.ed.gov/about/inits/ed/earlyliteracy/tools.html

12

Working With Administrative Partners

This chapter differs from previous chapters because it is written specifically for administrators and/or supervisors who will be supporting an SFC coach. We invite administrators/supervisors reading this chapter to reflect on what they expect to gain from working with an SFC coach, as well as how they will protect the coach's time and what they plan to do to protect the coach from being seen as an administrator/supervisor by their teacher colleagues. Our primary goal throughout the earlier chapters in this book has been to provide guidance and support for instructional coaches using the SFC model and describe their responsibilities so that they can be successful. This chapter, however, focuses on administrators/supervisors—the essential partners for successful SFC. We created the Best Practices Checklist for SFC Administrator/Supervisor Partners located in Appendix 12.1 to assist with this partnership. We recommend that you review this checklist and use it as a guide while you read this chapter.

Before reading this chapter, consider the following questions. Jot down some notes on your current understanding, and then at the end of the chapter, we will revisit these questions to assess the knowledge and insight you gained during your reading.

- What do you hope to gain by having an SFC coach at your school or district?

- How will you protect the SFC coach's time from becoming administrative work?

- How will you communicate the SFC coach's roles and responsibilities to stakeholder groups?

- What system(s) will you put in place so that your SFC coach can be productive and successful?

APPLICATION EXERCISE

Dear Classroom Teachers,

In November, Kristin will begin providing SFC by grade level. Kristin is here to coach and not evaluate. Her role is to work collaboratively with you to support your PDL to enhance student learning. Kristin's goals are to answer your questions, listen to your concerns, and help you find solutions. The work you do with her is confidential.

When it is your grade level's week to work with the coach, each teacher needs to choose a time slot for Kristin to come into your classroom. During this time, Kristin can coteach a lesson, observe your literacy block or intervention, help plan, or provide support with a specific topic or resource.

Soon I will be e-mailing a schedule for you to select a time and list what coaching service you would like Kristin to provide. Kristin will reach out to you prior to your selected time to discuss how she can best support your coaching time.

The hope is that we will be able to make the most of colaboring this year!

Thanks,

Theresa

A Vancouver, Washington administrator wrote and sent this e-mail to classroom teachers to introduce them to the new SFC coach on their campus. From reading this e-mail, what tasks do you believe the coach will be doing in this school? What can you infer that the coach will not be doing? How do you think the administrator/supervisor will support the coach role? How might teachers feel when they receive this e-mail? What words, phrases, or sentences do you find compelling or important in this e-mail.

INTRODUCTION

Thank you for taking time from your busy schedule to read this chapter. Although our hope is that you will also read the other chapters in this book, we will not make that assumption. Therefore, we include highlights from earlier chapters that we believe administrators/supervisors must understand to best support an SFC coach and maximize the numerous benefits that working with a coach can provide. These highlights include our definition of coaching, sample roles and responsibilities for an SFC coach, and some specific ways that an administrator/supervisor can effectively collaborate with an SFC coach. We encourage you to read small sections of this chapter at the same time your coach does and schedule time for reflection. During these reflection times, respond to the question(s) posed and, if needed, ask your coach to share additional examples or explanations that were included in previous chapters. The administrator/supervisor and coach must be seen as partners to successfully implement an SFC coaching model, and these ongoing conversations will help you stay connected.

THE ROLE OF SFC COACHES (CHAPTERS 1–3; 6–10)

We have worked closely with administrators/supervisors who have the best of intentions for their SFC coach, but, unfortunately, something goes wrong somewhere along the way. What often starts as a minor request for the coach gradually morphs into many more requests. These requests too often shift their focus away from coaching and toward serving as something like a junior administrator, which will undermine the coach and diminish their effectiveness.

We have observed administrators/supervisors select teachers to take on the role as instructional coaches. Teachers chosen to be coaches are generally talented, knowledgeable, and experienced or whose students have performed well on standardized tests. Unfortunately, this approach does not always mean the teacher will be a good coach. "Being an effective classroom teacher is no guarantee that one will also be an effective coach" (Poglinco & Bach, 2004, p. 400). Teachers must often learn the basics of coaching their colleagues while also determining the intricacies of their new and unfamiliar role. This situation is further complicated by the fact that very few administrators/supervisors have received any preparation themselves to support or guide the coaches with whom they work (Hall et al., 2003). This may be true in your case too.

We have also watched many skillful, resourceful, and dedicated coaches work hard to help students who are struggling by sharing their knowledge and expertise with other teachers. Too often, however, we have watched these efforts fail. This failure is frequently due, at least in part, to a lack of support from an administrator/supervisor or coaching roles and responsibilities that are unclear. This chapter is designed to help you avoid similar pitfalls.

SFC Defined

We define *SFC* as a cooperative, ideally collaborative, professional relationship with colleagues mutually engaged in efforts that help maximize every teacher's knowledge and skills to enhance student learning. Coaches perform three roles in the SFC model:

- *Facilitator:* Helping effective and skillful teachers continue their success and create opportunities for professionals to collaborate toward the goal of school-wide success and building professional relationships with every colleague. The important work of supporting the effective systems within a school also falls under the Facilitator role (see Chapter 3).

- *Collaborative Problem-Solver:* Using a structured, systematic collaborative problem-solving process to work with teachers to address student's instructional needs and provide contextualized PDL. We spend four chapters on this role because this is the role in which we hope SFC coaches will spend most of their time because engaging with their colleagues in collaborative problem solving has the highest impact for change and positive outcomes (see Chapters 6–9).

- *Teacher/Learner:* Sharing effective and proven strategies, methods, and techniques with teachers through high-quality and sustained PDL opportunities while continuing to develop the coach's own professional knowledge and skills (see Chapter 10).

These roles are designed to help accomplish the four goals of SFC as outlined in Chapter 1:

- Goal 1: To enhance student learning
- Goal 2: To maximize every teacher's knowledge and skills
- Goal 3: To learn from each other
- Goal 4: To prevent future problems

Specific responsibilities for SFC coaches might include

- Helping teachers successfully address classroom concerns and challenges through collaborative problem solving

- Organizing and delivering personalized and sustained PDL activities for various stakeholder groups

- Guiding and supporting stakeholders in the collection and analysis of data to guide instructional decisions that improve student outcomes

- Observing teachers' lessons and providing feedback for instructional improvement and obtaining data for collaborative problem solving

- Helping teachers with the organization and management of instructional programs

- Working collaboratively with colleagues to support student needs and an equitable learning environment

- Assisting various stakeholders with planning and implementing with fidelity the delivery of instructional and intervention programs

- Modeling lessons and/or activities as requested by colleagues

- Helping identify and address grade-level, department, or schoolwide concerns

- Participating in PL activities or meetings to learn from each other and explore relevant topics of interest

- Expanding their own and their colleagues' knowledge base by staying up to date on relevant research and best practices

- Sharing effective and proven strategies with stakeholder groups

- Being aware of local, state, and federal rules, regulations, and policies

- Leveraging digital integration to enhance learning

- Advising administrators/supervisors on effective instructional practices based on research

This is clearly a long and ambitious list. We hope it indicates to you that working with an SFC coach—if they are allowed to commit to their roles and responsibilities—can reap many benefits and help achieve ambitious goals for school success. The catch is that a coach needs sufficient training, time, and sustained support to make this happen.

REFLECTION

This would be a good stopping point for you to schedule time to talk with your coach. How, if at all, does the coach's current assignment relate to the three SFC roles? How are the coach's responsibilities similar or different from what we propose?

As an administrator, you play an essential role in a coach's success. This involves clearly understanding the role of the SFC coach and helping to communicate that to the other staff and determining how a coach can best provide sustained, differentiated support. An SFC coach is not a/an

- Administrator, supervisor, or evaluator of teachers

- Someone who works with struggling teachers and fixes them

- Substitute teacher or classroom cover

- Interventionist or tutor

- Classroom teacher

- Playground, bus, cafeteria, or hall monitor

- Test administrator, monitor, or coordinator

- Chaperone for field trips or discipline referrals

Someone other than an SFC coach should take on these roles and responsibilities. Consider assigning a paraprofessional or other administrator/supervisor to focus on some of the tasks listed here. Of course, we are not saying a coach can never teach an intervention group or take on any of these tasks occasionally. Some coaches have found success in teaching and coaching part time. In fact, it can be helpful for their teacher colleagues to see that the coach knows how to plan, prepare lessons, and work with students. This shows that the coach understands and does not lose sight of what teachers are required to do every day. However, an administrator/supervisor must keep in mind that every minute a coach is delivering instruction or intervention or taking on administrative duties means a teacher is not receiving support. Be cognizant of the fact that a teacher is not receiving coaching when a coach works with a small intervention group every day during the same time. Do you want someone in the coaching role, or is an intervention teacher a better fit for your needs? This is an important question and one worth thinking about.

Coaches Are Not Supervisors (Chapters 1–3)

As we have discussed, SFC coaches guide and support teachers to deliver the most effective instruction possible to every student. SFC coaches must know the teachers, content, standards and learn about and share evidence-based strategies and techniques. They analyze the implementation of evidence-based instructional practices, collaborate with teachers and leaders, differentiate support for individual teachers, and provide immediate and supportive feedback. They communicate with various stakeholder groups, lead team-building activities, maintain a positive attitude, and provide encouragement. During a classroom observation, meeting, or PDL session, they model instructional strategies, provide job-embedded assistance, adjust their delivery to meet individual teacher needs, challenge teachers to take risks, and more. After a classroom observation, meeting, or PDL session, they debrief, review feedback, consider future adjustments, prepare for their next coaching session with a teacher, and much more.

CONFIDENTIALITY AND TRUST (CHAPTER 2)

SFC coaches support teachers. They cannot legally, and should not, act as supervisors of teachers. Specifically, SFC coaches do not 1) formally evaluate teaching, 2) require teachers to work with them, 3) rate teacher performance or effectiveness, 4) determine or play any role in influencing decisions about teacher tenure, 5) determine schedules, or 6) mandate policies. Related to the previous topic of coaches not being involved in the supervision or evaluation of their peers, an instructional coach cannot be an administrator's/supervisor's eyes and ears in the classroom. They must not engage with a teacher or visit a classroom and then report their observations or conversations to the administrator/supervisor. Remember, an administrator/supervisor evaluates and supervises; a coach provides support. There must be a clear distinction to build trust between coaches and teachers.

It is essential for an administrator/supervisor to understand that a coach cannot share any information about a teacher's performance that may be obtained during the process of coaching. This extreme level of confidentiality may not seem to make much sense at first glance. You may be thinking that coaching is all about helping students become the best they can be: "If my coach happened to work with teachers who are having difficulty providing adequate instruction to their students, isn't that important information for me to know about?" Yes, it is. It is your role as an administrator/supervisor, however, to find this out for yourself. You are the evaluator and supervisor.

Trust and confidentiality, which are the cornerstones of coaching, are violated when a coach reports what they see or hear from a teacher. Coaching can occur only within a cooperative professional relationship built on trust and mutual respect. If a coach is perceived as a spy for the administration or as someone who talks about one teacher to another, then that coach will soon be unable to provide any coaching services at all. Few teachers will work with a coach if they do not believe the coach will maintain their privacy and keep all communication strictly confidential.

Of course, there are certain areas in which this level of complete confidentiality must be breached. Those would be the same areas in which any professional educator would be ethically and legally obligated to report evidence of cruelty, abuse, or neglect. If a coach witnesses a teacher being emotionally or physically abusive to any student at any time, then an administrator/supervisor should be immediately notified of this, and the coach must inform the teacher that the incident is being reported. The issue becomes a bit less clear in other situations. A coach may observe a colleague who has low expectations for their students or who provides little, if any, meaningful instruction in the classroom. What should a coach do about this? Does this fall into a category that could reasonably be called academic neglect or abuse of students? Some may argue that it does. The line is less obvious, however. How poorly does a teacher have to teach before a coach is justified in reporting this to an administrator/supervisor? How will this level of poor instruction be defined? This may be an agenda item to add to future conversations with your coach.

This confidentiality goes both ways. Although it may be very tempting to request the help of a coach to address concerns you have about a struggling teacher, you simply cannot do this directly without compromising your role as an evaluator and the confidentiality of the teacher about whom you have a concern. You cannot say, "I'm worried about Dave in the math department. I've visited his classroom a couple of times, and he is clearly in over his head with those seventh graders. And his lessons seem really poorly organized to me. I'd like you to go work with him." This brings the coach into the evaluation process by disclosing your concerns about this teacher. What you can do as an administrator/supervisor is let Dave know directly that you have concerns about his classroom management and his teaching and that you expect to see improvement. Then suggest some resources to Dave that he can use to make these changes and improvements, such as online training(s), a relevant conference to attend, and/or the services and support of the coach. Presenting the option of working with the coach to the teacher preserves the necessary requirement that teachers have a choice to work with a coach and also protects Dave's confidentiality. If Dave chooses to tell the coach that you suggested he work with them, then that is Dave's choice.

REFLECTION

This would be a good time to pause and reflect with your coach. How will you communicate to others that the coach is a resource who provides support and has no role in teacher evaluation? If your coach currently engages in ways that fall into an evaluator role, then what change(s) need to be made?

INTRODUCING THE COACH (CHAPTER 2)

Now that you have a good understanding of the role of an SFC coach, we recommend that you take the responsibility to formally introduce the coach to the colleagues that the coach will be supporting. This is important for you to do because you bring a level of power and authority to the conversation that coaches do not have—and should not have It is imperative that teachers view the coach as a peer colleague.

Informing teachers about the role of the coach, what they will be doing (and will not be doing), and what their roles and responsibilities are when working with a coach provides a significant jump start to successful outcomes. As we say in Chapter 2, this helps the coach enroll their colleagues into the coaching process. In Chapter 2 and on our Best Practices Checklist we also mention that it is helpful to actually mandate that teachers share their most current student performance data with the coach when asked. This data could include attendance records, any office referrals, grades, recent assessment results, and samples of classwork. If this discussion is making you think that you want to do a reset in the way that coaching has been implemented, then we want to assure you that this can be done successfully. We provide guidelines for doing this in Chapter 2.

MANAGING TIME (CHAPTER 5)

Chapter 5 provides the coaches with some recommendations and suggests some procedures for managing and tracking their time. Being in a position that allows for more control over their own time is a new professional experience for many coaches, and some express the need for some guidance for how to do this. We created a time tracking system (3T-SFC: Time Tracking Tool for Student-Focused Coaches in Appendix 5.2) that we encourage SFC coaches to use occasionally to monitor how they are spending their time. You might want to suggest that coaches collect this kind of information on a certain time line or schedule and then you can review the results together to make any adjustments in their schedule as a result of the findings.

For example, if the coach's time is mostly spent reviewing or analyzing data, then you might ask them why they are not spending more time meeting with teachers and determining instructional strategies to target areas of need. Could the coach instead be building capacity in teachers to review and analyze data?

How should the coach support teachers in determining appropriate interventions based on findings from the data? If the coach spends a lot of time copying or organizing materials, then you might revisit their roles and responsibilities. Making copies for a teacher might be a positive gesture and useful to build the necessary trusting professional relationship between teachers and the coach, but it is not going to directly affect a teaching practice. If the coach attends a lot of PDL, then you might ask them how they share their learning or how the PDL session will influence a teacher's practice (i.e., "How will this session lead to ongoing professional learning at the campus? Who benefits from the coach attending PDL?) Know what you expect from your coach, monitor their roles, and make adjustments to their schedules as needed. Using the 3T SFC form can assist you.

ONGOING FORMAL CONVERSATIONS (CHAPTERS 2 AND 4)

We often hear coaches express frustration that they do not get to provide coaching support like they know they should, and this frustration almost always can be traced back to an administrator/supervisor who does not understand the role of the coach or does not protect the coach's time. "Ms. Johnson, the fifth-grade math teacher, needs to be part of a parent meeting this morning, so please cover her class from this morning. We don't have anyone else to cover." "Mr. Navarro, our reading interventionist, called in sick this morning, so you'll need to teach his intervention groups. There wasn't time to get a substitute, and classroom teachers don't like it when we cancel an intervention group." We know administrators/supervisors usually have a rationale as to why the coach must take on an added responsibility, and coaches usually abide by the directive because they want to be a team player. Here is a good rule of thumb: Requests should not take a coach away from their primary responsibilities of supporting and maximizing every teacher's knowledge and skills to enhance student learning.

We encourage you to meet regularly with your coach to ensure that they are getting the support they need from you and they are accomplishing the tasks assigned to them. Regular meetings can help you maintain a clear sense of what the coach is doing, while still respecting the confidential coach/teacher relationship, so you can help define and protect the coach's role. We suggest holding these formal conversations about the role and schedule of the coach at least three times per year initially (see Chapter 3). Asking the coach to bring the results of their recent time tracking could inform this conversation. And three times is definitely a minimum. You should decide how often these meetings should be held to optimize your collaborative partnership with the coach.

SUPERVISING COACHES (CHAPTER 2)

Although we stated that SFC coaches should never be involved in the supervision or evaluation of their peer colleagues in any manner, coaches themselves, like every professional, deserve to receive helpful and encouraging supervision on a regular basis to encourage their professional growth. If you have never worked with or been an instructional coach before, then you may be unsure how it works. The regular conversations we previously discussed could help with this activity. We also developed an Evaluation Checklist for SFC Coaches that you may find helpful. A copy is included in Appendix 2.1.

REFLECTION

What plan do you have in place or will you put in place to ensure that you regularly communicate with your coach to analyze how they spend their time, understand support they need, or provide feedback on their roles or responsibilities? If a plan is in place, then what adjustments, if any, need to be made?

THE ROLE OF COACHING IN SUPPORTING SYSTEMS (CHAPTER 3)

Coaches can have a major impact on helping to improve the academic, behavioral, and social-emotional outcomes of schools when they spend part of their time (within the Facilitator role) helping identify or put in place effective systems of support. Various structures and systems in a school help ensure optimal outcomes when they are working optimally (see Chapter 3). Great things occur when faculty has time to collaborate effectively, appropriate data is regularly collected and used strategically to enhance instructional decisions, and instructional time and materials and human resources are used wisely. Encouraging the coach to partner with you in identifying and supporting these systems is an important role for the administrator/supervisor.

SUPPORT COACHES' CONTINUED PROFESSIONAL GROWTH (CHAPTERS 4–11)

SFC coaches have a responsibility to know about the best practices for providing instructional coaching using the parameters of the SFC model and using them effectively to achieve the goals of SFC coaching: Enhance student learning, maximize every teacher's knowledge and skills, continue to learn with and from their colleagues, and prevent future problems. That is a lot of knowledge and skills we expect coaches to bring to the table. And, of course, it is not possible to expect any coach to know everything about skillful coaching and effective instruction, and knowledge keeps advancing. As part of the Teacher/Learner role, SFC coaches are expected to continue to seek out their own PDL to continue to skillfully bring best practices into the classrooms of their colleagues and the school or district at large. We hope that you will support these efforts as their supportive professional partner.

THE SAILS FRAMEWORK FOR EFFECTIVE SCHOOLS (CHAPTER 11)

Chapter 11 described research supporting the need for explicit, targeted, and intensive interventions, especially for struggling students. In that same chapter, we described key elements that make up the research-based framework for effective schools that we call *SAILS*. We highlight these elements again in this chapter because we believe an administrator/supervisor and instructional coach must have a strong knowledge base of what it means to support explicit instruction in the classroom. We also believe that an administrator/supervisor and coach must have a shared understanding in all elements included in the SAILS framework to ensure a consistent message when communicating with teachers.

Standards

Ornstein and Hunkins (2013) said the following about standards.

> Standards, and particularly national standards, assume that all students, all communities, all teachers, and all school districts are alike and that they face the same challenges, possess the same values, and have students of the same intellectual abilities, the same intellectual interests, the same behavioral dispositions, and the same cultural and ethnic backgrounds. Standards imply that all school districts define the worth of a particular objective with the same metric. This is not reality. (p. 193)

An instructional coach can help teachers identify and understand essential learning standards for the grade level(s) they teach. A coach can collaborate with teachers to determine ways to extend learning for students who already mastered the concepts or skills being covered, as well as determine intervention strategies for students needing remediation.

REFLECTION

What should it look like and sound like when a coach supports a teacher with standards? Is a focus on standards clearly addressed in your coach's roles and responsibilities? If not, should this be included? How will you communicate to teachers that a coach can guide them when working with standards?

Assessment

Educators administer various assessments to gauge student performance and guide instructional planning. Although many assessments are administered, are they reliable and valid? Hargreaves and Fullan (2012) told us to "be informed by the evidence, not numbed by the numbers" (p. 173) and to "decide what data you need and use it judiciously" (p. 172).

A coach might support teachers with understanding how to 1) analyze data, 2) use data to plan instruction or intervention, 3) monitor student performance, 4) differentiate instruction, 5) set goals, or 6) communicate findings to various stakeholder groups. In our experience, we found that many teachers have had minimal to no formal training in assessments. Thus, a coach might need to help teachers understand the various types of assessments, create test blueprints, or write test items to measure essential standards.

REFLECTION

This would be a good time to pause and reflect with your coach. What are your coach's responsibilities in assisting teachers with assessments? Is a focus on assessments clearly addressed in your coach's roles and responsibilities? If not, should this be included? How will you communicate the coach's role to teachers when supporting them with assessments?

Instruction or Intervention

High-quality instruction and behavioral support for all students enhances learning. The American Institutes for Research (2017) highlighted the following levels of intensity or prevention.

- *Tier 1*: High-quality core instruction and school- and classroomwide behavior system for all students, staff, and settings

- *Tier 2:* Evidence-based intervention in addition to high-quality core instruction and specialized grouping systems for students with at-risk behavior

- *Tier 3:* Individualized, evidence-based intervention in addition to high-quality core instruction for students who show minimal response to the secondary prevention and individualized systems for students with high-risk behavior

A coach can help teachers understand the importance of early prevention for students who may be at risk, not relying on a wait-to-fail model, and can provide instruction on the effective and appropriate intervention strategies that have the most impact on teacher success and student learning.

Coaches should understand and support evidence-based practices, including explicit instruction, as a "systematic method of teaching with emphasis on proceeding in small steps, checking for understanding, and achieving active and successful participation by all students" (Rosenshine, 2012, p. 34). Hasbrouck and Denton (2005) referred to *explicit instruction* as "telling it like it is" (p. 8). Archer and Hughes (2011) defined *explicit instruction* as an "unambiguous and direct approach to teaching that incorporates instruction design and delivery" (p. 1). All definitions reinforce the need to be systematic and direct. A coach must be able to guide teacher colleagues with understanding and putting into practice explicit instruction principles, including how these principles relate to other instructional practices or models such as problem- or project-based learning.

REFLECTION

This would be a good time to pause and reflect with your coach. What are your coach's responsibilities in assisting teachers with instruction and intervention? Is a focus on instruction and intervention clearly addressed in your coach's roles and responsibilities? If not, should this be included? How do you ensure that your definition or description of evidence-based instruction and intervention are aligned to the coach's definition or description?

Leadership

Langley et al. (2009) defined a *system* as "an interdependent group of items, people, or processes working together towards a common purpose" (p. 37). A leadership team made up of teachers and other campus personnel can play a critical role in helping to establish the climate and culture for school success that is an essential foundation for growth and improvement. For example, after analyzing student achievement data, the school finds that ELs are performing significantly below the achievement of other subpopulation groups and decides that this needs to be their focus. The leadership team then sets out to further understand why there is a discrepancy in achievement.

The team seeks to learn more about the following elements through classroom observations and conversations with teachers or other school personnel (Hiebert & Stigler, 2017):

- Are learning goals being written for students at each stage of their school careers and specified as precisely as possible?

- Does the curriculum support the learning goals, and is it improved as teachers implement lessons and experiment with alternative techniques?

- Is data collected and analyzed, including qualitative data, to examine evidence of implementation or quantitative data to monitor student achievement?

- Are teachers receiving differentiated, sustained PDL that is focused on improving the methods of teaching and their outcomes?

If this team finds a lack of clarity or that discrepancies exist for one or more of the elements in the previous above, then this could be why ELs are performing lower than other subgroups. With data in hand, an instructional coach should now be able to collaborate with others to clarify misunderstandings and determine next steps that target the system's common purpose.

REFLECTION

This would be a good time to pause and reflect with your coach. What leadership roles or responsibilities do you expect from your coach? Are these leadership roles and responsibilities clearly addressed in your coach's roles and responsibilities? If not, should this be included?

Sustainability

Hasbrouck and Denton (2005) referred to *sustainability* as a "lasting agreement among all school faculty and administrators to adopt a no-excuses intervention model, making a firm pledge to work together to help every student" (p. 18). They went on to highlight terms such as *relentless, sense of urgency, passionate, realistic, high expectations, collaboration,* and *transparent communication* that can lead to successful reform. This aligns well with Li's (2017) findings about successful reform processes:

- *Focus and build:* Set direction and vision as well as identify a pilot group to experiment.

- *Manage resistance:* Use various strategies to address resistance against the reform and maintain focus on the direction and vision.

- *Transfer of skills:* External support guides the pilot group to develop new skills and celebrates successes to strengthen commitment and entice others to join.

- *Scale up:* Engage other teachers in the reform, and use pilot teachers as leaders in the reform area.

- *Deepen and broaden reform:* Expand reform to other areas within the organization, deepen knowledge of leaders, enhance collaboration opportunities, and share or model practices internally or externally.

- *Address new challenges:* Continue to deepen and broaden reform through leadership, flexibility, immediate response to concerns, or cohesiveness.

A coach acts as a catalyst for change who can build capacity and guide implementation practices. Thus, a reason why their schedule needs to be protected.

REFLECTION

This would be a good time to pause and reflect with your coach. What are your coach's roles and responsibilities with supporting change initiatives? Is this clearly addressed in your coach's roles and responsibilities? If not, should this be included? What is your sustainability plan should an instructional coaching position no longer be funded? How, if at all, does your coach build capacity among your teachers?

CREATING A CLIMATE AND CULTURE FOR STUDENT SUCCESS (CHAPTER 12)

Working to create a climate and culture for student success so that teachers will be inspired with desire to teach every student effectively is the final recommendation on our Best Practices Checklist for administrators/supervisors as the professional partners to SFC coaches. What do we mean by that? This idea came out of some work that Jan Hasbrouck and Carolyn Denton did with a district in Kansas that strategically and systematically implemented the SFC coaching model in their K–12 schools. This implementation involved many visits by Hasbrouck and Denton to the district and many meetings and trainings, with district leadership, principals, the coaches of course, and even the school board. The district leadership was deeply committed to having this work.

At the end of the first full year of implementation, we asked the coaches if they felt that their coaching had indeed been successful. About two thirds said it had, but about one third said they did not feel as if coaching had had much of a positive impact. After discussing this a bit, it was clear that the two thirds of coaches who felt successful had the support of their administrators/supervisors. By support they meant that the administrators/supervisors understood their role, helped communicate the role to the teachers, protected their time to actually provide coaching, and had open lines of communication. The administrators/supervisors worked as professional partners to the coaches. The coaches who felt less successful universally stated that their administrators/supervisors had ignored the guidelines of the SFC model and used the coaches to complete a myriad of miscellaneous tasks that left little time for actual coaching.

When we asked the coaches to brainstorm what they would like for us to say to the administrators/supervisors when we would be meeting with them later that day, they came up with this statement: If administrators/supervisors created a climate and culture for student success and inspired all teachers with a desire to do their very best to help all students, then the job of the coaches would be far easier. They could then work with these inspired teachers as their partners to achieve this challenging but important goal of student success.

CONCLUSION

Successful coaches must have sufficient training, time, and support, and administrators/supervisors must "enter into a partnership with coaches if the coaching model is going to succeed in their schools" (Poglinco & Bach, 2004, p. 399). We hope this chapter will assist you in forming a partnership with your coach, and we wish you all the best in achieving the vital goal of meeting the needs of all students. Remember to establish a plan for your coach, protect their time, and clearly communicate their role to others. We encourage you to revisit the e-mail at the beginning of this chapter, as well as take a look at a sample list of responsibilities in the Introduction. These can be helpful tools when preparing how you will communicate your coach's responsibilities.

Remember to focus the coach's roles and responsibilities on supporting teachers and not on administrative duties. If the former is what you need, then let the coach commit to their roles and responsibilities. If the latter is what you need, then we recommend that you not allocate funds for a coach. We sincerely hope that this chapter has provided you with a clear understanding of the SFC model and the utmost importance of having a well-functioning professional partnership with the administrators/supervisor and the coaches. Best of luck in your work.

VIRTUAL COACHING TIP

We included several reflection checkpoints throughout this chapter and encourage you to take your time to reflect with your coach. There are many systems to put in place to ensure the coach is successful in their role, and there are likely many responsibilities that need to be thought about and clearly defined. Use a virtual platform to

- Revisit the letter at the beginning of this chapter that was sent from an administrator/supervisor to her classroom teachers. Work with your coach to draft a letter that you can send to your teachers.

- Review the sample list of responsibilities included in the book's Introduction. Identify the coach's responsibilities for your school or district and define each responsibility. For example, create a looks-like and sounds-like chart for each responsibility and prepare to share with teachers.

- Reflect on one element of the SAILS framework. Discuss and decide how you will respond to the questions that we posed for each element. Include additional learning that is needed for your coach and how you will communicate a consistent message to demonstrate your administrator/supervisor and coach partnership.

REFERENCES

American Institutes for Research. (2017). *Multi-level prevention system.* Retrieved from https://mtss4success.org/essential-components/multi-level-prevention-system

Archer, A., & Hughes, C. (2011). *Explicit instruction: Effective and efficient teaching.* Guilford Press.

Hall, L., O'Neill, K., Hasbrouck, J., & Parker, R. (2003). *The best of both worlds: Texas Master Reading Teachers as teachers and mentors* [Poster presentation]. International Reading Association, Orlando, FL, United States.

Hargreaves, A., & Fullan, A. (2012). *Professional capital: Transforming teaching in every school.* Teachers College Press.

Hasbrouck, J., & Denton, C. (2005). *The reading coach: A how-to manual for success.* Sopris West Educational Services.

Hiebert, J., & Stigler, J. (2017). Teaching versus teachers as a lever for change: Comparing a Japanese and a U.S. perspective on improving instruction. *Educational Researcher, 46*(4), 169–176.

Langley, G., Moen, R., Nolan, K., Nolan, T., Norman, T., & Provost, L. (2009). *The improvement guide: A practical approach to enhancing organizational performance* (2nd ed.). Wiley.

Li, Y. (2017). Processes and dynamics behind whole-school reform: Nine-year journeys of four primary schools. *American Educational Research Journal, 54*(2), 279–324.

Ornstein, A., & Hunkins, F. (2013). *Curriculum: Foundations, principles, and issues* (6th ed.). Pearson.

Poglinco, S., & Bach, A. (2004). The heart of the matter: Coaching as a vehicle for professional development. *Phi Delta Kappan, 85,* 398–400.

Rosenshine, B. (2012). Principles of instruction: Research-based strategies that all teachers should know. *American Educator, 36*(1), 12–39.

Best Practices Checklist for SFC Administrator/Supervisor Partners

Background information: The primary role of instructional coaches is to provide professional development (PD) and professional learning (PL) opportunities to support to their peer colleagues. Coaching has the potential to be an especially effective form of professional development and learning (PDL) because it can be personalized and sustained over time.

Student-Focused Coaching (SFC) is one model of coaching. *SFC is defined as a cooperative, ideally collaborative, professional relationship with colleagues mutually engaged in efforts that help maximize every teacher's knowledge and skills to enhance student learning.*

- *Cooperative:* Coaching cannot be forced on a colleague. Coaches have no power and no authority over their peer colleagues. They are not supervisors and cannot participate in supervision or evaluation decisions, either directly or indirectly.

- *Relationship:* Coaches can only provide effective PDL when they have established a trusting and mutually respectful professional relationship with their colleagues. This is facilitated when the coach and teachers focus on partnering for student success. Establishing and maintaining mutual trust requires that coaching interactions be completely confidential unless specific permission is granted by the teacher.

- *Mutually engaged:* SFC coaches work with all teachers focused on enhancing student learning. Coaches primarily spend their time engaged in activities categorized as Facilitator, Collaborative Problem-Solver, or Teacher/Learner.

Coaches are most effective when they work in partnership with their administrator(s) and/or supervisor(s). To maximize this partnership, we recommend that administrators/supervisors

1. *Understand the role of coaches.* The coach's job is to provide support for PDL. The most effective way to do this is to engage in systematic, collaborative problem solving, rather than simply observation and feedback (coaching cycle) (Chapters 1–3; 6–10).

2. Understand that coaches are not supervisors. Coaches cannot ethically or legally be involved in the evaluation of teachers, either directly or indirectly. Coaches have no power or authority over their peer colleagues. They work as peer partners to their teacher colleagues to support effective classroom practices to promote positive student outcomes (Chapters 1–3).

3. Fully honor the confidentiality of the coaching/teacher relationship as appropriate. Although administrators/supervisors cannot mandate coaching to any teacher, they can strongly suggest to a teacher that they seek support from a coach. Such a suggestion would be confidential and cannot to be shared with the coach without the permission of the referred teacher (Chapter 2).

4. Take responsibility to clearly define and describe the coach's role to the teaching staff. State any obligations of the staff for working with the coach (e.g., a mandate to share current student performance data with the coach is highly recommended). Make clear the limitations of the coach's role (Chapter 2).

5. Help coaches find sufficient time to design and provide effective PDL to peer colleagues (Chapter 5).

6. Work to strengthen the coach and administrator/supervisor partnership by having regularly scheduled formal conversations with coaches about 1) their role, 2) how they are spending

their time, and 3) how you can be an effective professional partner to support their work. Initially, aim for a minimum of three times per year for these collaborative conversations. Consider using time-tracking data to support these conversations (Chapters 2 and 4).

7. Effectively supervise coaches by regularly providing specific feedback for professional growth (Chapter 2).

8. Support the coach's efforts to successfully implement systems of support, such as leadership teams (Chapter 3).

9. Ensure that coaches keep learning about instructional practices supported by the best possible research. Coaches should continue to read and study, seek out their own PDL opportunities, and access the support of colleagues and outside resources to gain new knowledge about effective teaching and effective coaching (Chapters 4–11).

10. Understand and work to implement the elements of the SAILS framework for effective schools. Coaches must possess a strong knowledge base of what it means to support explicit and effective instruction in the classroom (Chapter 11).

11. Work to create a climate and culture for student success so teachers will be inspired with the desire to teach all students effectively. Coaches then provide collegial support to help teachers achieve this goal (Chapter 12).

Index

*Page numbers followed by *f* indicate figures; page numbers followed by *t* indicate tables.